OVER 100 RECIPES FROM SIMPLE TO SHOWSTOPPING BAKES AND CAKES

THE GREAT BRITISH
BAKE OFF

PERFECT CAKES & BAKES TO MAKE
At Home

OVER 100 RECIPES FROM SIMPLE TO SHOWSTOPPING BAKES AND CAKES

THE GREAT BRITISH
BAKE OFF

PERFECT CAKES & BAKES TO MAKE

At Home

Linda Collister

WITH RECIPES BY

MARY BERRY & PAUL HOLLYWOOD

AND THE BAKERS OF 2016

CONTENTS

WELCOME

Who doesn't love a home-made cake or biscuit? It's always a special joy, and doesn't need to be extravagantly decorated to light up someone's face.

From the *Bake Off* tent to your own kitchen, here you will learn how to make a wide variety of bakes, from small, everyday snacks to special-occasion party delights. You'll quickly discover that baking just makes you incredibly happy (and very popular).

To prove that the simplest recipes can be just as impressive as the trickiest molecular gastronomy, every chapter kicks off with some deliciously easy bakes. The Greek Lemon-Yoghurt Loaf Cake on page 28 tastes and looks like the classiest Madeira sponge, but is really a fast, no-fuss, all-in-one mix. The crunchiest of granola bars (page 89), rich with nuts, seeds and dried cherries, and scrumptious Peanut Butter, Chocolate Chip and Oat Cookies (page 94) that just melt in your mouth can also be whipped up in a flash.

Catering for a party at home can appear a bit daunting, so why not approach it sideways? Rather than making your own pastry, you can use ready-made puff pastry to turn out a great batch of Spicy and Simple Lamb Rolls (page 282), or make quick canapés from a sliced white loaf (page 278).

If you're a pastry novice, shortcrust is a good place to start – so simple to whiz up in a processor for the Roasted Apple Brown Sugar Pie on page 230. If you've mastered this, and are looking to extend your pastry repertoire, there are plenty of more challenging recipes to try, which will interest home bakers of all levels.

It's fun to make a Pistachio Chocolate Baklava (page 233) using ready-made filo, but if you are looking for a new baking project why not try making your own filo pastry at home? You can choose from several different ways to prepare and then fill the filo (both sweet and savoury) – these lovely recipes come from our enthusiastic *Bake Off* bakers. They've also come up with some showstoppers to dazzle, such as mirror-glazed cakes (pages 72 and 76), which achieve their glamorous appearance from a final sweet coating of a gelatine-based icing. You can meet this year's bakers on pages 8–11, and find more of their recipes throughout the book.

Mary and Paul, our judges, have also added some great ways to stretch your kitchen repertoire, from pretty lace-patterned pancakes on page 184 to an unusual poached dumpling dessert called Dampfnudeln (page 139) and a spectacular layered Marjolaine (page 211). There are some well-loved classics too that you will definitely want to try: Jaffa Cakes (page 62), Viennese Whirls (page 113) and Bakewell Tart (page 228). These may seem simple, but the judges seek perfection – in taste, texture and appearance – and that comes with practice and experience.

Whether the recipe is easy or requires immense skill and creativity, you'll find baking tremendously gratifying, and you will want to bake more, share more – and more often. Baking is irresistible, one of the pleasures of life that's designed to share.

MEET THE 2016 BAKERS

Benjamina

Disappointed that her mum never made desserts, Benjamina took matters into her own hands at the age of 14 and started baking for the family for fun. She's self-taught and gets inspiration from online trends, using stylish flavours like matcha or salted caramel and trying out new techniques she reads about.

Benjamina serves up her creations to her grateful siblings, younger brother Nathan and non-identical twin sister Bo, who she says is her biggest critic. It's all about the extra wow-factor: 'All cakes should look fabulous. Always. Whether it's just for you and your mum, or for someone's birthday. Even if you're just baking at home, cakes should always be showstoppers.'

Andrew

Aerospace engineer Andrew enjoys perfecting techniques - both at work and in the kitchen - and experimenting with flavours. 'Trial and error is the foundation of engineering,' he says, just like baking. He loves dates (almost as much as his dad, who used to keep them in the car glove-box) so has tried dates in all kinds of bakes for his housemates in Derby to try.

Back in Northern Ireland for Christmas, Andrew reconnects with his family through baking. Everyone has a speciality to prepare over the festive period, and coming together over good food is what makes the family tick. 'As much as I enjoy eating what I've made, it's really about sharing with others.'

Candice

Vintage-loving Candice's main baking inspiration was her nan, who she always stayed with during the school holidays. She rarely saw her nan use weighing scales - everything was done by eye. One of Candice's prize possessions is a little 1960s recipe book she inherited from her grandmother with lots of jottings 'all in a jumble - ounces mixed with grams because that's how she worked.'

Candice likes to take a classic cake or pastry recipe from her nan's book and change things round a little bit, for example adding coconut and pineapple to carrot cake as coconut is a favourite family ingredient. But some she still makes exactly as her nan wrote them, in her honour.

Jane

Baking runs in Jane's family - her grandfather owned a bakery in Hastings, and her father was trained to take over. She can remember Easters during her childhood when the grown-ups would work all night to make the hot cross buns ready for Good Friday. Hating her time at boarding school, Jane would always look forward to coming home and baking with her dad in the family kitchen. He was the one who first showed her how to royal-ice a cake and make sugar flowers and other decorations.

Baking continues to be central to her home life. Her bakes aren't too sweet or fussy, 'although if it's a special occasion and I can throw glitter at it, I will.'

Kate

Kate describes herself as a farmhouse cook, but loves a bit of glamour in her baking. She's often up at 5am baking muffins, biscuits or flapjacks for her children's lunchboxes before heading out for her part-time nursing job, but also enjoys the intricate art of sugar craft.

'My mum gave me a wooden spoon and a bowl from the minute I could hold one.' As soon as she could read a recipe on her own, her mother stood back and let Kate do it herself.

Even though she's a perfectionist, Kate accepts that disasters will happen. 'When a sponge cake goes wrong, it just becomes a trifle; if a meringue gets broken, you'll have a delicious Eton Mess.'

Lee

Lee started baking in the 1980s. He'd hurt his back and was off work for quite a while. Not liking just sitting around while his wife and children were out all day, he decided to teach himself to bake.

He's now a church minister and hosts baking demos at church, making madeleines, tarts and little cakes. 'All the ladies are accomplished bakers, and I pick up tips and recipes from them. Occasionally something might go wrong, but we just have a laugh.'

He's even made a few wedding cakes. The first was a three-tiered showpiece for his daughter Dawn's big day. 'It's nice when people like it, and you can say that you made it.'

Michael

North London boy Michael's family is from Cyprus and his main baking influence was his nan, who taught him how to make filo pastry the traditional way. 'All the recipes in older Greek families are shared by word of mouth. [Nan] didn't have anything written down. So I'd stand there, watching and scribbling on a piece of paper.'

Michael's heritage is reflected in the flavours he loves – the likes of cinnamon, nutmeg and the classic Greek spice mahlepi. One of his favourite things to make is olive bread, following his grandma's recipe. When he made the bread for his flatmates at uni, one said that they would pay him to make it every week.

Louise

'When I'm baking, I call that my bliss,' says Cardiff hair-stylist Louise. 'What's better than enjoying that feeling and then having the satisfaction of pleasing your family?'

Like her mother, she always cooks everything from scratch, though she admits her Welsh Cakes will never be as good as her mum's.

Cooking is a hobby she shares with her fiancé Simon. They've even been on a cooking holiday in Andalusia, making orange cake and almond biscuits along with paella and tortillas. A lot of her friends say that they couldn't cook with their partner. 'Obviously we have the odd bicker, but it's something that we really love doing together.'

Rav

You wouldn't think that baking could help you lose weight, but for Rav baking and weight loss go hand in hand. In the last two years Ravinder has shrunk seven stone as he found that the creative process of baking and sharing can encourage a healthy lifestyle.

'It's usually the woman in an Indian family who does the cooking, but my mother raised my sister and me to be equals.' One of Rav's earliest memories is of his mum making chapatis and him wanting to avoid helping with what he thought of as a chore. 'But then when I had the dough in front of me and was getting my hands stuck in, with my mum encouraging me and telling me the correct technique, I loved it.'

Selasi

Banker Selasi works long hours, yet he still finds time to bake – sometimes into the early hours. 'My girlfriend thinks I'm addicted to baking, but I'd rather spend time in the kitchen than in front of the TV.'

Selasi grew up in Ghana, looked after by aunties and his grandma while his parents worked in the UK. There is no tradition of home baking in Ghana, so it wasn't until he was at university in the UK that baking piqued his interest – when his best friend Sally taught him to bake fairy cakes. Now he likes to challenge himself with complicated gâteaux and pâtisserie. 'It's funny growing up not knowing that much about baking and then all of a sudden loving it so much.'

Tom

Oxford graduate Tom works for the Royal Society of Arts. He's a creative soul and sees baking and cooking as an important outlet: 'If I haven't got the time to make the family loaf on a Sunday, I know that's when things are going wrong in my life.'

In the village where he grew up, just outside Rochdale, there was an annual horticultural society show, 'which was the height of the social calendar'. Tom's parents would enter their home-grown vegetables and when he was a teenager he started bringing along his home-made breads, cakes and pies. 'I was the only person under 30 and only male entering the baking competition judged by the WI. The slight rebel in me liked that.'

Val

Former headmistress Val took over the family baking at the age of 15. She worked her way through the cookbooks of each generation of celebrity chefs, and she learned from her grandma, mum and in-laws too. 'I'm the sum of several bakers,' she says.

She's known husband Ian since she was 17 and remembers going to his grandmother's house to bake. They would cook on a Yorkshire Range, made up of two ovens next to a fire. 'We'd test the oven's temperature with a piece of brown paper, watching how long it took to char.'

She always takes a home-made cake with her wherever she travels, be it to England, Europe or America.

BAKING TIPS

NOTE
In the recipes, an asterisk is used to refer you back to these instructions and information.

What Does This Mean?

• fold This is a way to delicately combine 2 (or more) ingredients so you don't knock out all the air you've carefully beaten or whisked into a mixture – for example, adding sifted flour to a creamed mixture of butter, eggs and sugar for a cake, or adding sugar or other ingredients to whisked egg whites for meringue. A large metal spoon or plastic spatula is best for folding. Turn the spoon so one side cuts down through the mixture. When you touch the bottom of the bowl, turn the spoon upwards and draw it up through the mixture to the top, then flip the spoon over so the mixture flops on to the surface. Give the bowl a quarter turn (so you start folding from a different place) and repeat. Using a light touch and as few movements as possible, keep lightly cutting down, lifting and flopping over until you can no longer see any streaks of unmixed ingredients.

• rub in This is how you combine butter and flour when making pastry and simple cake mixtures (like that for plain fruit cakes). Use the fingertips and thumbs of both hands – try to keep your palms clean (your fingertips are cooler than your palms). Pick up a little of the butter and flour mixture, lift your hands up to the top of the bowl and gently rub your fingers and thumbs together so the mixture is combined as it falls back down into the bowl. Continue doing this until the mixture has an even crumb-like consistency. The rubbing-in will add air, which will make the resulting pastry or cake mixture lighter.

• sift This means shaking flour, a raising agent, cocoa powder, icing sugar, ground spices or other dry ingredients through a sieve into a bowl. Sifting will remove any lumps, as well as adding air, and it helps to combine ingredients – important for raising agents added to flour to be sure they are evenly dispersed (you can also do this in a food processor by 'pulsing' the flour with the raising agents a few times).

• work This is a way of saying to mix, stir, blend or combine ingredients using a spoon, plastic spatula or your hands until they have come together (or look smooth, or soft, or thickened, as the recipe directs).

How Do I Do This?

PREPARING TINS
• grease and base-line a springclip tin, a deep round or square tin, a sandwich tin or a traybake/brownie/rectangular cake tin Lightly and thoroughly brush the base and sides of the tin (including the rim) with melted

butter. Set the tin on a sheet of baking paper and draw around it, then cut out the disc (or square or rectangle). Turn the baking paper over, to be sure any pencil or pen marks are underneath, and press it on to the base of the tin.

• grease and line a springclip tin or a round, deep cake tin
Brush the base and sides with melted butter, then cut out 2 discs of baking paper very slightly smaller than the base of the tin (measure as for base-lining, above, then cut inside the drawn line). Also cut out a double-thickness strip of baking paper long enough to go around the tin and stand about 5cm above its rim. Make a 2.5cm fold along one edge of this strip, then snip diagonally up to the fold at 1cm intervals (it will look like a thick fringe). Press one paper disc on to the base of the tin, then place the strip around the inside of the tin so the snipped edge lies flat on the base and the paper is pressed smoothly to the sides of the tin (no creases). Brush the paper on the

base and the snipped edge of the side strip with a little more melted butter, then press the second paper disc on top. Lightly brush the paper on the base and sides with melted butter to hold it all in place.

• grease and line a loaf tin with a long strip of baking paper
Lightly brush the base, sides and rim of the tin with melted butter. Cut a strip of baking paper the same width as the tin and long enough to cover the base and 2 short sides. Press the paper into the greased tin to line it. The paper will help you lift out the loaf after baking.

COOKING WITH CHOCOLATE

• melt chocolate Chop or break up the chocolate into even pieces so it will melt at the same rate. Put it into a heatproof bowl and set this over a pan of steaming hot but not boiling water – the base of the bowl shouldn't touch the water. As the chocolate starts to soften, stir gently so it melts evenly. It is ready as soon as it is liquid and smooth. *Take care not to leave it over the heat any longer because if the chocolate overheats it will 'seize up' – turn grainy and hard – and be unusable.* White chocolate melts at a lower temperature and seizes more readily than dark chocolate.

• temper chocolate This process of melting and cooling chocolate makes it shiny and very smooth, and will give a professional finish when you are covering or coating a cake or dessert, or when you are making decorations such as chocolate curls. You'll need a cooking thermometer or a special digital chocolate and

caramel thermometer. First melt the chocolate (see above), then put in the thermometer. Slightly increase the heat under the pan of water so the temperature of the chocolate rises. Keep stirring so the chocolate heats evenly. As soon as the temperature reaches 45°C/113°F (no higher) remove the bowl from the pan and set it in a larger bowl of cold but not icy water to quickly cool the chocolate (take care not to let any water get into the chocolate bowl). Gently stir until the temperature falls to 27°C/81°F. Set the bowl over the pan of steaming hot water again and reheat the chocolate, stirring, until it reaches 29–30°C/85°F. When the chocolate gets up to temperature, remove the bowl from the pan. The tempered chocolate is now ready to use.

COOKING WITH EGGS

• whisk egg whites Separate your eggs carefully – *any trace of yolk (or speck of grease in the bowl) will stop the whites from being whisked*

to their full volume – and use the whites at room temperature. Put them into a large, spotlessly clean and grease-free bowl. Whisk, on low speed if using a hand-held electric whisk or mixer whisk attachment, for about 30 seconds until frothy. If you add a pinch of cream of tartar, or dash of vinegar or lemon juice at this point, the slight acidity will help the structure of the whites to stiffen. Then increase the speed and continue whisking – the whites will become a mass of tiny bubbles, with a very smooth and fine texture. *Soft peak* is when you lift the whisk and the peak of whites on it slightly droops down. The next stage, after more whisking, is *stiff peak* when the peak stands upright. You should also be able to turn the bowl upside down without the whites falling out.

• **whisk to the ribbon stage**
Whisked sponges, eggs and sugar must be whisked thoroughly to build up a thick mass of tiny air bubbles that forms the structure of

the cake. Use a large bowl – after 4 or 5 minutes of whisking on high speed, the initial volume of eggs and sugar will increase five-fold. Using a large free-standing electric mixer is the easiest and quickest way to whisk eggs and sugar to the ribbon stage, but you can also use a hand-held electric whisk or, if you're not making a large quantity, a rotary whisk. The ribbon stage is reached when the whisked mixture becomes very thick: if you lift the whisk out of the bowl, the mixture on it will fall back on to the surface of the mixture in the bowl to make a distinct thick, ribbon-like trail.

COOKING WITH CREAM

• **whip cream** Make sure the cream is well chilled before you start (in warm weather, pop the bowl and whisk into the fridge to chill too). This will prevent the butterfat from separating and the mixture from curdling as you whip. You can use a hand-held electric

whisk, a rotary whisk or a wire hand whisk. If you are going to fold the cream into another mixture, whip the cream to *soft peak* stage (see 'whisk egg whites', above). For piping, whip the cream to a slightly firmer peak.

• **fill a piping bag** Put the piping bag in a large glass or tall mug and fold the top of the bag over the rim (the glass/mug will support the piping bag, making it easier to fill). Spoon the whipped cream (or icing or meringue) into the bag, filling it about two-thirds full. Unfold the bag from the glass/mug, then twist the top to push the cream down to the tip or nozzle end, getting rid of any air pockets. Twist the top again to compact the cream.

MAKING A PASTRY CASE

• **line a flan tin or pie plate**
Roll out the pastry dough on a lightly floured worktop to a disc about 8cm larger than your tin. Roll up the pastry around the rolling pin and lift it over the flan tin, then unroll the pastry gently so it drapes over the tin. Flour your fingers and gently press the pastry on to the base and up the side of the tin, smoothing out any pockets of air. Leave the excess pastry hanging over the rim if you are going to trim it after chilling or baking, or roll the pin over the top of the tin to cut off the excess (if there are any holes in the pastry case, use these dough trimmings to patch them). With your thumbs, ease the pastry up the side of the tin, just slightly higher than the rim, to allow for shrinkage during baking. Curve your forefinger inside this new rim and gently press the pastry over your finger so it

curves slightly inwards – this will make it easier to unmould the case after baking. Prick the base of the pastry case well with a fork, then chill for 20 minutes. If you need to keep the pastry case in the fridge for any longer, loosely cover with clingfilm to prevent the pastry from drying out.

• **bake a pastry case blind**
Crumple up a sheet of baking or greaseproof paper, then flatten it out (this makes the paper easier to fit). Line the pastry case with the paper and fill with ceramic baking beans or dried beans. Place in the heated oven and bake for 12–15 minutes (or as the recipe directs) until the pastry is firm. Carefully remove the paper and beans, then return the tin to the oven and bake for a further 5–7 minutes (or as the recipe directs) until the pastry is thoroughly cooked and starting to colour (this is vital to avoid the dreaded 'soggy bottom'). *Pastry containing sugar or*

cocoa powder needs to be watched carefully as it can burn on the edges before the base is cooked through. If this happens, reduce the oven temperature slightly, or cover the rim with a long strip of foil.

• **'knock up' a pastry edge**
Use the back of a small knife to make small horizontal cuts in the pastry rim all around.

• **flute or scallop a pastry edge**
Place 2 fingers on the pastry edge to press it down and draw a small knife between them. Continue all around the edge.

BAKING CAKES

• **skewer test** For richer, heavier cakes, fruit cakes and dense chocolate cakes, the way to test if the cake is done is to insert a wooden cocktail stick or fine skewer into the centre of the cake. If the stick or skewer comes out clean rather than damp with cake mixture adhering, the cake has finished baking. Note though that for some recipes, such as brownies,

the cocktail stick should come out slightly sticky; this is to avoid over-cooking a cake that is supposed to be moist and fudgy.

• **fingertip test** For delicate sponge cakes the most reliable test to check if the cake is done is to gently press the top, in the centre, with your fingertip, then lift it up – the cake is ready if the sponge springs back into place. If a slight dent is left, the mixture is still soft, so bake for a couple of minutes more and test again. When done, a sponge will also have started to shrink from the side of the tin.

• **cool a sponge on a wire rack**
To avoid a wire rack leaving marks on the top of a sponge, cover a clean board (or a second wire rack) with a clean, dry tea towel. Hold the upturned towel-covered board over the sponge (in its tin) and turn the whole thing over so the sponge falls out on to the tea towel. Lift off the tin and remove the lining paper. Set the upturned wire rack on the sponge base and turn the whole thing over again. Carefully remove

the board and tea towel and leave the sponge to cool, now the right way up, on the wire rack.

• cut a sponge into 2 layers First, make a small vertical nick in the side of the sponge with the tip of a sharp knife (this will help you align the layers when sandwiching). Gently but firmly press the top of the sponge with the flat of your hand and, using a long serrated knife (such as a bread knife), carefully saw the sponge horizontally in half to make 2 equal layers.

MAKING BREAD
• mix a non-yeasted dough Doughs raised with a mixture of bicarbonate of soda and buttermilk need to be mixed, shaped and baked without delay. It's important to work quickly because once the acidic buttermilk starts to react with the alkaline bicarbonate of soda, bubbles of carbon dioxide gas are produced and it is these that will raise the dough as it bakes.

• mix a yeasted dough Many doughs raised with yeast specify lukewarm liquid (milk, water, etc). It's important that the liquid not be too hot or it could kill the yeast. After warming the liquid, check the temperature by dipping your little finger into it: it should feel comfy. For lukewarm water, you can mix half boiling water with half cold water from the tap.

• hydrate the flour If you leave the mixed yeasted dough in its bowl for 5 minutes (uncovered) before you start to knead, you'll find it an easier process because the flour will have had time to absorb the liquid properly – a particularly important step for wholemeal and rye flours, which are slow to hydrate. You can judge whether or not the dough needs a touch more flour or water at this point.

• knead dough Working a dough develops the gluten in the flour's protein and turns it from a messy ball into neat bundles of strands

that are capable of stretching around the bubbles of carbon dioxide gas produced by the growing yeast. The dough will then rise slowly, thanks to the yeast and gluten, and set in the oven. You can knead by hand or in a free-standing electric mixer fitted with the dough hook attachment. Note that some unyeasted quick doughs are also kneaded, just to mix them but not to develop the flour's gluten.

• knead yeasted dough by hand First lightly dust the worktop with flour to prevent the dough from sticking. Turn the dough out on to the worktop. Stretch the ball of dough away from you by holding down one end with your hand and using the other hand to pull and stretch out the dough as if it were an elastic band. Gather the dough back into a ball again and give it a quarter turn (so you start from a different section of the dough), then repeat the stretching and gathering-back movements. As you knead you'll notice the dough gradually changes in the way it looks and feels – it will start to feel pliable and then stretchy and very elastic, and silky smooth. Most doughs need about 10 minutes of thorough kneading by hand.

• knead yeasted dough in an electric mixer Set the mixer on the lowest possible speed and knead with the dough hook for about 5 minutes. While it's almost impossible to over-knead by hand (your arms will give out first), *take care when using a mixer because you can stretch the gluten beyond repair,* which means the dough won't rise well at all.

• **knead a rye flour dough** If you are having a hard time kneading a dough made with rye flour, give the dough (and your arms) a break: cover the dough with the upturned bowl and have a rest for 5–10 minutes, then continue. Rye flour has very little gluten, which means it doesn't really become stretchy as a wheat flour dough does.

• **test if yeasted dough has been kneaded enough** Take a small piece and stretch it between your fingers to make a thin, translucent sheet. If it won't stretch out or it tears easily, continue to knead for a while longer.

• **bake a loaf with a good crust** Make sure the oven is thoroughly heated so the dough quickly puffs (this is called 'oven-spring') and then sets, bakes evenly and forms a good crust. If you are worried about the oven temperature dropping dramatically as you load the bread in the oven, heat it slightly higher

than the recipe says, then turn it down to the specified temperature once the oven door is closed again.

• **bake a loaf with a crisp crust** Creating a burst of steam in the oven at the start of baking will help give your loaf a crisp crust – the steam keeps the surface moist, helping the bread to rise easily; once the surface has set the moisture evaporates, leaving a crisp finish. To do this, put an empty roasting tin on the floor of the oven when you turn it on to heat it. Then, when you're putting the loaf in to bake, pour cold water – or throw a handful of ice cubes – into the hot tin. Quickly close the oven door to trap the resulting steam inside.

• **bake a loaf with a crisp bottom crust** When you turn on the oven, put a baking sheet or baking stone in to heat up. Then carefully transfer your loaf (in a tin or on a sheet of baking paper) on to the hot baking sheet or stone for baking.

• **test bread to see if it is done** Carefully remove the bread from the oven and turn it over or out of its tin, upside down, on to one hand (thick oven gloves needed here). Tap the underside of the loaf with your knuckles. If the bread sounds hollow, like a drum, then it is cooked through. If you just get a dull 'thud', put the bread back into the oven – straight on to the oven shelf. Bake for a few more minutes, then test again. *A rule of thumb: a slightly over-baked loaf will taste far better than an undercooked one.* Cool on a wire rack, not in the tin or on a baking sheet, so the steam from the loaf cannot condense during cooling and turn the crust soggy.

Cook's Notes

SPOON MEASURES
All teaspoons and tablespoons are level unless otherwise stated.

EGGS
Some recipes contain raw or partially cooked eggs. Pregnant women, the elderly, babies and toddlers, and people who are unwell should avoid these recipes.

SALT
If a recipe calls for a small or hard-to-weigh amount of salt, remember that ½ teaspoon fine salt weighs 2.5g and ¼ teaspoon weighs 1.25g. If you are using sea salt it is best to crush the flakes into a fine powder before measuring and adding to your recipe (unless otherwise specified).

OVEN TEMPERATURES
Recipes give temperatures for a conventional oven. If your oven is fan-assisted, set the temperature 20°C lower than specified in the recipe. Don't forget that ovens vary – from the front to the back of the oven, as well as between top and bottom shelves – so an oven thermometer is very useful. Get to know your oven, and where the 'hot spots' are. Always preheat the oven, and be sure your oven gloves are dry.

BASIC RECIPES

CRÈME CHANTILLY

Serve this whipped sweetened cream flavoured with vanilla to accompany desserts and sweet pastries, as well as for piping. Before you begin, make sure the bowl, whisk and cream are thoroughly chilled for maximum volume.

makes about 350g

250ml whipping cream, well chilled
2 tablespoons icing sugar
I teaspoon vanilla extract

Pour the cream into a chilled mixing bowl and add the sugar and vanilla. Whip* using a hand-held electric whisk or a hand wire whisk until the cream becomes just stiff enough to hold a peak when the whisk is lifted out. Use immediately or cover and keep in the fridge for up to an hour.

VANILLA EGG CUSTARD

For the best flavour, you need rich, high-fat milk and a vanilla pod to make a real egg custard, or crème anglaise.

makes about 475ml to serve 4-6

425ml creamy milk (such as Jersey or Guernsey)
I vanilla pod, split lengthways
4 egg yolks, at room temperature
2½ tablespoons caster sugar

1. Put the milk into a medium pan (non-stick for choice). Scrape some of the seeds from the vanilla pod into the milk, then add the pod too. Bring to the boil, stirring frequently with a wooden spoon, then remove from the heat, cover and leave to infuse for about 20 minutes.

2. Meanwhile, put the yolks and sugar into a heatproof mixing bowl. Set the bowl on a damp cloth, to stop it wobbling, then beat with a wooden spoon until the mixture is very smooth and much paler – this will take about a minute.

3. Remove the vanilla pod from the warm milk, then slowly pour it on to the yolk mixture in a thin, steady stream, stirring constantly with the wooden spoon. Tip back into the pan and stir constantly over medium heat until the custard thickens enough to coat the back of the spoon – don't let the custard come to the boil or the eggs will scramble!

4. Pour the custard into a serving jug. Serve immediately, or to serve it cold, sprinkle the surface with a thin layer of caster sugar to prevent a skin from forming, then cover the top of the jug with clingfilm; stir gently before serving. The custard can be kept, tightly covered, in the fridge for up to 2 days.

VANILLA CRÈME MOUSSELINE

This is basically crème pâtissière - a thick custard - enriched with butter and lightened with whipped cream. It makes an indulgent filling for brioche doughnuts (see page 156).

makes about 300ml

200ml creamy milk (such as Jersey or Guernsey)
1 vanilla pod, split lengthways
3 medium egg yolks, at room temperature
50g caster sugar
15g cornflour
30g unsalted butter, at room temperature
75ml double cream, well chilled

1. Heat the milk with the split vanilla pod in a medium pan until bubbles start to form around the edge, then remove from the heat and leave to infuse for 15 minutes. Fish out the vanilla pod and scrape a few seeds back into the milk (the pod can be rinsed, dried and used again or to flavour sugar), then reheat the milk.

2. Meanwhile, whisk the egg yolks with the sugar and cornflour in a heatproof bowl for 1–2 minutes until smooth and light. Whisk in the hot milk. When thoroughly combined, pour the mixture back into the pan and set over medium heat. Whisk constantly until the mixture boils and thickens to make a smooth custard, taking care it doesn't scorch.

3. Remove from the heat and whisk in the butter – the custard will become glossy. Tip into a bowl and press a piece of clingfilm or dampened greaseproof paper on to the surface to prevent a skin from forming. Cool, then chill for 6 hours or overnight.

4. Whip the cream* until it holds a soft peak. Whisk the chilled custard until smooth, then fold* in the whipped cream. Use immediately or cover tightly and keep in the fridge for up to 4 hours.

FRESH RASPBERRY SAUCE

A vibrantly coloured sauce that is made in minutes. You can use either fresh or frozen fruit, and serve it chilled or warm (reheat gently, stirring constantly).

makes about 300ml

250g raspberries
1 teaspoon lemon juice OR raspberry liqueur
  OR kirsch
4 tablespoons icing sugar, or to taste

1. If using frozen raspberries, remove the pack from the freezer and leave to thaw for 15–20 minutes.

2. Put all the ingredients into a food processor and run the machine until the mixture becomes a very thick purée. Taste and add a little more sugar if you think it's needed.

3. For a very smooth, seedless sauce, push the purée through a fine sieve into a bowl. Cover and chill until needed — it can be kept in the fridge for 4 days.

HOT BITTER CHOCOLATE SAUCE

A really good, top-quality dark chocolate is essential for this simple sauce, to give that special intense and just-bitter chocolatey flavour you need to contrast with sweet meringues, ice creams and brownies. Any leftover sauce can be kept, covered, in the fridge, then gently reheated the next day.

serves 4-6

100g dark chocolate (about 70% cocoa solids),
   broken up
25g unsalted butter
2 tablespoons icing sugar
100ml water

Simply put all the ingredients into a small pan, preferably non-stick, and heat gently, stirring frequently, until melted and smooth. Keep warm until ready to serve by setting the pan in a larger pan of hot water (like a bain-marie).

LEMON CURD

The unique flavour of home-made lemon curd has a vividly fresh, sweet sharpness. When you've made some Swiss-meringue buttercream or meringues, use the leftover egg yolks for this divine treat.

makes about 400g

70g unsalted butter, diced
125g caster sugar
finely grated zest of 3 medium unwaxed lemons
100ml lemon juice
2 medium eggs, plus 2 yolks, at room temperature

2 sterilised jars or containers with wax discs
   (optional) and lids

1. Put the butter, sugar, lemon zest and juice into a heatproof bowl. Set the bowl over a pan of simmering water (the base of the bowl shouldn't touch the water) and stir with a wooden spoon until the sugar has completely dissolved.

2. Remove the bowl from the pan and set it on a heatproof surface. Beat the whole eggs with the yolks in a small bowl until well mixed, then strain into the lemon mixture and combine thoroughly. Set the bowl back over the pan of simmering water and stir the lemon mixture until it becomes very thick and opaque. Don't be tempted to turn the heat up because the eggs will scramble if the mixture gets anywhere near boiling. The lemon curd is ready when you can draw a finger through the curd on the wooden spoon and make a clear path.

3. Immediately lift the bowl from the pan and spoon the lemon curd into the jars or containers. Cover with wax discs, if using, then leave until cold before covering tightly with lids. Store in the fridge and use within 2 weeks.

QUICK AND EASY RASPBERRY JAM

You can easily make jam with a small amount of fruit. The result is an almost instant treat: vibrant, deeply flavoured, fruit-packed jam for sandwiching biscuits and sponge cakes, as well as topping scones.

makes about 425g (1 jar)

250g raspberries
250g jam sugar (a ready-made combination
   of sugar and pectin)

1 x 500g jam jar, sterilised and gently warmed, with
   wax disc (optional) and lid or covering

1. Put an old saucer in the freezer to help with the setting test. Tip the berries into a large heavy-based pan and add the sugar. Gently squash the berries with a potato masher or the back of a wooden spoon, keeping a bit of texture in the mash. Set the pan over low heat and stir gently with a wooden spoon as the juice starts to run. Keep the heat low, and stir gently until the sugar has completely dissolved – this won't take long.

2. Turn up the heat and boil rapidly, stirring to prevent the jam from 'catching' around the base of the pan, until setting point is reached: this is 105°C/220°F on a sugar thermometer. If you are not using a thermometer to test, start checking after about 4 minutes of boiling: draw the pan off the heat, put about ½ teaspoon of jam on to the chilled saucer and let it cool and set for a few seconds, then draw your finger through it. If the jam forms a skin that wrinkles, it has reached setting point. If not, boil for another minute or so and test again.

3. Carefully pour the jam into the warm jar. Put a wax disc on the surface, if using, then leave until cold before tightly covering with a lid or cellophane disc. Store in a cool spot and use within a month; keep in the fridge after opening.

MAPLE PECAN PRALINE

Praline is usually based on sugar, but here maple syrup provides the 'caramel' as well giving the praline a unique delicious flavour. Once the praline is cold and set, you can use the pecans whole for decoration, or chop them to flavour buttercreams, butter icings and ice cream mixtures or to press around the sides of large iced cakes.

makes about 60g

50g pecan halves
25g pure maple syrup

1 baking sheet, greased with a flavourless oil

1. Tip the nuts into a small heavy-based pan. Measure the maple syrup on top of the nuts and set over low heat. Stir with a metal spoon so all the nuts are thoroughly coated in syrup, then leave until the syrup boils and bubbles up. Cook, frequently stirring and shaking the pan, for about 3 minutes until the syrup has almost disappeared (the pan will look quite dry) and the nuts are heavily coated with the 'caramel'.

2. Tip on to the oiled baking sheet and spread out so the nuts are not sticking together. Leave until completely cold. Use immediately or store in an airtight container for up to a day.

chocolate-dipped maple pralines:
Melt 75g dark chocolate* (about 75% cocoa solids), then temper* it if you like. If necessary transfer the melted or tempered chocolate to a small bowl. Use 2 forks for the dipping: balance a whole maple pecan praline on the forks and dip into the chocolate to coat all over, then place on a baking sheet lined with baking paper. Leave until completely set. Use the same day.

QUICK HERB BUTTER SAUCE

This easy, delicious and impressive sauce is basically a warm mayonnaise of egg yolks and melted butter (instead of oil) whizzed up in a food processor or blender. The result is very light yet rich-tasting and buttery.

serves 6

3 medium egg yolks, at room temperature
2 tablespoons water
juice of ½ medium lemon, or to taste
175g unsalted butter
3 tablespoons finely chopped fresh herbs (such as parsley and chives, with a few optional sprigs of thyme or oregano)
salt and pepper to taste

1. Put the egg yolks, water and lemon juice into the bowl of a food processor or blender. Add a little salt and pepper and process briefly until just combined – about 10 seconds.

2. Melt the butter in a small pan over low heat. Skim the froth off the surface with a small spoon, then heat the butter until very hot but not quite boiling.

3. With the machine running, gradually pour the hot butter through the feed tube into the processor or blender, in a thin, steady stream. Stop the machine as soon as all the butter has been added and the sauce is creamy and thick.

4. Taste and add more salt or pepper (or lemon juice) if needed, then add the herbs and 'pulse' briefly just to combine. Transfer to a serving jug and serve as soon as possible (to keep warm, stand the covered jug in a pan of just-hot water, off the heat).

PUFF PASTRY

This is the lightest, richest and flakiest of all pastries - and the trickiest. What makes it so delicious is its butteriness. Save all the trimmings: to use, just stack them up, then re-roll - don't knead them together.

makes about 750g

300g plain flour
½ teaspoon fine sea salt
300g unsalted butter, cold but not rock-hard
1 teaspoon lemon juice
about 140ml icy cold water

1. Put the flour and salt into a food processor and 'pulse' to combine. Cut 50g of the butter into small pieces and add to the bowl, then blitz until the mixture looks like fine crumbs. Mix the lemon juice with the water. With the machine running, add the liquid through the feed tube to make a ball of slightly moist dough.

2. You can also make the pastry by hand: rub* the butter into the flour, then stir in the liquid with a round-bladed knife. Shape into a ball.

3. Turn out the ball of dough on to a lightly floured worktop and score a deep cross in the top of it. Wrap and chill for 15 minutes.

4. Meanwhile, sprinkle a little flour on the remaining piece of butter, then place it between sheets of clingfilm. Pound it with a rolling pin until it is half its original thickness. Remove the film and fold the butter in half, then re-cover and pound again. Keep doing this until the butter is pliable but still cold. Beat it into a 13cm square.

5. Put the ball of dough on the floured worktop again and roll out the dough 'flaps' from the scored cross in 4 directions – the dough will end up looking like a cross with a thick rough square in the centre.

6. Dust the butter lightly with flour, then place on top of the central square. Fold the flaps of dough over the butter to enclose it and gently press the seams with the rolling pin to seal.

7. Turn the dough upside down, brush off excess flour and lightly press with the rolling pin to flatten – don't squeeze the butter out. Gently roll out the dough away from you to a rectangle about 54 x 18cm. Fold it in thirds – fold up the bottom third to cover the centre third, then fold down the top third to cover the other layers and make a neat square. Lightly press the open edges with the rolling pin to seal. This is your first 'turn'. Brush off excess flour.

8. Lift up the dough and give it a quarter turn anti-clockwise so the folded edges are now to the sides. Roll out the dough to a rectangle and fold it in 3 again, just as before. Wrap and chill for 15 minutes.

9. Give the dough 2 more turns, alternating the position of the folded edges each time, then wrap and chill as before. Finish with 2 more turns, to make a total of 6, and chill well before using.

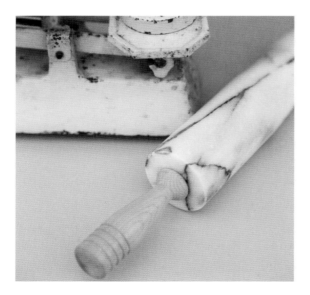

A few tips

• It is important not to develop the gluten in the flour, as you don't want overworked, over-stretched pastry that shrinks in the oven, so don't 'manhandle' the dough (like you have to do when making yeasted bread). Also, stick to the chilling times, particularly before baking.

• Don't let the butter get warm - make sure it's chilled before you begin. If it starts to ooze out of the dough, wrap and chill the dough or it will be hard to handle and end up greasy and heavy.

• Keep a dry pastry brush next to the rolling pin and brush off the excess flour before folding the dough - this will stop the pastry becoming dry.

• It's difficult to make puff pastry in small quantities, but it keeps well: after the fourth turn, store in the fridge for 4 days, or freeze (thaw before using). Complete the last 2 turns when you want to use the dough.

CAKES

A cake doesn't need to be tricky to be impressive. Take the humble Greek Lemon-Yoghurt Loaf Cake on page 28: it's a basic all-in-one mix, made in a trice with a light olive oil (meaning no butter to cream); it's packed with flavour; and it turns out like the classiest Madeira cake.

If you're fond of drizzle cakes (and who isn't?) you're in for a real treat! There's a layered St Clement's Orange and Lemon Drizzle Cake (page 33), an unusual gluten-free Raspberry, Rhubarb and Custard Drizzle Cake (page 48) and a lovely ring-shaped Lemon and Poppyseed Drizzle Cake (page 35).

Jaffa Cakes (page 62) – a hard-to-resist classic – may seem simple enough but it takes skill to achieve a light, fluffy sponge base, a perfectly smooth, non-rubbery layer of orange jelly and a nicely finished melted chocolate topping.

Exquisite mirror-glazed cakes – layers of a light genoise sponge filled and then very smoothly coated with an ultra-shiny icing – are a test for any keen baker. Working with the gelatine glaze to get the finish just right, as well as baking a fine sponge, are challenging. There's a dark chocolate-glazed Ultimate Indulgence Mirror-glaze Cake (page 72) and a Praline and White Chocolate Mirror-glaze Cake (page 76) for you to try.

There's more chocolate in the very adult (and appealingly easy) Bitter Chocolate Stout Cake (page 40), a creamed sponge infused with the malty flavour of chocolate milk stout. For sheer prettiness, plus the chance to show off some piping, it's hard to beat the Little Pink Rose Cakes on page 56, where individual truffle cakes are finished with delicate swirls of fresh raspberry buttercream. Tiramisu, that much-loved Italian dessert, is transformed into a beautiful, easy-to-slice cake (see page 68). It still has the traditional coffee- and brandy-soaked sponge layers and mascarpone cream, and is decorated with an elegant white-chocolate ribbon.

Our Black and White Celebration Cake (page 64) is the real showpiece here: a perfect and delicious blank canvas for you to design your own fabulous decorations. The dark chocolate sponges are coated with a white-chocolate Swiss-meringue buttercream, which will take piping, chocolate work, moulded flowers, candles or, as we have done, bunting made from edible rice paper. Make it for a very special occasion to delight and impress your guests.

GREEK LEMON-YOGHURT LOAF CAKE

A slice of this quick and easily mixed loaf cake - you just need a bowl and wooden spoon - is perfect with a cup of tea. The sponge has a bright yellow crumb with a moist texture and tangy flavour thanks to the inclusion of thick creamy yoghurt and light olive oil plus lemon zest. While the cake is still hot, a lemon and yoghurt glaze is added to give a shiny finish with a slight crunch.

serves 8

150g plain flour
2 teaspoons baking powder
good pinch of salt
50g ground almonds
200g caster sugar
finely grated zest of 1 large
    unwaxed lemon
3 medium eggs, at room
    temperature
125ml Greek-style yoghurt
125ml mild light olive oil

FOR THE LEMON GLAZE
125g icing sugar, sifted
finely grated zest of 1 large
    unwaxed lemon
1–1½ tablespoons Greek-style
    yoghurt

you will need
1 x 450g loaf tin, about
19 x 12.5 x 7.5cm, greased
with butter and lined with
a long strip of baking paper*

1. Heat the oven to 180°C/350°F/gas 4. Sift the flour, baking powder, salt and ground almonds into a mixing bowl (tip in any almonds remaining in the sieve). Stir in the sugar and lemon zest, then make a well in the mixture.

2. Combine the eggs, yoghurt and oil in a measuring jug and beat well with a fork until well mixed. Pour into the well in the bowl, then beat everything together with a wooden spoon until thoroughly combined.

3. Scrape the mixture into the prepared tin, spreading evenly and making sure the corners are well filled. Bake in the heated oven for 55–65 minutes until well risen and a deep golden brown; a skewer inserted into the centre of the cake should come out clean*.

4. Towards the end of the baking time make the lemon glaze so it will be ready when you need it. Sift the icing sugar into a bowl. Mix in the lemon zest, then stir in enough yoghurt to make a smooth, shiny glaze with the consistency of double cream.

5. As soon as the cake is ready, remove from the oven and set the tin on a wire rack. Leave the cake to firm up for 5 minutes. Run a round-bladed knife around the inside of the tin to loosen the loaf, then carefully lift it out, using the ends of the lining paper strip, and set the cake on the wire rack. Place a plate underneath the rack to catch drips. Spoon the glaze over the hot cake, letting the glaze slowly drip down the sides. Leave until the cake is cold and the glaze has set.

6. Serve cut in thick slices. Store, wrapped in foil or baking paper, in an airtight container and eat within 4 days – the flavours and aromas will be even more pronounced a day or so after baking.

FRESH MANGO LOAF CAKE

This dairy-free cake is packed with fresh fruit: diced mango, crushed bananas and lime as well as soft-dried cranberries and coconut, so you don't need to add much sugar. The lime water icing is optional. For the best texture pick a mango that is just about ripe because a very soft or juicy one will give a slightly heavy and damp (but still delicious) result.

serves 12 | dairy free

50g desiccated coconut
1 medium-large mango, just ripe
finely grated zest and juice
    of 1 large unwaxed lime
250g peeled, very ripe bananas
    (about 3 medium)
300g plain flour
good pinch of fine sea salt
1 teaspoon baking powder
1 teaspoon bicarbonate of soda
100g light muscovado sugar
50g soft-dried cranberries
175ml sunflower oil
3 medium eggs, at room
    temperature

FOR THE ICING AND DECORATION
(OPTIONAL)
100g icing sugar
finely grated zest and juice of
    1 large unwaxed lime
soft-dried mango pieces OR
    small curls of lime peel

you will need
1 x 900g loaf tin, about
26 x 12.5 x 7.5cm, greased
with sunflower oil and
lined with a long strip
of baking paper*

1. Heat the oven to 180°C/350°F/gas 4. Tip the desiccated coconut into a small tin and toast in the oven for 3–4 minutes until lightly coloured – keep an eye on the coconut to be sure it doesn't get too dark. Leave to cool.

2. Meanwhile, peel the mango and cut the flesh away from the stone. Cut the flesh into 1cm cubes. Weigh out 275g (save any leftovers for a fruit salad or smoothie). Put the weighed mango into a bowl and add the lime zest and 1 tablespoon of the squeezed juice. Mix well, then set aside. In another bowl, mash the bananas coarsely with a fork so some lumpy bits remain.

3. Sift the flour, salt, baking powder and bicarbonate of soda into a large mixing bowl. Stir in the sugar (press out the lumps with your fingers), cooled toasted coconut and cranberries. Make a well in the mixture.

4. Combine the sunflower oil and eggs in a jug and beat together with a fork, then pour into the well in the flour mixture. Give the ingredients in the bowl a couple of stirs with a plastic spatula or wooden spoon, then add the mango/lime mixture and the bananas. Stir gently to mix everything together until thoroughly combined, without beating or over-working the mixture.

5. Scrape the mixture into the prepared tin and spread evenly, making sure the corners are well filled. Bake in the heated oven for 1–1¼ hours until well risen and golden brown; a skewer inserted into the centre should come out clean* (test in several places in case you hit a lump of fruit).

6. Remove from the oven and set the tin on a wire rack. Leave the cake to cool and firm up for 20 minutes. Run a round-bladed knife around the inside of the tin to loosen the cake, then carefully lift it out using the ends of the lining paper. Set the cake on the wire rack and leave until cold.

7. If you want to ice the cake, sift the icing sugar into a bowl and stir in the lime zest, followed by 1½–2 tablespoons lime juice – enough to make a smooth, spreadable icing. Spread over the top of the cake and decorate with the mango pieces or small curls of fresh lime peel. Leave to set.

8. Cut into thick slices to serve. Best eaten the same or the next day (store in an airtight container in a cool spot but not the fridge).

ST CLEMENT'S ORANGE AND LEMON DRIZZLE CAKE

Two layers of classic creamed lemon sponge are spiked with lemon drizzle, then filled with a tangy orange curd and finished with a lemon glacé icing and home-made candied peel decoration.

serves 12

FOR THE SPONGE
450g unsalted butter, softened
450g caster sugar
finely grated zest of 4 medium
  unwaxed lemons
8 medium eggs, at room
  temperature, beaten to mix
450g self-raising flour

FOR THE CANDIED PEEL
1 medium unwaxed lemon
1 large orange

300ml water
200g caster sugar, plus extra
  for sprinkling

FOR THE DRIZZLE SYRUP
75g caster sugar
juice of 6 medium lemons

FOR THE ORANGE CURD
6 medium egg yolks, at room
  temperature
175g caster sugar

finely grated zest of 3 large
  oranges
300ml orange juice
2 teaspoons lemon juice
120g unsalted butter, at room
  temperature, diced

FOR THE LEMON ICING
300g icing sugar
about 5 tablespoons lemon juice

you will need
2 x 23cm springclip tins,
greased with butter
and base-lined*

1. Heat the oven to 180°C/350°F/gas 4. To make the sponge, put the butter into a large mixing bowl, or the bowl of a free-standing electric mixer fitted with the whisk attachment, and beat until creamy with a hand-held electric whisk, or the whisk attachment. Add the sugar and zest and beat in thoroughly, scraping down the sides of the bowl from time to time, until the mixture is light and fluffy.

2. Gradually add the eggs, beating well after each addition, and scraping down the sides as before – it's a good idea to add a tablespoon of the weighed flour with each of the last 3 additions of egg. Sift the rest of the flour into the bowl and gently fold* in using a plastic spatula.

3. Transfer the mixture to the prepared tins, dividing it equally, and spread evenly. Bake in the heated oven for about 35 minutes until well risen, golden brown and springy when gently pressed in the centre; a skewer inserted into the centre should come out clean*.

4. While the cakes are baking, make the candied peel and the drizzle. For the candied peel, carefully remove strips of peel from the lemon and orange using a vegetable peeler – leave as much white pith behind on the fruit as possible (squeeze the juice from the fruit to use in the curd).

5. Trim the peel to neaten the edges, then put it into a medium pan of cold water. Bring to the boil and simmer for about 10 minutes until tender. Drain. Put the measured water and sugar into the empty pan and stir over low heat until the sugar has dissolved. Bring to the boil, then add the drained peel. Simmer for 20–30 minutes until the peel looks translucent. Drain the peel thoroughly, then spread out on a sheet of baking paper and dust with caster sugar. Leave until cold.

6. To make the drizzle, stir the sugar with the lemon juice in a bowl until dissolved. Set aside.

7. When the cakes are baked, run a round-bladed knife around the inside of each tin, unclip the side and turn out the sponge on to a wire rack. Place a plate underneath the rack to catch drips. Prick the sponges well with a cocktail stick, then spoon over the drizzle syrup. Leave to cool.

8. Meanwhile, make the orange curd. Put the egg yolks, sugar, orange zest and juice, and lemon juice into a medium-sized heavy-based pan and whisk with a hand wire whisk until thoroughly combined. Set over low heat and stir constantly with a wooden spoon until the sugar has completely dissolved, then turn up the heat to medium and continue stirring as the mixture comes to a simmer. Keep stirring as the mixture simmers and thickens to a consistency that will coat the back of the spoon – this will take 8–10 minutes; if necessary, move the pan on and off the heat so the mixture keeps to a gentle simmer. Remove the pan from the heat and gradually stir in the butter. Transfer to a heatproof bowl, press a sheet of clingfilm on the surface (to prevent a skin from forming) and leave to cool, then chill until firm enough to spread easily.

9. To make the icing, sift the icing sugar into a mixing bowl and gradually stir in enough lemon juice to make a smooth, thick but flowing icing. Keep covered until needed.

10. To assemble the cake, set one sponge, crust-side down, on a plate or board. Spread the orange curd over the surface, then set the other sponge on top, crust-side up. Spoon the icing over the top and allow it to flow gently to the edge and just over it. Add the candied peel decoration. Leave to firm up before serving.

LEMON AND POPPYSEED DRIZZLE CAKE

This all-in-one sponge is baked in a fluted ring mould or bundt tin, with lemon syrup drizzled on to the base as well as the top of the cake, making it extra flavoursome and moist. The poppyseeds add a nice and just-bitter crunch.

serves 8–10

FOR THE SPONGE
250g self-raising flour
2 teaspoons baking powder
250g salted butter, softened
250g caster sugar
50g ground almonds
4 medium eggs, at room
 temperature, beaten to mix
finely grated zest of 4 medium
 unwaxed lemons
3 tablespoons poppyseeds

FOR THE SYRUP
125ml lemon juice
80g caster sugar
2 tablespoons limoncello OR
 extra lemon juice

FOR THE LEMON DECORATION
1 medium unwaxed lemon
caster sugar, for sprinkling

FOR THE ICING
125g icing sugar, sifted
1 tablespoon limoncello OR extra
 lemon juice
about 1 tablespoon lemon juice

TO FINISH
2 tablespoons toasted flaked
 almonds
poppyseeds, for sprinkling

you will need
1 x 23–24cm fluted, deep,
non-stick ring mould/
bundt tin, well greased
with non-stick baking
spray or butter; a baking
sheet

1. Heat the oven to 190°C/375°F/gas 5. Sift the flour and baking powder into a large bowl. Add the soft butter, sugar, ground almonds, beaten eggs, lemon zest and poppyseeds. Whisk using a hand-held electric whisk just until the mixture is very creamy and smooth – start slowly, then gradually increase the speed, and scrape down the sides of the bowl from time to time. Check the consistency – the mixture should drop easily off a wooden spoon when you give it a little shake. If the mixture is too stiff, beat in boiling water a teaspoon at a time.

2. Transfer the mixture to the prepared mould/tin and spread evenly. Tap the tin on the worktop to settle the contents, then bake in the heated oven for about 35 minutes until the cake is golden and starts to shrink away from the sides of the tin; a skewer inserted into the sponge halfway between the sides and the central funnel should come out clean*.

3. While the cake is baking make the syrup for the drizzle. Put the lemon juice and sugar in a small pan and heat gently, stirring frequently, until the sugar has dissolved. Turn up the heat slightly and simmer for about a minute until syrupy. Stir in the limoncello (or extra juice). Bring back to the boil, then remove from the heat.

4. Thinly slice the lemon for the decoration into neat discs, discarding the ends. Pick 6 discs that look a similar size. Gently remove any pips, then lay the slices in the lemon drizzle syrup. Reheat the syrup and simmer for 1–2 minutes until the lemon slices soften. Remove from the heat. Lift out the lemon slices with a slotted spoon or kitchen tongs (keep the syrup hot) and drain well on kitchen paper, then place the slices on a piece of baking paper set on a baking sheet. When cool enough to handle, make a cut or snip in each, from the outer edge into the centre, using a small knife or kitchen scissors, then twist the ends of the cut in opposite directions so each lemon slice looks a bit like a bow. Set aside.

5. When the cake is ready, remove from the oven and make holes with a skewer over the top surface (which will become the bottom of the cake). Brush or spoon about a third of the hot drizzle syrup over the cake. Leave to cool for 5 minutes, then turn the cake out on to a wire rack. Place a plate underneath to catch any drips. Gently prick holes all over what is now the top of the cake (these will eventually be covered with icing), then brush or spoon the rest of the syrup over the whole cake. Allow to cool completely. Reduce the oven temperature to its lowest setting.

6. Sprinkle the twisted lemon slices with a little caster sugar. Place the baking sheet in the oven and leave the slices to dry out for 20–30 minutes. Watch carefully as you want the slices to be chewy not crisp. Leave to cool.

7. When the cake is cold, transfer it to a plate or a board. Mix the icing sugar with the limoncello (or juice) and enough of the lemon juice to make a thick icing that is just fluid. Pour or spoon over the top of the cake, encouraging the icing to drip down the sides a little. Decorate with the lemon slices, toasted flaked almonds and poppyseeds.

HONEY LOAF CAKE

This very simple melt-and-mix cake is sure to become a regular addition to the tea table. For the best taste, pick a well-flavoured honey, rather than a bland blend, because the cake is dense with honey - in the mixture, added to infuse the cake straight from the oven, and again in the easy cream-cheese icing. Cut it into thick slices to show off the golden sponge, dark crust and white icing.

serves 10

275g clear honey
225g unsalted butter
125g light muscovado sugar
300g self-raising flour
good pinch of fine sea salt
2 teaspoons ground ginger
3 medium eggs, at room
   temperature, beaten to mix

FOR THE GLAZE
3 tablespoons clear honey
1 tablespoon water

FOR THE ICING
50g full-fat cream cheese
1 tablespoon clear honey
165g icing sugar
few drops of lemon juice

you will need
1 x 900g loaf tin, about 26 x
12.5 x 7.5cm, greased with
butter and lined with a long
strip of baking paper*

1. Heat the oven to 180°C/350°F/gas 4. Weigh the honey, butter and sugar into a medium pan. Set over low heat and leave until melted and smooth, stirring occasionally. Remove the pan from the heat.

2. Sift the flour, salt and ground ginger into a mixing bowl and make a well in the middle. Pour the melted honey mixture into the well in the flour, then add the beaten eggs. Beat everything together with a wooden spoon to make a smooth, runny mixture like a thick batter.

3. Scrape the mixture into the tin, easing it into the corners. Bake in the heated oven for 50–55 minutes until the cake is a rich brown on top and a skewer inserted into the centre comes out clean*. Start checking after 45 minutes and, if necessary, lightly cover the tin with a sheet of baking paper or foil to prevent the top of the cake from getting too dark.

4. Towards the end of the baking time, make the glaze. Gently heat the honey with the water until smooth, then bring to the boil. Remove from the heat and keep hot (or reheat when needed).

5. When the cake is ready, remove the tin from the oven and set it on a wire rack. Prick the cake all over with a cocktail stick or skewer, then brush or spoon the honey glaze over the top, allowing it to seep into the sponge and trickle down the sides. Leave to cool and firm up for 20 minutes before carefully removing the cake from the tin (use the ends of the lining paper to help you) and setting it on the rack. Leave until cold.

6. Meanwhile, make the honey icing. Beat the cream cheese with the honey in a mixing bowl using a wooden spoon or a hand-held electric whisk until thoroughly combined. Sift the icing sugar into the bowl and beat in (use slow speed with the whisk). Continue beating until smooth and fluid like double cream – add a few drops of lemon juice, if necessary. Cover the bowl and chill for about 1 hour until the icing is firm enough to spread.

7. Spread the icing over the top of the cake, allowing it to gently creep over the edges. Leave to firm up before transferring the cake to a serving plate. Store in an airtight container and eat within 4 days.

BITTER CHOCOLATE STOUT CAKE

Here a simple creamed sponge cake mixture is turned into an adults-only chocolate cake,
with chocolate milk stout (or porter) adding a smooth, dark malty flavour. Malted-milk powder –
the kind used for bedtime drinks – boosts the slightly sweet, rich taste of the stout.
As always with chocolate cakes, this one is even better a day or so after baking.
Delicious with a cup of coffee after dinner.

serves 10-12

FOR THE SPONGE
40g cocoa powder
1 tablespoon malted-milk drink
   powder (use 'original', not diet
   or flavoured versions)
150ml chocolate milk stout
   OR porter
150g unsalted butter, softened
120g caster sugar
120g light muscovado sugar
2 medium eggs, at room
   temperature, beaten to mix

4 tablespoons buttermilk, at room
   temperature
250g self-raising flour
¼ teaspoon bicarbonate of soda
good pinch of fine sea salt

**FOR THE CHOCOLATE FILLING
AND FROSTING**
85g dark chocolate (about 70%
   cocoa solids), broken up
1½ tablespoons malted-milk
   drink powder ('original')

2 teaspoons cocoa powder
2 tablespoons boiling water
115g unsalted butter, softened
25g light muscovado sugar
75g icing sugar
good pinch of sea salt flakes, or
   to taste

TO FINISH
15g dark chocolate (about 70%
   cocoa solids)

you will need
2 x 20.5cm round, deep
sandwich tins, greased with
butter and base-lined*

1. Heat the oven to 180°C/350°F/gas 4. Measure the cocoa and malted-milk powders into a small pan, add the milk stout and set over low heat. Whisk constantly with a small hand wire whisk until the mixture is smooth and comes to the boil – take care it doesn't catch on the base of the pan. Remove from the heat and leave until cooled to room temperature.

2. Meanwhile, put the softened butter into a mixing bowl, or the bowl of a free-standing electric mixer fitted with the whisk attachment. Beat well with a hand-held electric whisk, or the whisk attachment, until creamy and mayonnaise-like. Scrape down the side of the bowl, then beat in the caster sugar. As soon as it is thoroughly amalgamated, beat in the muscovado sugar (press out any lumps first). Once combined, scrape down the side of the bowl again, then beat for 2 minutes to make a soft, light creamed mixture.

3. Gradually add the eggs, beating well after each addition and scraping down the side of the bowl from time to time. Beat in the buttermilk a tablespoon at a time, adding a tablespoon of the weighed flour with the last 2 additions. Sift the remaining flour with the bicarbonate of soda and salt into the bowl. Add the cooled cocoa mixture. Mix in using the whisk on its lowest speed, stopping as soon as the mixture is very smooth.

4. Divide the mixture equally between the 2 sandwich tins and spread evenly. Bake in the heated oven for 20–25 minutes until the sponges are well risen and springy when gently pressed in the centre*. Remove from the oven and run a round-bladed knife around the inside of each tin to loosen the sponge, then turn it out on to a wire rack and leave to cool.

5. When the sponges have cooled to room temperature, make the chocolate mixture for the filling and frosting. Gently melt the chocolate*, then leave to cool until needed. Put the malted-milk powder and cocoa powder into a small heatproof bowl, add the boiling water and stir to make a smooth paste. Leave to cool.

6. Beat the butter in a mixing bowl until very creamy using a wooden spoon or hand-held electric whisk, then beat in the muscovado sugar (press out any lumps first). Add the cooled melted chocolate and beat well, then beat in the cooled cocoa liquid. Sift the icing sugar into the bowl and beat, slowly at first, until the mixture is very smooth and light in texture. Sprinkle over the salt and stir in.

7. Now set one sponge, crust-side down, on a serving plate. Spread over half the chocolate mixture. Set the other sponge on top, crust-side up. Spread and swirl the rest of the chocolate mixture over the surface. Grate the dark chocolate on top – or decorate with chocolate curls shaved off with a vegetable peeler. Leave the frosting to firm up for at least 2 hours before cutting the cake. Store in an airtight container and eat within 4 days.

CARIBBEAN RUM CAKE

Toasted slices of fresh pineapple make a vivid, attractive topping for this golden sponge cake. A dark rum syrup, spooned over the cake after baking, adds a subtle kick without making the sponge heavy or soggy. Serve it with crème Chantilly for dessert, or take it on a picnic.

serves 12

1. Heat the oven to 180°C/350°F/gas 4. Break the eggs into a large mixing bowl, or the bowl of a free-standing electric mixer fitted with the whisk attachment. Whisk with a hand-held electric whisk, or the whisk attachment, for a few seconds until combined. Gradually whisk in the sugar, followed by the vanilla. Now whisk, on full speed, for several minutes until the mixture is very thick and pale and has reached the ribbon stage*.

2. Continuing to whisk, slowly pour in the cream followed by the rum – the mixture will lose some volume and become thinner. Sift the flour and salt into the bowl and carefully fold* in using a large metal spoon or plastic spatula. Trickle the butter into the bowl around the sides and gently fold in. When the mixture is thoroughly combined, transfer to the prepared tin and spread out evenly so the corners are well filled.

3. Bake in the heated oven for 40–45 minutes until the cake is well risen and a rich golden brown; a skewer inserted into the centre should come out clean*. Check after 35 minutes and, if the top is browning too quickly, cover it loosely with a sheet of baking paper or foil.

4. While the cake is baking make the soaking syrup. Put the water, lemon peel and sugar into a small pan and heat gently, stirring occasionally, until the sugar has completely dissolved. Bring to the boil and simmer for 30 seconds, then remove from the heat and set aside to infuse until needed.

5. When the cake is ready, remove from the oven and set the tin on a wire rack. Leave to cool and firm up for 10 minutes before gently unmoulding. Peel off the lining paper and set the cake on the rack placed over a large plate (to catch the drips). Reheat the syrup until boiling, then remove the strip of lemon peel and stir in the rum. Prick the cake all over with a skewer or cocktail stick, then spoon the hot syrup over the top, letting it trickle into the holes and down the sides. Leave until completely cold.

6. To make the toasted pineapple, heat the grill to maximum and line the grill pan with foil. Peel the fruit, cut it into quarters lengthways and cut out the core. Cut the quarters across into slices about 4mm thick and pat dry between several sheets of kitchen paper.

4 medium eggs, at room
  temperature
285g golden caster sugar
1½ teaspoons vanilla bean paste
100ml double cream, at room
  temperature
2 tablespoons dark rum
225g self-raising flour
¼ teaspoon fine sea salt
150g unsalted butter, melted and
  cooled until barely warm

FOR THE SOAKING SYRUP
75ml water
a long strip of peel from an
  unwaxed lemon
50g golden caster sugar
4 tablespoons dark rum, or
  to taste

FOR THE TOASTED PINEAPPLE
1 small, ripe pineapple
icing sugar, for dusting

TO SERVE
Crème Chantilly (see page 18)

you will need
1 x 20.5cm square, deep
cake tin, greased with
butter and lined*

7. Arrange the pineapple slices in a single layer on the foil-lined grill pan (you may have to work in 2 batches) and dust heavily with icing sugar. Slide under the grill, as close to the heat as possible, and toast until the icing sugar bubbles and the pineapple becomes flecked with golden and dark brown patches. Using a palette knife, quickly transfer the slices to the top of the cake (if you leave them to cool on the foil they will become difficult to dislodge) – start at one corner of the cake and slightly overlap the slices in a diagonal pattern.

8. Once all the toasted pineapple slices are on the cake, spoon over any rum syrup that has collected on the plate under the rack. Serve the same or the next day with crème Chantilly.

PRALINE-TOPPED TRAYCAKE

Here a simple all-in-one creamed-sponge mix is turned into a one-slice-isn't-enough cake by adding a surprise hidden layer of flavour and a crunchy caramel-nut topping. The dark seam running through the centre is made from dark muscovado sugar, coffee and cinnamon, and the impressive topping is a quick all-in-one praline, made in a frying pan - piece of cake!

cuts into 20 squares

1. Heat the oven to 180°C/350°F/gas 4. Put the butter, milk, flour, salt and sugar into a mixing bowl, or the bowl of a free-standing electric mixer fitted with the whisk attachment. In a small bowl beat the eggs with the vanilla using a fork until thoroughly combined. Pour into the mixing bowl and beat everything together with a wooden spoon or a hand-held electric whisk, or the whisk attachment of the mixer, until very smooth, scraping down the sides of the bowl a couple of times.

2. Spoon two-thirds of the cake mixture into the prepared tin and spread evenly, making sure the corners are well filled.

3. Make the filling mixture by stirring together the sugar, cinnamon and coffee granules/powder. Scatter evenly over the cake mixture in the tin. Spoon the remaining mixture over the top in small dollops, then gently spread to cover the filling evenly – an offset palette knife works best for this.

4. Bake in the heated oven for 30–35 minutes until golden and a skewer inserted into the centre comes out clean*. Remove the tin from the oven and set it on a wire rack. Run a round-bladed knife around the inside of the tin to loosen the cake, then leave it to cool before turning out.

5. To make the topping, dissolve the coffee in the boiling water, then pour into a non-stick frying pan. Add the icing sugar and stir well until smooth, then add the almonds. Set the pan over medium heat and cook for 1–2 minutes, carefully moving the pan back and forth constantly to swirl the mixture, rather than stirring it, until it bubbles up and forms a light caramel. Pour the mixture over the cold cake and, working quickly, spread it evenly over the top. Leave to set before cutting into squares. Store in an airtight container. Best eaten within 48 hours.

FOR THE SPONGE
225g unsalted butter, softened
2 tablespoons milk, at room temperature
225g self-raising flour
good pinch of fine sea salt
225g caster sugar
4 medium eggs, at room temperature
½ teaspoon vanilla extract

FOR THE FILLING
85g dark muscovado sugar
1 teaspoon ground cinnamon
2 teaspoons instant coffee (granules or powder)

FOR THE TOPPING
½ teaspoon instant coffee (granules or powder)
2 tablespoons boiling water
150g icing sugar, sifted
50g flaked almonds

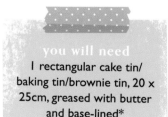

you will need
1 rectangular cake tin/ baking tin/brownie tin, 20 x 25cm, greased with butter and base-lined*

RASPBERRY, RHUBARB AND CUSTARD DRIZZLE CAKE

A bundt drizzle cake with a difference! This is a gluten-free version as it is made with ground pistachios, polenta and ground almonds instead of flour, and it's flavoured with fresh raspberries and pink rhubarb. As a final touch the cake is injected with a creamy egg custard and decorated with a rhubarb-pink glacé icing and frosted berries.

serves 10 | gluten free

FOR THE RHUBARB AND SYRUP
250g young, thin stems pink
  rhubarb, cut into 1cm chunks
50g golden caster sugar
100ml water
finely grated zest and juice of
  2 unwaxed limes

FOR THE SPONGE
100g unsalted pistachio nuts
  (shelled)
100g polenta or fine cornmeal
100g ground almonds
1½ teaspoons baking powder

good pinch of fine sea salt
200g unsalted butter, softened
200g golden caster sugar
3 medium eggs, at room
  temperature, beaten to mix
200g fresh raspberries

FOR THE CUSTARD
300ml double cream
50ml full-fat/whole milk
1 teaspoon vanilla bean paste
2 medium egg yolks, at room
  temperature
25g golden caster sugar

FOR THE DECORATION
50g unsalted pistachio nuts
  (shelled)
1 medium egg white
100g white caster sugar
100g fresh raspberries
9–10 fresh mint leaves
finely grated zest of 1 lime

FOR THE ICING
200g icing sugar
about 1 tablespoon fresh lime juice

---

you will need
1 x 20cm fluted, deep,
non-stick ring mould/bundt
tin, greased with butter;
a squeezy icing bottle
OR small disposable piping
bag fitted with a small
round nozzle

1. Heat the oven to 180°C/350°F/gas 4. Start by poaching the rhubarb so it has time to cool. Set aside 50g of the rhubarb chunks for later, and tip the rest into a medium pan. Add the caster sugar, water and lime juice (keep the zest for the sponge) and cook over low heat, stirring occasionally, until the sugar has dissolved. Turn up the heat slightly and simmer for 8–10 minutes until the rhubarb is just tender when pierced with the tip of a knife.

2. Using a slotted spoon, remove three-quarters of the poached rhubarb to a sieve and leave to cool and drain thoroughly. Simmer the rest of the rhubarb and syrup, stirring frequently, for about 5 minutes until it has formed a fairly thick purée. Leave this to cool.

3. Next make the sponge. Tip the pistachios and polenta into a food processor and blitz until the nuts are finely ground. Add the ground almonds, baking powder and salt and 'pulse' a couple of times until combined.

4. Put the softened butter and grated lime zest into a mixing bowl, or the bowl of a free-standing electric mixer fitted with the whisk attachment. Beat

well using a hand-held electric whisk, or the whisk attachment, then add the sugar and continue beating, scraping down the sides of the bowl from time to time, until the mixture is light and fluffy. Reduce the speed to medium and beat in the ground nut mixture, a heaped tablespoonful at a time, alternately with the beaten eggs. Using a large metal spoon or plastic spatula, fold* in the cooled poached rhubarb and the raspberries.

5. Transfer the mixture to the prepared mould/tin and spread evenly. Using the tip of a small knife, gently push the reserved chunks of uncooked rhubarb into the mixture so they are evenly distributed. Bake in the heated oven for about 1 hour until golden brown and starting to shrink away from the sides of the tin; a skewer inserted into the sponge halfway between the side and the central funnel should come out clean* (test in several places in case you hit a chunk of fruit). Check after 50 minutes and, if necessary, cover the top of the cake with a sheet of baking paper to avoid it over-browning. Remove the tin from the oven and set on a wire rack. Leave the sponge to cool and firm up for about 20 minutes before turning out on to the rack (the cake should still be warm when you inject the custard).

6. While the cake is baking make the custard. Heat the cream and milk with the vanilla paste in a heavy-based medium pan. As soon as the creamy milk starts to simmer, remove from the heat and set aside to cool slightly. Put the egg yolks and sugar into a heatproof bowl set on a damp cloth (to prevent wobbling) and whisk with a hand wire whisk until very pale. Slowly pour the hot cream mixture on to the yolks in a thin, steady stream while whisking constantly. As soon as the mixture is smoothly amalgamated, tip it back into

the pan. Set over low heat and stir the custard constantly with a wooden spoon until it thickens enough to just coat the back of the spoon – don't allow it to come anywhere near boiling point or the eggs will scramble. Strain into a heatproof jug, then press a sheet of clingfilm on the surface (to prevent a skin from forming). Leave to cool, then chill.

7. To make the decorations, add the whole pistachios to the rhubarb purée and stir until coated. Remove the nuts with a slotted spoon and leave to drain thoroughly on a plate. Whisk the egg white in a small bowl until frothy, and tip the sugar on to a large plate. One at a time, carefully brush the raspberries and mint leaves with a thin coating of egg white, then roll/coat in the sugar, shaking off the excess. Leave to dry on a sheet of baking paper. Once set, chop about 4 of the sugared mint leaves; leave the rest whole.

8. To make the icing, sift the icing sugar into a bowl and add 1 tablespoon of the rhubarb purée. Mix gently, adding enough lime juice to make a smooth, pourable consistency. Keep covered until needed.

9. Using a skewer, prick holes all over the top and sides of the cake. Gently warm the remaining rhubarb purée, then spoon it over the cake so it trickles into the holes. Leave for 5 minutes for the purée to be absorbed.

10. Spoon about a quarter of the custard into the icing bottle or piping bag. Inject or pipe custard into the cake around the top edge at regular intervals. Leave the cake to cool completely. Pour the remaining custard into a jug.

11. To decorate the cake, drizzle the icing over the top so it flows down the sides and along the grooves. Decorate with the glazed pistachios, frosted raspberries and the whole and chopped mint leaves. Finish with a sprinkling of lime zest. Serve with the custard.

TRIPLE GINGER CAKE

Lighter than the traditional style of gingerbread loaf, thanks to the addition of buttermilk, this dark, moist ring cake is rich and warm with ginger - root, spice and stem in syrup.

serves 10-12

60g piece fresh root ginger
170g black treacle
175g unsalted butter, softened
125g dark muscovado sugar
3 medium eggs, at room
   temperature, beaten to mix
250g plain flour
good pinch of fine sea salt
1 teaspoon bicarbonate of soda
1 tablespoon ground ginger
1 teaspoon ground cinnamon
½ teaspoon ground mixed spice
225ml buttermilk
3 lumps (about 60g) stem ginger
   in syrup, drained

FOR THE GINGER CREAM
FROSTING

200g full-fat cream cheese
50g unsalted butter, softened
50g icing sugar, sifted
2 tablespoons ginger syrup
   (from the jar)
3 lumps (about 60g) stem ginger
   in syrup, drained

you will need
1 x 20cm fluted,
deep ring mould, greased
with butter

1. Heat the oven to 180°C/350°F/gas 4. Peel the root ginger and finely grate it. Measure 2 rounded tablespoons into a small pan. Add the treacle, then set the pan over low heat and warm gently, stirring occasionally, until liquid. Remove from the heat and leave to cool.

2. Put the softened butter into a large mixing bowl, or the bowl of a free-standing electric mixer fitted with the whisk attachment. Add the muscovado sugar (press out any small lumps). Beat well with a hand-held electric whisk, or the whisk attachment, until very light in texture, scraping down the sides of the bowl from time to time. Gradually add the eggs, beating well after each addition – this mixture curdles easily so add a tablespoon of the weighed flour with each of the last 2 additions of egg.

3. Sift the rest of the flour, the salt, bicarbonate of soda, ground ginger, ground cinnamon and ground mixed spice into the bowl. Add the cooled treacle mixture and the buttermilk. Mix everything together with a wooden spoon or plastic spatula until roughly combined. Chop the stem ginger into medium-small chunks and add to the bowl, then stir the mixture very well so there are no streaks (check at the bottom of the bowl).

4. Pour and scrape the mixture into the prepared tin and spread evenly. Bake in the heated oven for 40–45 minutes until well risen and a skewer inserted into the cake halfway between the sides and the centre funnel comes out clean*. Leave to cool and firm up for about 5 minutes before running a round-bladed knife around the inside of the tin to loosen the cake. Turn it out on to a wire rack and leave to cool completely. (The cake can be stored in an airtight container for up to 2 days before finishing.)

5. To make the ginger cream frosting, put the cream cheese into a mixing bowl and microwave for 10 seconds to soften it. Cream the softened butter with the icing sugar in another mixing bowl using a wooden spoon until pale and fluffy. Add the softened cream cheese and the ginger syrup and beat well until very smooth and light. Finely chop 1½ lumps of the stem ginger and mix into the frosting. Cover and chill for about 20 minutes until firm but still spreadable. Roughly chop the rest of the stem ginger.

6. To finish the cake, spread and swirl the ginger cream frosting over the top of the cake and decorate with the roughly chopped ginger. Store in an airtight container at cool room temperature and eat within 3 days.

ITALIAN PEAR AND PINE NUT RING CAKE

The deliciously light, moist and very buttery crumb of this pretty ring cake is thanks to whipped cream - there's no butter in the mixture. Fresh diced pears, dark chocolate and pine nuts are folded into the delicate mixture just before baking in the pine nut-lined tin. With some crème Chantilly and a glass of Marsala or dessert wine, it makes a sophisticated dessert.

serves 12

FOR THE TIN
15g very soft butter
3 tablespoons pine nuts

FOR THE CAKE
2 medium just-ripe pears
60g pine nuts
50g dark chocolate (about 70% cocoa solids)
225ml double cream, well chilled
4 medium eggs, at room temperature
3 drops of almond extract
270g caster sugar
250g plain flour
good pinch of fine sea salt
2 teaspoons baking powder

TO FINISH
icing sugar, for dusting
Crème Chantilly (see page 18), to serve (optional)

you will need
1 x 20cm fluted, deep ring mould

1. Heat the oven to 180°C/350°F/gas 4. Using a pastry brush, coat the inside of the ring mould with the very soft butter – make sure the central funnel is thoroughly greased. Scatter the pine nuts over the base and sides, then put the mould in the fridge to firm up – this chilling will help to prevent the nuts from becoming dislodged when you add the cake mixture.

2. Meanwhile, peel, quarter and core the pears, then cut into 4–5mm chunks. Tip into a bowl and mix in the pine nuts. Chop the chocolate into chunks about the same size as the pears and mix in. Set aside for now.

3. Pour the cream into a mixing bowl and whip* with a hand-held electric whisk until it will stand in soft peaks. Set aside. Wash the whisk.

4. Break the eggs into another larger mixing bowl, or the bowl of a free-standing electric mixer fitted with the whisk attachment, and add the almond extract. Whisk with the hand-held whisk, or the whisk attachment, until frothy. Add the sugar and whisk on full speed until the mixture is very pale and thick and has reached the ribbon stage*.

5. Sift the flour, salt and baking powder into the whisked egg mixture and gently fold* in with a large metal spoon or plastic spatula. Once thoroughly combined, carefully fold in the whipped cream. When you can no longer see any blobs or streaks of cream, add the pear mixture and lightly fold in – at this point it's important not to overmix, so stop folding as soon as the pieces are almost evenly distributed.

6. Spoon the mixture into the mould and spread evenly. Bake in the heated oven for about 45 minutes until well risen and golden brown; a skewer inserted in the cake halfway between the side and the centre funnel should come out clean* (test in several spots in case you hit a chunk of pear).

7. Remove from the oven and set the mould on a wire rack. Leave the cake to firm up for about 5 minutes, then carefully turn out on to the rack and leave to cool completely. Dust with icing sugar just before serving. Store in an airtight container and eat the same or the next day.

LITTLE PINK ROSE CAKES

These tiny, ultra-glamorous chocolate sponges are made from a rich truffle-cake mixture, so they match up with the deeply flavoured, fresh raspberry buttercream and hold up well when split and filled. The same cakes (as unsandwiched layers) can also be served as petits fours or as part of a buffet table.

makes 12 (or 24 petits fours)

FOR THE CHOCOLATE SPONGES
100g dark chocolate (about 70% cocoa solids), broken up
100g unsalted butter, diced
2 medium eggs, at room temperature
½ teaspoon vanilla extract
150g caster sugar
90g self-raising flour
good pinch of fine sea salt
½ teaspoon baking powder
3 tablespoons cocoa powder

FOR THE RASPBERRY PURÉE
200g fresh raspberries
2 tablespoons caster sugar
2 tablespoons water

FOR THE RASPBERRY BUTTERCREAM
125g caster sugar
6 tablespoons water
3 medium egg yolks, at room temperature

225g unsalted butter, at room temperature, diced

TO FINISH AND DECORATE
24 pink rose petals
1 medium egg white
1 tablespoon cold water
4–5 tablespoons white caster sugar
24 fresh raspberries

you will need
1 x 12-cup loose-based mini sandwich tin or non-stick muffin/cupcake tray, greased with butter; a piping bag fitted with a medium star nozzle

1. The sugared rose petals are best made at least a day ahead so they have time to dry. First use a fine pastry brush to carefully remove any dust or pollen from each petal. Beat the egg white with the water in a small bowl until frothy. Gently paint the egg mix on to both sides of each petal and shake off the excess, then dip the petal in the sugar to coat evenly, again shaking off excess. Leave to dry overnight on a sheet of baking paper set on a wire rack in a cool, dry spot. (Once dry the petals can be stored in an airtight container for up to 5 days.)

2. Heat the oven to 180°C/350°F/gas 4. Before you make the sponge mixture, be sure your eggs are at room temperature – if they are cold the chocolate mixture will set in lumps as it is added. Gently melt the chocolate* with the butter, then set aside to cool until needed. Put the eggs and vanilla into a large mixing bowl, or the bowl of a free-standing electric mixer fitted with the whisk attachment. Whisk for a few seconds until frothy using a hand-held electric whisk, or the whisk attachment, then add the sugar and whisk on full speed until the mixture is very thick and pale, and has reached the ribbon stage*.

3. Whisk the just-warm chocolate mixture into the egg mixture on low speed, then scrape down the side of the bowl and whisk for another few seconds. Sift the flour, salt, baking powder and cocoa powder into the bowl and carefully fold* in using a large metal spoon or plastic spatula.

4. Spoon the mixture into the cups in the mini-sandwich tin or muffin tray, making sure they all have an equal amount (the cups will be half-full). Using a teaspoon, carefully level the surface of each little cake. Bake in the heated oven for 13–15 minutes until the sponges are just firm to the touch and have started to shrink away from the sides of the cups. Carefully unmould on to a wire rack and leave until cold.

5. Meanwhile, make the raspberry purée to flavour the buttercream. Tip the raspberries into a medium pan, add the sugar and water, and set over low heat. Stir gently until the sugar has dissolved, then bring to the boil and simmer, stirring frequently, for about 4 minutes until the mixture is very thick. Tip into a sieve set over a heatproof bowl and push the raspberries through the sieve to make a thick seedless purée. Leave to cool.

6. To make the buttercream, put the sugar and water into a small pan and heat gently, without boiling, until the sugar has completely dissolved. Bring the sugar syrup to the boil and boil for about 5 minutes until it reaches 110°C/225°F on a sugar thermometer. While the syrup is boiling put the yolks into a heatproof bowl set on a damp cloth (to prevent wobbling) and beat briefly with a hand-held electric whisk. As soon as the syrup has reached the correct temperature, slowly pour it on to the yolks in a thin, steady stream while whisking at full speed. Continue whisking until the mixture is thick and pale, and has reached the ribbon stage*. Whisk for a few minutes more until the mixture has cooled to room temperature (if it is warm the butter will quickly melt, turning the buttercream heavy and greasy).

7. Now gradually whisk in the butter, a few pieces at a time – don't add too much at once or the mixture will curdle (rather like with mayonnaise) – to make a thick, creamy icing. Whisk in about 8 tablespoons of the cold raspberry purée, a tablespoon at a time – stop as soon as you have the colour and flavour you want. Cover the bowl and chill for about 20 minutes until the buttercream is firm enough to pipe easily.

8. When you are ready to assemble the cakes, cut each little sponge in half horizontally. Transfer the buttercream to the piping bag fitted with the star nozzle. Pipe a ring of buttercream around the edge of each sponge bottom half and a small star in the centre. Set a raspberry on top of the star. Pipe a buttercream rosette in the middle of each top half.

9. To make 12 small cakes, re-assemble the sponges and decorate the top of each with a raspberry and 1 or 2 sugared rose petals. To make 24 petits fours, set the half-cakes on a serving platter and decorate with the rose petals and remaining raspberries. Once assembled serve the same day. If you want to serve them the next day, keep the sponges in a covered container in a cool spot (not the fridge), but add the raspberry and rose petal decoration at the last minute.

WALNUT-COFFEE SPONGE ROLL

If you've made a Swiss roll before, you'll find this more sophisticated version surprisingly easy. The very light crumb of the sponge comes from whisking egg whites until stiff and whole eggs with sugar until mousse-like, then folding these together with toasted ground walnuts. There's no flour or butter. The sponge is filled with a lovely, rich coffee butter icing made with *beurre noisette* (butter cooked until it turns a nut-brown colour).

gluten free | ——————————————————————— serves 8

1. Heat the oven to 180°C/350°F/gas 4. Tip the walnuts into a small baking dish or tin and toast in the heated oven for about 7 minutes until light golden. Leave until completely cold, then grind in a food processor with the baking powder until sandy-textured – stop the machine before the mixture turns into a paste. Turn up the oven temperature to 220°C/425°F/gas 7.

2. Separate the eggs, breaking the whites into a large mixing bowl, or the bowl of a free-standing electric mixer fitted with the whisk attachment, and the yolks into another mixing bowl; set the yolks aside. Whisk the whites* with the salt using a hand-held electric whisk, or the whisk attachment, on high speed until they stand in stiff peaks.

3. If your stand mixer has only one bowl, transfer the whisked whites to another bowl, then pour the yolks into the mixer bowl (no need to wash it or the whisk). Add the sugar and whisk on high speed for about 4 minutes until the mixture is very thick and pale and has reached the ribbon stage*.

4. Using a large metal spoon, very gently fold* the ground walnuts into the yolk mixture. Then add the stiffly whisked whites and carefully fold them in until you can no longer see any blobs of egg white or streaks of nuts – gently scrape down the sides of the bowl, and check the bottom of the bowl for any unmixed patches.

5. Carefully transfer the mixture to the prepared tin and spread evenly, making sure the corners are well filled. Bake in the heated oven for 10–12 minutes until the sponge is golden brown and springy to the touch*.

6. While the sponge is baking, lay a sheet of baking paper (about 30 × 40cm) on the worktop and sprinkle it with a little caster sugar. As soon as the sponge is ready, invert it on to the sugared paper and lift off the tin. Carefully and gently peel off the lining paper.

7. With a large sharp knife, make a shallow cut about 2cm in from one short end – this will help you roll the sponge into a neat spiral. Starting from the end with the cut, gently roll up the warm sponge, with the paper inside. Set the roll on a wire rack and leave until cold.

FOR THE SPONGE

75g walnut pieces
¼ teaspoon baking powder
3 medium eggs, at room
   temperature
good pinch of fine sea salt
75g caster sugar, plus extra
   for sprinkling

FOR THE FILLING

125g unsalted butter
300g icing sugar
3 tablespoons instant coffee
   (powder or granules)
2 tablespoons boiling water
3 tablespoons double cream

TO FINISH

8 walnut halves

you will need

1 Swiss roll tin, 20 × 30cm, greased with butter and base-lined*; a piping bag fitted with a medium or medium/large star nozzle

8. Meanwhile, make the coffee filling. Put the butter into a small pan and heat gently until melted, then turn up the heat slightly so the melted butter bubbles. Leave to bubble until it turns a light nut-brown colour – watch it carefully as you don't want it to become too dark or blackened, which would make the icing very bitter. Remove the pan from the heat. While the bubbles subside, sift the icing sugar into a heatproof mixing bowl, or the (washed) bowl of the free-standing electric mixer fitted with the (washed) whisk attachment, and dissolve the coffee in the boiling water.

9. Whisk the hot butter into the icing sugar using a (washed) hand-held electric whisk, or the whisk attachment of the mixer – leave the darkened, heavy specks of butter solids in the base of the pan. Next, whisk in the cream followed by enough of the coffee to give a flavour you like. Continue whisking, scraping down the sides of the bowl once or twice, for about 2 minutes until the mixture is very smooth and thick. Leave until cool and firm enough to spread (you can hurry this up by chilling the mixture for a few minutes, but don't leave it in the fridge to set firm).

10. When ready to fill, gently unroll the sponge and trim off the edges with a sharp knife. Give the coffee filling a really good stir, then transfer about a quarter of it to the piping bag fitted with the star nozzle. Spread the rest evenly over the sponge. Gently re-roll the sponge, starting once more from the end with the cut. Sprinkle the roll with a little more sugar, then transfer to a serving plate.

11. Pipe the reserved coffee filling in 8 rosettes along the top of the roll. Decorate each rosette with a walnut half. Serve immediately or keep in an airtight container in a cool spot – the sponge is best eaten the same or the next day.

another idea: For an extra glamorous touch, dip the walnut halves in caramel. Weigh 100g caster sugar into a small heavy pan, add 1 tablespoon of water and dissolve over low heat, stirring occasionally. When all the sugar has dissolved, increase the heat and boil the syrup, without stirring but carefully swirling it in the pan, until the syrup turns to a chestnut-coloured caramel. Remove from the heat, add the walnut halves and tilt the pan so the nuts are completely coated with caramel. Tip out on to an oiled baking sheet and carefully separate the nuts with a fork so they are not sticking together. Leave until set before using to decorate the piped rosettes.

JAFFA CAKES

A home-baked version of our much-loved classic teatime treat, the perfect combination of whisked sponge, ready-made orange jelly layer and melted dark chocolate.

makes 12 ———————————————————————— | dairy free

FOR THE JELLY
1 x 135g pack orange jelly
150ml boiling water
finely grated zest of 1 small orange

FOR THE SPONGE
2 large eggs, at room temperature
50g caster sugar
50g self-raising flour, sifted

FOR THE TOPPING
180g dark chocolate (about 46% cocoa solids), broken up

you will need
1 shallow 30 x 20cm baking tin; a 12-hole shallow bun tin/mince pie tin, greased with butter; a 5cm plain round cutter

1. Break up the jelly into pieces and place in a small heatproof bowl. Pour over the boiling water and stir until the jelly has completely melted. Stir in the orange zest. Pour into the shallow tin and chill for about 1 hour until set.

2. Meanwhile, heat the oven to 180°C/350°F/gas 4. To make the sponge, whisk the eggs and sugar together for 4–5 minutes until pale and fluffy, then fold* in the flour gently but thoroughly.

3. Spoon the sponge mixture into the bun tin to fill each hole three-quarters full (you will probably have some mixture left over). Bake in the heated oven for 7–9 minutes until the sponges are light golden and puffy, and they feel springy to the touch*. Remove from the oven and leave to cool for a few minutes before carefully transferring the sponges to a wire rack to finish cooling.

4. When ready to assemble, gently melt the chocolate*. Stir until smooth, then leave to cool and thicken slightly.

5. Turn the orange jelly out of the tin on to a sheet of baking paper. Cut out 12 discs from the jelly using the 5cm round cutter. Sit a jelly disc on top of each sponge.

6. Spoon the melted chocolate over the jelly discs – don't worry if a little chocolate dribbles down the sides. Allow to set slightly, then use a fork to create a criss-cross pattern on top of the chocolate. Leave to set completely before serving.

BLACK AND WHITE CELEBRATION CAKE

This is a tall, elegant cake to which you can add your own decoration ideas to match a theme or colour scheme, so it's the perfect showpiece for a big birthday. The three layers of chocolate chiffon sponge, made by whisking eggs with oil and then adding both chocolate and cocoa to give a deep colour and taste, are filled and iced with a white chocolate Swiss-meringue buttercream (egg whites warmed before whisking give it its fluffy texture). Temperature control is crucial for the buttercream - you'll need a sugar thermometer.

serves 12-14

FOR THE SPONGE LAYERS
65g dark chocolate (about 70% cocoa solids)
225ml boiling water
2 medium eggs, at room temperature
125ml sunflower oil
1 teaspoon vanilla extract
225ml buttermilk, at room temperature
425g caster sugar
225g plain flour
¼ teaspoon fine sea salt

125g cocoa powder
1½ teaspoons bicarbonate of soda
½ teaspoon baking powder

FOR THE BUTTERCREAM
4 medium egg whites, at room temperature
300g white caster sugar
450g unsalted butter, at room temperature
1 teaspoon vanilla extract

400g white chocolate (about 30% cocoa solids), broken up
100ml water

FOR THE DECORATION (OPTIONAL)
coloured edible wafer or rice paper sheets; edible icing colouring pens or paints; a fine cake-decorating paint brush; edible glue or a few drops of vodka; 2 bamboo skewers

you will need
3 x 20.5cm round, deep sandwich tins, greased with butter, base-lined* and dusted with cocoa powder; a thin card cake board

1. Heat the oven to 180°C/350°F/gas 4. Finely chop the chocolate into even-sized pieces and put into a heatproof bowl. Leave the boiling water to cool for a minute, then pour on to the chocolate in a thin, steady stream, whisking constantly with a hand wire whisk. Leave to cool for 5 minutes, then whisk again until smooth. Set aside to cool to room temperature.

2. Meanwhile, break the eggs into the bowl of a free-standing electric mixer fitted with the whisk attachment, or into a large mixing bowl set on a damp cloth (to prevent wobbling). Whisk with the whisk attachment, or a hand-held electric whisk, just until frothy. Starting at low speed (to prevent splashing) and gradually increasing the speed, whisk in the oil in a thin, steady stream so the mixture emulsifies and becomes light and creamy. Add the vanilla and whisk on high speed for a further minute.

3. Reduce the speed again and slowly whisk in the chocolate liquid. When it is thoroughly amalgamated, whisk in the room-temperature buttermilk in the same way (if it is fridge-cold the mixture will solidify and turn lumpy).

Gradually whisk in the sugar, increasing the speed when possible. Once all the sugar has been added, whisk the mixture on high speed for 2 minutes until very smooth.

4. Sift the flour, salt, cocoa, bicarbonate of soda and baking powder into the bowl and fold* in with a plastic spatula. The mixture will now look a bit lumpy so use a hand wire whisk to mix for a minute or so until you have a smooth, runny cake batter.

5. Divide the mixture equally among the 3 prepared tins, spreading it out evenly. Bake in the heated oven for 20–25 minutes until well risen and starting to shrink away from the side of the tin; a skewer inserted into the centre of the sponges should come out clean*.

6. Remove from the oven and run a round-bladed knife around the inside of each tin to loosen the sponge, then turn it out on to a wire rack and leave to cool completely. Once cold the cakes can be stored in an airtight container for 24 hours until ready to assemble.

7. Now make the Swiss meringue for the buttercream (it's a good idea to have a bowl of cold water and a clean pastry brush to hand). Put the egg whites into the washed bowl of the free-standing electric mixer, or a large heatproof bowl. Add the sugar and mix with a hand wire whisk for a few seconds to combine. Set the bowl over a pan of just-simmering water (the water should not touch the base of the bowl and should not be boiling). Stir using the whisk until the sugar has completely dissolved – you should not feel any gritty sugar crystals – and the mixture has warmed to a minimum of 60°C/140°F (maximum 70°C/160°F) on a sugar thermometer. Here you are aiming to dissolve the sugar and stabilise the mixture but NOT to cook the whites or make a meringue, so stir with the whisk just to keep the mixture moving and resist the urge to whisk vigorously. During the dissolving process, use the wet pastry brush to wash down the side of the bowl from time to time, to prevent any sugar crystals from sticking.

8. As soon as the mixture reaches the correct temperature, remove the bowl from the pan and set it on the mixer stand (or on a cold damp cloth). Whisk vigorously with the whisk attachment, or a hand-held electric whisk, until the mixture forms a very thick, white meringue – you will need to scrape down the side of the bowl frequently. Keep on whisking until the mixture has returned to room temperature – if it is at all warm it will melt the butter and turn greasy.

9. Make sure the butter is at room temperature – not warm or oily, and not fridge-hard either – then cut it into dice. Whisk into the meringue a couple of pieces at a time. When all the butter has been incorporated, whisk in the vanilla. Cover and set aside (the buttercream can be left at room temperature for 1–2 hours until ready to assemble).

10. Gently melt the white chocolate* with the water, then leave it to cool to room temperature – it should still be fluid but not at all warm (or it will melt the buttercream), so stir it frequently as it cools.

11. Uncover the buttercream and gradually whisk in the cooled white chocolate a tablespoon at a time to make a very smooth, thick and spreadable icing. The buttercream can be used immediately or covered and left at room temperature for 1–2 hours.

12. To assemble the cake, divide up the buttercream (to avoid contaminating it with dark sponge crumbs): put aside a third for sandwiching the sponges, then put a bit less than half of the remaining buttercream into another bowl for the crumb-catcher layer of frosting. Cover the rest of the buttercream and set it aside for the top layer of frosting.

13. Set one sponge crust-side down on the cake board. Layer up with the other 2 sponges using the sandwiching buttercream. Cover the top and sides of the layered cake with the crumb-catcher buttercream, spreading it in a thin, even layer. Chill for about 20 minutes until firm.

14. Now, before you finish the icing, make sure the worktop and all equipment (and your hands) are completely free of dark chocolate sponge crumbs. Cover the top and sides of the cake with the remaining buttercream, spreading it so the sides are smooth and straight and the top is flat and even. Leave the buttercream icing to firm up, uncovered, on the worktop (if necessary, you can hurry this up in the fridge) before adding the decorations. At this point the cake can be stored in a covered container at cool room temperature overnight.

15. To make the edible bunting, use edible icing colouring pens, or edible paints and a fine brush, to draw designs on the wafer or rice paper (you could also buy ready-printed rice paper). Cut into strips about 2cm wide (you can make them larger or smaller if you wish). Cut into triangles. Cut strips of the paper about 3mm wide and 20cm long. Attach the triangles to the strips using tiny dabs of edible glue or vodka, then attach to the cake by gently pressing the ends of the strips into the icing. (As some strips may break, and you may want extras for the top of the cake, it's worth making a few more than you need.) Here, we wrapped the fine strips of paper around bamboo skewers, stuck them into the cake and then attached a string of bunting.

16. Once the cake is decorated, serve the same day.

TIRAMISU CAKE

A feather-light sponge layered with a mascarpone mousse and gently flavoured with coffee and brandy – this is the cake version of the Italian 'pick-me-up'. Once assembled, it's chilled overnight, which not only makes slicing easier but really boosts the taste and texture. A white chocolate ribbon adds an elegant finishing touch to this delectable showstopper.

serves 12

FOR THE SPONGE LAYERS
5 medium eggs, at room temperature
large pinch of fine sea salt
150g caster sugar
2 teaspoons instant coffee (granules or powder)
1 tablespoon boiling water
150g plain flour

FOR THE FILLING
4 medium egg yolks, at room temperature
65g caster sugar
4 tablespoons brandy
250g full-fat mascarpone, chilled
125ml double cream, well chilled
60g dark chocolate (about 70% cocoa solids), grated

FOR THE BRUSHING SYRUP
85g caster sugar
130ml water
1 tablespoon instant coffee (granules or powder)
3 tablespoons brandy

FOR THE CHOCOLATE RIBBON
50g white chocolate (about 32% cocoa solids), broken up

you will need
3 x 20.5cm round, deep sandwich tins, greased with butter and base-lined* then dusted with flour; a thin card cake board (optional); a chocolate-transfer sheet (acetate printed with an edible cocoa butter design)

1. Heat the oven to 180°C/350°F/gas 4. To make the sponge layers, separate the eggs, putting the whites into a large mixing bowl, or the bowl of a free-standing electric mixer fitted with the whisk attachment, and the yolks into another large bowl; set the yolks aside. Add the salt to the whites, then whisk* using a hand-held electric mixer, or the whisk attachment, until the whites stand in soft peaks when the whisk is lifted. Whisk in half of the sugar, then whisk for a few seconds more until the mixture stands in stiff peaks.

2. If your stand mixer has only one bowl, transfer the whisked whites to another bowl, then pour the yolks into the mixer bowl (there is no need to wash it or the whisk attachment/hand-held electric whisk).

3. Dissolve the instant coffee in the boiling water, then add to the yolks with the remaining sugar and whisk until the mixture is very thick and mousse-like and has reached the ribbon stage*. Fold* the whites into the yolk mixture in 4 batches using a large metal spoon. Sift the flour over the mixture and gently fold in.

4. Divide the mixture equally among the 3 prepared tins (do this by weight or by eye) and spread evenly. Bake in the heated oven for 13–15 minutes until the sponges are golden and starting to shrink away from the sides of the tins, and they feel springy to the touch*. Remove from the oven and run a round-bladed knife around the inside of each tin to loosen the sponge, then turn out on to a wire rack and peel off the lining paper. Leave to cool.

ULTIMATE INDULGENCE MIRROR-GLAZE CAKE

Four layers of orange genoise sponge are layered and coated with a whipped salted caramel cream, then finished with a very dark chocolate mirror-glaze. The cake is embellished with a stunning decoration of caramelised hazelnut 'spikes', piped beads and tempered chocolate ribbons.

serves 12

FOR THE GENOISE SPONGE
5 medium eggs, at room
  temperature
165g caster sugar
finely grated zest of 2 large
  oranges
165g plain flour
pinch of fine sea salt
40g unsalted butter, melted and
  cooled

FOR THE SALTED CARAMEL CREAM
55g unsalted butter
135g light muscovado sugar
85ml double cream
1 teaspoon sea salt flakes,
  or to taste
600ml double cream, well chilled
ivory edible food colouring gel

FOR THE MIRROR-GLAZE
150ml double cream

150ml water
135g caster sugar
55g cocoa powder
3 leaves gelatine (from
  a 13g/8-leaf pack)

FOR THE DECORATION
100g Belgian milk chocolate chips
75g granulated sugar
1 tablespoon water
12 blanched hazelnuts

you will need
2 x 20.5cm round, deep
sandwich tins, greased with
butter and base-lined*; a
thin card cake board; acetate
sheet; 12 wooden cocktail
sticks; a piece of thick, stiff
foam; 2 small piping bags;
a medium star nozzle and
a small round nozzle

1. Heat the oven to 180°C/350°F/gas 4. To make the sponge mixture, break the eggs into a large heatproof bowl, add the sugar and orange zest, and whisk with a hand-held electric whisk until combined. Set the bowl over a pan of barely simmering water (the base of the bowl should not touch the water) and whisk on full speed for about 10 minutes until the mixture is very pale, thick and mousse-like and has reached the ribbon stage* – don't let the egg mixture become too hot (you should be able to dip in your little finger and not find it uncomfortable). If the mixture begins to feel too hot, move the pan and bowl off the heat, if necessary. Once ribbon stage has been reached, remove the bowl from the pan and whisk the egg mixture until it cools to room temperature.

2. Sift the flour and salt into another bowl, then sift a third of the flour on to the egg mixture. Carefully fold* in. Repeat 2 more times to fold in the remaining flour. Slowly trickle the cooled melted butter down the inside of the bowl and fold in until there are no streaks visible in the mixture.

3. Gently spoon the mixture into the prepared tins, dividing it equally, and spread evenly. Bake in the heated oven for 14–16 minutes until the sponges are well risen, golden and starting to shrink away from the sides of the tins – they should feel springy when gently pressed in the centre*.

4. Remove from the oven and leave the sponges to cool and firm up for 3 minutes, then run a round-bladed knife around the inside of each tin and turn out the sponges on to a wire rack to cool completely.

5. Meanwhile, make the salted caramel sauce to flavour the cream filling. Put the butter and sugar into a small, heavy-based pan and heat gently until the butter has melted, stirring frequently. Slowly pour in the 85ml cream, stirring constantly (take care as the mixture may splutter). Bring to the boil, still stirring, and simmer for 1 minute. Remove from the heat and stir in the salt. Leave to cool, stirring frequently.

6. Once the sauce is cold, whip the 600ml chilled cream* using a hand-held electric whisk until it is floppy – the stage before soft-peak. Using a hand wire whisk, beat the cold caramel sauce for a minute to lighten it, then fold in a couple of tablespoons of the whipped cream. Now add this mixture to the remaining whipped cream and whip with the electric whisk for a few seconds until combined to make a thick, spreadable mixture. Fold in a drop or two of food colouring – dip a wooden cocktail stick into the tiny pot, then shake drops into the mixture – to make an attractive golden-orange colour. Set aside 4 tablespoons of the caramel cream in a small bowl for the decoration. Cover both bowls and keep in the fridge until needed.

7. To assemble the cake, cut each sponge horizontally into 2 layers*. Set one layer cut-side up on the cake board. Spread over a layer of caramel cream about 4mm thick. Lay a second sponge layer on this. Repeat to sandwich together the 4 layers, making sure the cake is even and straight.

8. Use just under half the remaining caramel cream to cover the top and sides of the cake – this is the 'crumb-catcher' coat so make sure to fill in any gaps/holes and to make the sides and top as flat and straight as possible. Chill for about 30 minutes until firm.

9. Cover the top and sides of the cake with the rest of the caramel cream (except the 4 tablespoons reserved for the decoration), using a palette knife to give the smoothest possible finish. Keep the cake in the fridge while you make the mirror-glaze.

10. Put the cream, water, sugar and cocoa into a small heavy-based pan and heat gently, stirring constantly, until the sugar has dissolved. Bring to the boil and simmer, stirring, for 2 minutes. Strain through a fine sieve into a heatproof bowl and leave to cool for 10 minutes. Meanwhile, soak the gelatine leaves in a bowl of cold water for 5 minutes until softened.

11. Squeeze the excess water from the gelatine leaves, then gently whisk them into the chocolate mixture until completely melted. Pass through a sieve into a measuring jug. Leave until the glaze is cold and thickened but still fluid before using.

12. Place the chilled cake on a wire rack set over a baking tin (to catch the drips). Slowly pour the glaze evenly over the cake to cover the top and sides completely. Return the cake to the fridge to set.

13. To make the chocolate decoration, cut the acetate into strips of different widths and lengths – 1 x 10cm, 2 x 10cm, 1 x 8cm, for example – and have some small bits of masking tape already cut. Gently melt the chocolate* chips, then temper* the chocolate. Set the acetate strips on a clean worktop. Using an offset palette knife, spread the tempered chocolate over the acetate. One at a time, lift the strips off the worktop and form into rings or curls, using the bits of masking tape to secure the ends of the strips in place. Place on a sheet of baking paper and leave in a cool spot or the fridge until the chocolate has set.

14. To make the caramelised hazelnuts, put the sugar and water into a small, heavy-based pan and heat gently until the sugar has melted – don't stir but swirl it in the pan from time to time. Meanwhile, push a cocktail stick into the base of each hazelnut. Place the piece of foam at the edge of the worktop and secure it firmly with a chopping board. When the sugar has melted to a syrup, bring to the boil and cook rapidly, without stirring, until it turns into a rich chestnut-coloured caramel.

15. Remove the pan from the heat and, one at a time, dip the hazelnuts into the caramel (holding the stick), then push the end of the stick into the foam so that the caramel on the tip of the nut will drip down and set to form a 'spike'. (If you like, gather up all the 'spare' threads of caramel – spun sugar – left from dipping the nuts and gently form them into a loose ball, then set on a sheet of baking paper; use for an extra decoration.) Leave the hazelnuts until hard before trimming the 'spikes' to the same height with kitchen scissors. Carefully pull out the cocktail sticks and set the caramelised nuts, spike up, on a sheet of baking paper. (You only need 8 caramelised hazelnuts, but it's a good idea to make more, to allow for breakages.)

16. Transfer the cake to a serving platter. Spoon about two-thirds of the reserved 4 tablespoons caramel cream into a piping bag fitted with the star nozzle and pipe 8 small swirls, evenly spaced, around the top edge of the cake. Set a caramelised nut on each (pick the best-looking), spike pointing up. Put the rest of the reserved caramel cream in the other piping bag fitted with the small round nozzle and pipe small beads around the base of the cake where it meets the board. Peel the chocolate ribbons away from the acetate strips and arrange, nest-like, in the centre of the cake.

PRALINE AND WHITE CHOCOLATE MIRROR-GLAZE CAKE

Two layers of light vanilla genoise sponge are sandwiched and coated with a salted praline-flavoured Swiss-meringue buttercream and topped with a fine and glamorous mirror-glaze made with white chocolate.

serves 12

FOR THE GENOISE SPONGE
60g unsalted butter
6 medium eggs plus 2 yolks, at room temperature
120g caster sugar
1 teaspoon vanilla bean paste
150g plain flour
30g cornflour
good pinch of fine sea salt

FOR THE PRALINE PASTE
120g blanched hazelnuts
225g caster sugar
4 tablespoons water
½ teaspoon sea salt flakes, or to taste

FOR THE BUTTERCREAM
5 medium egg whites, at room temperature
180g caster sugar
250g unsalted butter, at room temperature, diced

FOR THE SYRUP
75g caster sugar
150ml water
½ teaspoon vanilla bean paste

FOR THE MIRROR-GLAZE
2 gelatine leaves (from a 13g/8-leaf pack)
180g white chocolate (about 30% cocoa solids), broken into even pieces
130ml double cream
100ml glucose syrup
20g caster sugar
2 tablespoons water

TO DECORATE
1 sheet or fragments of gold leaf

you will need
2 x 20.5cm round, deep sandwich tins, greased with butter and base-lined*; a baking sheet, lightly oiled; a card cake board; a small piping bag fitted with a small plain nozzle

1. Heat the oven to 180°C/350°F/gas 4. To make the sponge mixture, melt the butter, then pour into a medium bowl and set aside to cool. Put the eggs, egg yolks, sugar and vanilla into the heatproof bowl of a free-standing electric mixer and whisk with a hand wire whisk until combined. Set the bowl over a pan of simmering water (the base of the bowl should not touch the water) and whisk, using the hand whisk, for a couple of minutes, just until the mixture feels warm when you dip in your little finger, and the sugar has dissolved – you shouldn't feel any gritty grains of sugar. Remove the bowl from the pan and put it in place in the mixer fitted with the whisk attachment. Whisk on high speed until the mixture is thick and mousse-like and it has reached the ribbon stage*.

2. Sift the flour, cornflour and salt 3 times into another bowl. Once the egg mixture is at ribbon stage, scoop out a cupful and stir it into the cooled butter; set aside. Sift a third of the flour mixture on to the rest of the egg mixture and gently fold* in. Repeat twice to mix in the rest of the flour, then fold in the butter mixture.

3. Divide the mixture equally between the prepared tins and spread evenly. Bake in the heated oven for 20–25 minutes until the sponges are well risen and golden, and they feel springy when gently pressed in the centre*. Run a round-bladed knife around the inside of each tin and turn out the sponge on to a wire rack. Leave to cool. Reduce the oven temperature to 170°C/325°F/gas 3.

4. To make the praline paste, tip the hazelnuts into a small baking dish or tin and toast in the oven for 10–15 minutes until they turn a light golden brown. Leave to cool, then chop roughly and spread out on the oiled baking sheet. Put the sugar and water into a medium pan and heat gently, stirring occasionally, until the sugar has dissolved. Turn up the heat and bring the syrup to the boil, then boil rapidly until it turns into a rich chestnut-coloured caramel. Immediately pour the caramel over the nuts on the baking sheet to cover them. Quickly sprinkle with the sea salt, then leave until cold. Once set, break the praline into shards. Save a few of the best-looking shards for the decoration, and grind the rest in a food processor to make a paste.

5. Now make the Swiss-meringue buttercream. Put the egg whites and sugar into the (clean) heatproof bowl of the electric mixer and whisk with a hand wire whisk until combined. Set the bowl over a pan of simmering water (the base of the bowl should not touch the water) and stir constantly with the whisk until the mixture reaches 65°C/150°F on a sugar thermometer. Remove the bowl from the pan and put it in place on the mixer fitted with the whisk attachment. Whisk on high speed to make a thick white meringue. Keep whisking until the meringue has cooled to room temperature, then gradually whisk in the butter. Switch to the paddle/beater attachment and beat for a couple of minutes until the mixture is very smooth and silky-textured. Add 5 tablespoons of the praline paste to the bowl and fold* in with a plastic spatula (save the rest of the praline paste for the decoration). Keep the buttercream covered until needed.

6. To make the brushing syrup, put the sugar, water and vanilla into a small pan and heat gently until the sugar has dissolved. Bring to the boil, then simmer for a minute. Remove from the heat.

7. Set one sponge layer, crust-side down, on the cake board and brush thoroughly with about half of the syrup. Leave to soak in for 10 minutes.

8. Transfer 4 tablespoons of the buttercream to a small bowl, for the piped decoration; cover and set aside. Spoon about a quarter of the remaining buttercream on top of the syrup-brushed sponge and spread evenly. Set the other sponge on top, crust-side up, and brush with the rest of the syrup. Leave to soak in for 10 minutes, then use half the remaining buttercream to evenly coat the top and sides of the cake – this is the 'crumb-catcher' layer. Chill until firm.

9. Repeat to cover the cake with the rest of the buttercream (except for that reserved for decoration) – make sure this coating is completely smooth so the mirror-glaze doesn't have bumps. Now give the cake a thorough chilling in the fridge for about 30 minutes (or freezer if time is short).

10. To make the mirror-glaze, put the gelatine in a bowl of cold water to soak for about 5 minutes until softened, and put the chocolate into a heatproof bowl. Gently heat the cream, glucose, sugar and water in a medium pan, stirring constantly, until melted and smooth, then bring to the boil. Pour over the chocolate in a thin, steady stream, stirring gently until smooth. Squeeze excess water out of the gelatine, then add to the chocolate cream mixture and stir in until melted. Blitz with a hand blender to make sure the mixture is completely smooth – take care not to introduce froth or bubbles. Leave until cool and thickened but still fluid, stirring frequently.

11. Remove the cake from the fridge/freezer and place on a rack set over a tray to catch the drips. Carefully pour the white chocolate mirror-glaze over the cake to completely and evenly cover the top and sides. Leave to set before transferring to a cake stand.

12. To decorate the cake, spoon the reserved buttercream into the piping bag and pipe small 'dots' on to the top of the cake in a slightly diagonal line. Add the shards of praline and a little of the praline paste to this line, then finish with small pieces of gold leaf.

BISCUITS
&
TEATIME
TREATS

Making biscuits is easy!
Ask the best baker you
know and there's a very good
chance that biscuits are the
first thing they ever made.
A home-baked biscuit can be
a simple homely treat or a
small luxury - it's up to you
- but the majority are really
easy to achieve.

Most biscuits and little bakes can be quickly whipped up with the minimum of ingredients and equipment, perfect for a heavenly wet-afternoon treat or midnight snack. But you do need first-class ingredients for the best results: nothing can match the taste of really good unsalted butter in a rich, short Viennese Whirl (page 113), or the flavour and texture of dark chocolate made with 70 per cent cocoa solids when you bake the Bitter Extremely Rich Chocolate Cookies (page 97).

A good bake if you – or the children in your life – are just starting out is the Peanut Butter, Chocolate Chip and Oat Cookies recipe on page 94. It's a wooden spoon and bowl affair, lots of hands-on. If you enjoy rolling out and cutting dough shapes, or want a bit of practice, there are some pretty Linzer Sablés (page 100) – crisp, crumbly, flower-shapes sandwiched with home-made jam. Unusual shapes, neatly cut and baked, then iced and decorated, can be terrific fun to make. Take a look at the Malt, Chocolate and Orange Iced 'Beer' Biscuits (beer mug shapes) on page 103 and the Bhaa Bara Brith Biscuits (sheep shapes) on page 105.

In addition to simply rolling biscuit dough into balls or cutting it into shapes, it can be piped. Piping looks simple but it takes a little experience to make neat, even and pretty shapes, which is what makes piped Viennese Whirls such a challenge – deliciously crisp, evenly baked biscuits are a given, but also beautiful piping for both the dough and the buttery filling. There's home-made jam to make as well!

Muffins and bakes like Easy Espresso Traybake (page 86) or Rum 'n' Raisin Brownies (page 99) can be quickly made to share with friends and family. They're ideal too for lunchboxes or to take on a picnic, as are the Posh Granola Bars on page 89 – you can customise these with your own favourite nuts and seeds.

MEXICAN WEDDING COOKIES

Made like shortbread, these light cookies have an appealing sandy texture and are finished with a 'double-dusting' of icing sugar. The simple recipe has just five ingredients and depends on fresh nuts for the richest flavour - use an unopened pack for best results.

makes 16

100g pecan halves
115g unsalted butter, softened
35g icing sugar
½ teaspoon vanilla extract
125g plain flour

TO FINISH
50g icing sugar, for dusting

you will need
2 baking sheets, lined
with baking paper

1. Heat the oven to 180°C/350°F/gas 4. Pick out the 16 best-looking pecan halves and keep on one side to decorate the cookies. Weigh out 50g of the remaining nuts and tip into a small baking dish or tin (save any leftover nuts for another recipe). Toast in the heated oven for about 8 minutes until slightly darker with a good 'toasty' smell. (You can turn off the oven for now.)

2. Leave the nuts to cool, then chop coarsely: use a large sharp knife rather than a food processor as you want small chunks, and it's easier to control size with a knife. Set aside.

3. Put the softened butter into a mixing bowl (set on a damp cloth to prevent it from wobbling). Beat with a wooden spoon, or a hand-held electric whisk, for a couple of minutes until the butter becomes creamy and mayonnaise-like. Sift the icing sugar into the bowl and add the vanilla, then beat thoroughly until the mixture is very fluffy and smooth.

4. Sift the flour into the bowl and mix in using the wooden spoon or a plastic spatula. Tip the chopped nuts into the bowl and mix in until evenly distributed. Tightly cover the bowl with clingfilm and chill the dough for about 30 minutes until firm and stiff.

5. Reheat the oven to 180°C/350°F/gas 4. Divide the dough into 16 equal portions and roll each one into a walnut-sized ball with your hands (you don't need to flour your hands if the dough is well chilled and firm). Set the balls on the lined baking sheets, well apart to allow for expansion. Gently place a pecan half on top of each ball.

6. Bake in the heated oven for 16–18 minutes until the cookies are a light gold colour with darker edges – check after 15 minutes and rotate the sheets, if necessary, so the cookies bake evenly. Once baked, lift out the baking sheets and set them on a wire rack, then quickly dust the cookies with icing sugar – you won't need it all but save the rest. Leave the cookies to cool and firm up on the baking sheets for 3–4 minutes before carefully transferring to the wire rack to cool completely.

7. Store in an airtight container and eat within 5 days. Dust with the rest of the icing sugar just before serving – the cookies will look like snowballs.

EASY ESPRESSO TRAYBAKE

You can make the mixture for this straightforward traybake in the time it takes to heat up the oven! The all-in-one coffee sponge is baked with a layer of cinnamon-spiced chocolate, then finished with a rich, fudgy chocolate frosting. Older children can help to make this, to enjoy as an after-school treat.

cuts into 16 squares

FOR THE SPONGE MIX
100ml milk
4 teaspoons instant coffee (granules or powder)
225g self-raising flour
½ teaspoon ground cinnamon
225g light muscovado sugar
200g unsalted butter, softened
3 medium eggs, beaten to mix

FOR THE FILLING
100g chocolate chips (dark with 70% cocoa solids OR milk chocolate)
2 tablespoons light muscovado sugar
½ teaspoon ground cinnamon

FOR THE FROSTING
125g dark chocolate (about 70% cocoa solids)
30g unsalted butter
1 tablespoon golden syrup

you will need
1 x 20.5cm square baking/
cake tin, 2.5cm deep,
greased with butter
and base-lined*

1. Heat the oven to 180°C/350°F/gas 4. Heat half the milk until steaming hot, then add the coffee and stir until dissolved. Stir in the remaining cold milk. Set aside to cool until needed.

2. Sift the flour and cinnamon into a mixing bowl, or the bowl of a free-standing electric mixer fitted with the whisk attachment. Add the sugar (if necessary, press out any lumps), soft butter and eggs. Beat well with a wooden spoon or hand-held electric whisk, or with the whisk attachment – slowly at first and increasing the speed – until thoroughly combined and smooth. Beat in the milky coffee.

3. Spoon half of the sponge mixture into the prepared tin and spread evenly, making sure the corners are filled. Combine all the ingredients for the filling in a small bowl. Sprinkle over the sponge mixture in the tin, then spread the remaining sponge mixture evenly on top.

4. Bake in the heated oven for about 35 minutes until golden and well risen; a skewer inserted into the centre should come out clean*. Remove the tin from the oven and set it on a wire rack. Run a round-bladed knife around the inside of the tin to loosen the sponge, then leave to cool completely before carefully turning out of the tin on to the wire rack.

5. To make the frosting, gently melt the chocolate* with the butter and syrup. Leave to cool, stirring frequently, until the frosting is thick enough to spread easily. Spoon the frosting on top of the cold sponge, and spread and swirl to cover evenly. Leave until set and firm before cutting into squares. Store in an airtight container and eat within 4 days.

POSH GRANOLA BARS

Crisp, crunchy and utterly addictive, these bars contain plenty of nuts and seeds (you can make up your own combinations) and juicy sour cherries, with puffed-rice cereal to ensure the mixture isn't too dense. A piped white chocolate decoration makes the bars especially attractive. Ideal to pack for picnics and sports outings.

gluten free | ———————————————————— cuts into 14 bars

1. Heat the oven to 180°C/350°F/gas 4. Tip the oats into the roasting tin (ungreased) and sprinkle the oil over them. Rub the oats between the palms of your hands until they are all lightly coated with oil. Shake the tin to level the oats, then toast in the heated oven for 15 minutes until lightly coloured. Remove from the oven, add the chopped nuts, seeds and puffed rice, and mix thoroughly.

2. Return the tin to the oven and toast for a further 5–7 minutes until the mixture is golden. Remove from the oven, add the cinnamon and cherries, and give the mixture a good stir. Leave to cool until needed. Reduce the oven temperature to 170°C/325°F/gas 3.

3. Measure the honey and butter into a small pan and set over low heat. Leave to melt gently, then bring to the boil. Pour the hot mixture over the oat mixture and stir well until the oat mixture is thoroughly coated. Tip into the prepared baking tin and spread evenly, right into the corners. Gently level the surface without compressing the mixture.

4. Bake in the heated oven for 18–20 minutes until lightly golden with slightly darker edges. Remove the tin from the oven and set it on a wire rack. Run a round-bladed knife around the inside of the tin to loosen the granola 'cake', then leave until it is barely warm.

5. With a sharp knife, gently cut the 'cake' in half down the length of the tin, then cut across to make 14 bars. Leave until they are cool and firm before slicing again along the cut lines and removing the bars from the tin.

6. To finish, gently melt the white chocolate*, then stir in the oil. Leave to cool until thick enough to pipe. Spoon into the piping bag and snip off the tip, then pipe the chocolate over the bars in a zig-zag pattern (you could also do this by drizzling the chocolate from a spoon). Leave until set. Store in an airtight container and eat within 5 days.

200g porridge oats
3 tablespoons rapeseed oil
160g coarsely chopped nuts
  (a mix of almonds, pecans,
  pistachios, brazils)
50g seeds (a mix of pumpkin
  and sunflower)
25g puffed-rice breakfast cereal
½ teaspoon ground cinnamon
25g soft-dried sour cherries
  OR cranberries
150g clear honey
40g unsalted butter

TO FINISH

100g good white chocolate
  (about 30% cocoa solids)
2 tablespoons sunflower oil

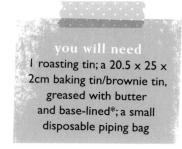

you will need
1 roasting tin; a 20.5 x 25 x
2cm baking tin/brownie tin,
greased with butter
and base-lined*; a small
disposable piping bag

another idea: For a bigger chocolate kick without adding more sugar, replace the cherries with cacao nibs, and use 70% dark chocolate instead of white chocolate for the piped zig-zag finish.

LEMON-GLAZED LEMON AND POPPYSEED MUFFINS

Muffins are the ideal easy bake when you're in a hurry because they need to be mixed up quickly and baked without delay. These are light and lemony spelt muffins with a lemon curd centre. Lemon-drizzle fans will love them - they're finished while still hot with a lemon glaze.

makes 12

250g white spelt flour
2 teaspoons baking powder
¼ teaspoon bicarbonate of soda
125g caster sugar
2 teaspoons poppyseeds
finely grated zest and juice
    of 1 large unwaxed lemon
2 medium eggs, at room
    temperature
about 175ml natural yoghurt
100g unsalted butter, melted and
    cooled
4 tablespoons lemon curd
    (for a recipe, see page 20)

FOR THE GLAZE
100g icing sugar
finely grated zest and juice
    of 1 large unwaxed lemon

you will need
1 x 12-hole muffin/
cupcake tray, lined with
paper muffin/cupcake cases

1. Heat the oven to 200°C/400°F/gas 6. Sift the flour, baking powder and bicarbonate of soda into a mixing bowl. Add the caster sugar, poppyseeds and lemon zest. Mix thoroughly, then make a well in the centre.

2. Pour the lemon juice into a measuring jug, add the eggs and mix gently with a fork. Add enough yoghurt to make up to 300ml and mix well. Pour the mixture into the well along with the butter. Mix everything together using a wooden spoon or plastic spatula – stop stirring as soon as the ingredients have come together (overmixing risks developing the gluten in the flour, which would make the muffins tougher, with a less tender crumb).

3. Spoon half of the mixture into the paper cases in the muffin tray, dividing equally (the cases will be about a third full). Spoon a teaspoon of lemon curd on to the centre of each, then carefully top with the rest of the muffin mixture, again taking care to divide it equally.

4. Bake in the heated oven for 20–25 minutes until the muffins are golden brown and feel firm when gently pressed in the centre – check after 15 minutes and, if necessary, rotate the tray so the muffins bake evenly.

5. While the muffins bake, make the lemon glaze. Sift the icing sugar into a bowl and stir in the lemon zest followed by enough lemon juice (1–1½ tablespoons) to make a smooth, runny consistency – it should just flow off the spoon when it is lifted out of the bowl.

6. As soon as the muffins are ready, remove the tray from the oven and set it on a wire rack. Working quickly, while the muffins are still very hot, add the glaze: it is easiest to ice the muffins one at a time. Dollop a teaspoon of the lemon glaze on to the centre of the muffin (it will be slightly domed) and let it flow over the top. The glaze will melt slightly and then set.

7. When all the muffins have been glazed, transfer them to the wire rack and leave to cool completely. They are best eaten the same or next day (store in an airtight container).

MAPLE WALNUT BISCUITS

These very rich, crumbly biscuits are flavoured with a heavenly combination of maple syrup and walnuts. The dough needs to be thoroughly chilled before baking so this isn't an obvious impulse bake, but - being an ultra-convenient 'fridge' dough - once made it can be stored in the fridge for several days so you can slice off and bake just a few biscuits at a time.

makes 30

100g walnut pieces
5 tablespoons maple syrup
225g slightly salted butter, softened
55g light muscovado sugar
250g plain flour

TO FINISH
100g walnut pieces

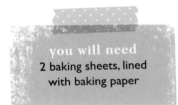

you will need
2 baking sheets, lined
with baking paper

1. Heat the oven to 180°C/350°F/gas 4. Tip the nuts into a baking dish or small roasting tin and toast in the heated oven for 5–8 minutes until they turn a light gold colour. Leave to cool (you can turn off the oven for now).

2. Meanwhile, measure the maple syrup into a small pan and set over medium/low heat. Simmer gently until reduced to 3 tablespoons (slightly more than half). Transfer to a mixing bowl and leave until barely warm.

3. Add the butter and sugar to the bowl and beat with a wooden spoon for a couple of minutes until smooth and creamy. Tip the cooled walnuts into a food processor and grind to a fine, sandy powder – watch carefully because if you grind them too far they will form an oily paste. Add the nuts to the butter mixture along with the flour and mix well with the wooden spoon or a plastic spatula. Turn out the dough on to the worktop and form into a log shape about 5cm across and 30cm long. The dough will be a bit soft and sticky but the log doesn't need to be neat at this point.

4. Chop the remaining 100g walnut pieces with a large knife until they are like fine gravel. Scatter evenly over a large sheet of baking paper. Lift the log on to the paper and gently roll back and forth until the log is completely coated with chopped nuts (except the 2 ends). Use your hands to make sure the log is a neat and even 5 x 30cm cylinder. Tightly wrap up the log in the baking paper and then in clingfilm. Set it on a baking sheet or tray. Chill until solid – this will take at least 4 hours, but as long as the dough is well wrapped it can be kept in the fridge for up to 5 days.

5. When ready to bake, heat the oven to 170°C/325°F/gas 3. Using a large, sharp knife, cut the log across into 1cm slices and set them on the lined baking sheets, slightly apart to allow for expansion. You don't have to bake all the dough at once – you can cut off as many slices as you need, then re-wrap the remaining dough and put it back in the fridge (or freeze for up to a month, then thaw before slicing and baking).

6. Bake the biscuits for 15–17 minutes until lightly golden with slightly darker edges. Remove from the oven and leave the biscuits to cool and firm up on the baking sheets for about 3 minutes before transferring to a wire rack to cool completely. Store in an airtight container and eat within 5 days.

PEANUT BUTTER, CHOCOLATE CHIP AND OAT COOKIES

A great bake for children - this is simple and fun, with lots of hands-in-the-bowl work, and little needed in the way of equipment. Be sure to use a top-quality crunchy peanut butter, made without any sugar, palm oil or butter. The chocolate chips can be replaced with raisins if you prefer. These cookies make the best ice cream sandwiches!

makes 24

130g good, chunky peanut butter
115g unsalted butter, softened
100g caster sugar
75g light muscovado sugar
1 medium egg, at room temperature
½ teaspoon vanilla extract
150g porridge oats
70g plain flour
½ teaspoon bicarbonate of soda
½ teaspoon ground cinnamon
100g chocolate chips (milk or plain) OR raisins

you will need
2 baking sheets, lined
with baking paper

1. Combine the peanut butter, softened butter and both sugars in a mixing bowl. Set the bowl on a damp cloth to prevent it from wobbling, then mix everything together with a wooden spoon. Once all the ingredients are amalgamated, beat the mixture well for about 2 minutes until it turns paler in colour and becomes lighter in texture.

2. Break the egg into a small bowl, add the vanilla extract and beat with a fork just until broken up. Pour the egg into the peanut butter mixture and beat well for a minute.

3. Add the oats to the bowl, then sift in the flour, bicarbonate of soda and cinnamon. Stir everything together with the wooden spoon. Finally, add the chocolate chips and mix into the dough until evenly distributed. Cover the bowl with clingfilm and chill for 45 minutes to 1 hour to firm up the dough.

4. Towards the end of this time, heat the oven to 180°C/350°F/gas 4.

5. Using a tablespoon measure, scoop out a spoonful of the dough and roll it into a ball in your hands. Set the ball on a lined baking sheet. Repeat with the rest of the dough, placing the balls well apart to allow for spreading. Bake in the heated oven for about 15 minutes until golden with darker brown edges. For the best results, check after 11 minutes and rotate the baking sheets, if necessary, so the cookies bake evenly.

6. Remove from the oven and leave the cookies to cool and firm up on the baking sheets for 2 minutes before transferring them to a wire rack to cool completely. Store in an airtight container and eat within 5 days.

CRISP SPICED WAFERS

Scandinavian spice biscuits, very thin, crisp and dark, these smell as good as they taste. Perfect with a cup of coffee after a special meal, or to pack up as a gift. They make an excellent biscuit base for a cheesecake too (see page 196) - you'll need about half this batch, but the extra wafers will keep well in an airtight container.

makes about 60

115g unsalted butter, softened
200g dark muscovado sugar
1 medium egg, at room
   temperature, beaten to mix
250g plain flour
4 teaspoons ground cinnamon
2 teaspoons ground ginger
¼ teaspoon ground cloves
good pinch of fine sea salt

you will need
2 baking sheets, lined
with baking paper

1. Beat the softened butter with a wooden spoon or hand-held electric whisk until very light and creamy. Break up any lumps in the muscovado sugar, then add to the butter and beat until thoroughly combined. Add the egg and beat well to make a smooth, light mixture. Sift the flour, cinnamon, ginger, cloves and salt on top, then mix in with the wooden spoon or a plastic spatula. As soon as the mixture starts to clump together, use your hands to bring it together into a dough.

2. Turn out the dough on to an unfloured worktop and knead gently for a few seconds to make a smooth ball. Divide it in half and shape each portion of dough into a neat 12 x 7.5cm brick that is 3cm thick. Wrap each brick in clingfilm and chill for about 30 minutes until firm. (The dough can be kept in the fridge for up to 3 days; or freeze for up to a month, then thaw before cutting and baking.)

3. When ready to bake, heat the oven to 180°C/350°F/gas 4. Unwrap one brick of dough and cut into very thin (slightly thinner than a pound coin) slices with a sharp knife. You will have about 30 rectangular slices. Arrange these on the lined baking sheets, slightly apart to allow for spreading, and bake in the heated oven for 9–10 minutes until the biscuits are slightly darker and firm. Remove from the oven and leave on the sheets for a minute, then transfer to a wire rack to cool completely.

4. Once the baking sheets are cold, you can cut and bake the second batch of biscuits in the same way (or whenever you want to have some freshly baked biscuits). Stored in an airtight tin the wafers will keep for a week.

BITTER EXTREMELY RICH CHOCOLATE COOKIES

Almost like a baked chocolate mousse or soufflé, based on eggs and sugar whisked until thick, these cookies have a tender, melt-in-the-mouth texture. It's vital to chill the mixture before baking to ensure the cookies keep a good shape in the oven. Try these with ice cream and Chocolate-dipped Maple Pralines (see page 21) for a summertime dessert.

makes 12

1. First gently melt the chocolate* with the butter and stir until smooth. Set aside to cool until needed.

2. Measure the coffee into a mixing bowl, or the bowl of a free-standing electric mixer fitted with the whisk attachment. Add the boiling water and leave for a couple of minutes to dissolve. Break the egg into the bowl, then add the sugar and whisk with a hand-held electric whisk, or the whisk attachment, on high speed until the mixture is very thick and mousse-like – almost but not quite to the ribbon stage*. This will take about 3 minutes.

3. Using slow speed, whisk in the melted chocolate until thoroughly combined. Sift the flour and baking powder into the bowl and fold* in with a large metal spoon or plastic spatula. Add the chocolate chips and salt and fold them in gently. Cover the bowl and chill for about 1 hour until the cookie mixture is firm.

4. Towards the end of this time, heat the oven to 180°C/350°F/gas 4.

5. Using a tablespoon measure, scoop out 12 portions and roll each one briefly between your hands to make a neat, walnut-size ball. Set these on the lined baking sheet, well apart to allow space for spreading. Bake in the heated oven for 15 minutes until the cookies are cracked and just firm to the touch with darker edges.

6. Remove from the oven and allow the cookies to firm up on the baking sheet for 2 minutes, then transfer to a wire rack and leave to cool completely. Store in an airtight container and eat within 5 days.

125g dark chocolate (about 70% cocoa solids)
20g unsalted butter
⅓ teaspoon instant coffee (powder or granules)
½ teaspoon boiling water
1 medium egg, at room temperature
75g caster sugar
25g plain flour
¼ teaspoon baking powder
100g dark chocolate chips (about 70% cocoa solids)
large pinch of sea salt flakes

you will need
1 baking sheet, lined with baking paper

RUM 'N' RAISIN BROWNIES

The perfect little treat - moist chocolate brownies studded with rum-soaked raisins. The light, silky texture is achieved by whisking the eggs and sugar to a very thick, mousse-like consistency before the melted chocolate is whisked in, and by taking care to avoid over-baking. You can turn the brownies into a luscious dessert by serving with Crème Chantilly and a Hot Bitter Chocolate Sauce (see pages 18 and 20).

cuts into 25 squares

1. Heat the oven to 170°C/325°F/gas 3. Put the raisins, cinnamon stick and rum (or water) into a small pan, set over low heat and bring to the boil. Remove from the heat and leave to cool and soak until needed.

2. Gently melt the chocolate* with the butter, stirring now and then until smooth. Leave to cool until needed.

3. Break the eggs into a mixing bowl, or the bowl of a free-standing electric mixer fitted with the whisk attachment, and add the sugar (be sure it is lump-free) and vanilla. Whisk using a hand-held electric whisk, or the whisk attachment, on high speed for about 4 minutes until the mixture is very thick and mousse-like and has reached the ribbon stage*.

4. Whisk in the melted chocolate mixture until you can't see any streaks. Sift the flour and salt into the bowl, and gently fold* in using a large metal spoon or plastic spatula. Remove the cinnamon stick from the raisins, then add them with their soaking liquid to the bowl and fold in.

5. Transfer the mixture to the prepared tin and spread evenly, making sure the corners are well filled. Bake in the heated oven for about 30 minutes until a wooden cocktail stick inserted into the mixture halfway between the sides and the centre comes out clean (the centre will still be moist, but the brownie will continue cooking for a few minutes after it is removed from the oven, and you want to avoid over-baking as that would dry out the mixture).

6. Set the tin on a wire rack and leave until cold before cutting into squares and removing from the tin. Store in an airtight container and eat within 5 days.

50g jumbo raisins
1 small cinnamon stick
2 tablespoons dark rum OR water
175g dark chocolate (about 70% cocoa solids)
175g unsalted butter, diced
3 medium eggs, at room temperature
200g light muscovado sugar
½ teaspoon vanilla extract
65g plain flour
good pinch of fine sea salt

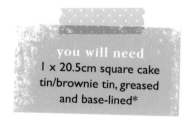

you will need
1 x 20.5cm square cake tin/brownie tin, greased and base-lined*

another idea: Make petits fours topped with piped rum cream to enjoy with coffee after dinner. Cut the brownie into small bite-sized squares. Flavour Crème Chantilly (see page 18) with 1 tablespoon dark rum, adding it after the cream has thickened but has not yet reached soft peak stage. Whip to a stiff peak, then spoon into a piping bag fitted with a 1cm plain nozzle. Pipe a large 'kiss' on top of each brownie. Serve as soon as possible.

LINZER SABLÉS

The super-rich almond dough for these continental-style biscuits is made with cream cheese and butter - it's easy as you use a food processor. Once baked, the crisp flower shapes are sandwiched with a high-fruit raspberry jam for a good fresh berry flavour. Home-made jammy dodgers with an elegant twist.

makes about 12

FOR THE DOUGH
50g unblanched almonds
  (still with brown skins on)
200g plain flour
¼ teaspoon baking powder
1 teaspoon finely grated lemon
  zest (from about 1 small
  unwaxed lemon)
large pinch of ground cinnamon
140g caster sugar
125g unsalted butter, chilled
  and diced
30g full-fat cream cheese
1 medium egg yolk

TO FINISH
about 200g raspberry jam (for a
  recipe, see page 21)
icing sugar, for dusting

you will need
1 x 8cm flower-shaped
cutter; a 2.5cm plain round
cutter; 2 baking sheets,
lined with baking paper

1. Grind the almonds in a food processor to make a fine powder, then add the flour, baking powder, lemon zest, cinnamon and sugar to the bowl and 'pulse' a few times until thoroughly combined.

2. Add the butter and cream cheese to the processor bowl and blitz just until the mixture looks like fine crumbs. Add the egg yolk and run the machine again until everything comes together to make a soft dough. Remove the dough from the bowl, shape it into a thick disc and wrap it tightly in clingfilm. Chill for 15–20 minutes until firm.

3. Unwrap the dough on to a lightly floured worktop and roll out to the thickness of a pound coin. Dip the flower cutter in flour and stamp out shapes. Arrange half the flower shapes on a lined baking sheet. Stamp out the centre from the rest of the shapes using the small plain cutter dipped in flour. Set these flowers-with-a-hole on the other baking sheet.

4. Gather up all the dough trimmings, then re-roll them and cut more flower shapes – make sure you have an equal number of those with and without a hole. Set these on the baking sheets. Chill for 10–15 minutes while you heat the oven to 180°C/350°F/gas 4.

5. Bake the biscuits in the heated oven for about 10 minutes until they are a pale gold colour with slightly darker edges – check after 8 minutes and rotate the sheets, if necessary, so the biscuits bake evenly. Remove from the oven and leave to cool on the baking sheets for a minute to allow the fragile biscuits to firm up, then transfer to a wire rack and leave until cold.

6. When ready to finish, spread jam over the flat underside of the biscuits without a hole, then sandwich with the flowers-with-a-hole biscuits (flat underside against flat underside) so the jam shows through. Dust with icing sugar before serving.

7. Once the biscuits are sandwiched they are best eaten the same day. Keep in an airtight container until serving. Without the jam filling, the biscuits can be stored in an airtight container for up to a week.

MALT, CHOCOLATE AND ORANGE ICED 'BEER' BISCUITS

Crisp and deliciously flavoured biscuits - sweetly malty to suggest beer's maltiness - these are flecked with dark chocolate. The biscuits are decorated in a cartoon fashion with coloured royal icing so they look like foaming beer mugs.

makes 24-28

1. Break up the chocolate and put into the bowl of a food processor. Add the orange zest and run the machine until the mixture looks like fine grit. Set aside for now.

2. Put the softened butter and sugar into a mixing bowl and beat with a hand-held electric whisk or wooden spoon until light and fluffy. Scrape down the sides of the bowl, then gradually add the egg, beating well after each addition. Beat in the malt extract until thoroughly combined.

3. Sift the flour into the bowl. Add the malted drink powder, vanilla extract and 1 teaspoon of orange juice. Mix everything together with a wooden spoon, then use your hands to bring the mixture together into a ball of firm dough – if there are crumbs in the base of the bowl or the dough feels stiff and dry, work in a little more orange juice, a teaspoon at a time.

4. Turn out the dough on to a lightly floured worktop and roll out to about 3mm thick. Dip the cutter in flour, then stamp out shapes. Arrange the beer-mug-shaped biscuits on the lined baking sheets, setting them slightly apart to allow for spreading during baking. Gather up the trimmings, re-roll and cut out more shapes. Prick each biscuit 2–3 times with a fork, then chill while you heat the oven to 180°C/350°F/gas 4.

5. Bake the biscuits, in batches if necessary, for 12–14 minutes until a light golden brown – check after 10 minutes and rotate the baking sheets, if necessary, so the biscuits cook evenly. Take care not to let them become dark brown, or for the edges to get dark brown, as this would make the biscuits taste bitter. Remove from the oven and leave the biscuits to cool and firm up on the baking sheets for 5 minutes before transferring to a wire rack to cool completely.

6. To make the icing, sift the icing sugar into a mixing bowl and stir in the cold water with a wooden spoon to make a smooth, thick icing. Divide the icing into 3 equal portions, transferring 2 of the portions to separate bowls. Cover these with clingfilm.

FOR THE BISCUITS

75g dark chocolate (about 72% cocoa solids)
finely grated zest and juice of 1 medium orange
125g unsalted butter, softened
125g golden caster sugar
1 medium egg, at room temperature, beaten to mix
60g malt extract
375g self-raising flour
45g malted-milk drink powder (use 'original', not diet or flavoured versions)
½ teaspoon vanilla extract

FOR THE ICING

about 600g royal icing sugar
about 75ml water
black and yellow-gold edible food colourings (gels or pastes)

you will need

1 beer-mug-shaped biscuit cutter, about 7.5–8cm long; 2 baking sheets, lined with baking paper; 3 small disposable piping bags; a fine writer-piping nozzle (no. 1.5 or 2)

7. Add enough black food colouring to the icing remaining in the original bowl to tint it a deep black. Check to be sure the icing is thick enough to pipe smoothly and hold a good shape – add a little more royal icing sugar if it is a bit runny, or a drop or two of extra water if it is too stiff – then transfer to a piping bag fitted with the writer-piping nozzle. Use the black icing to pipe the outline of a beer mug, handle and foam just inside the edge on each biscuit. Leave to set and dry for about 1 hour.

8. Tint the second portion of icing a golden beer-like colour. This icing needs to have a smoothly flowing, 'flooding' consistency (add a few drops of water if necessary). Spoon into a second piping bag and snip off the tip to make a 3mm opening, then pipe the icing into the bottom part of the outlined beer mug to 'flood' it smoothly (this represents the beer). Set aside to set.

9. Leave the remaining portion of icing white, but check that it too has a smoothly flowing consistency. Transfer to the last piping bag. Snip off the end and pipe/flood within the black outline above the 'beer' to represent the 'foam' head. Leave to set for about 1 hour.

10. To finish the decoration, pipe black lines vertically on the 'beer' to add definition, plus squiggles on the 'foam' if you like. Leave to set before serving. Store in an airtight tin and eat within 4 days.

BHAA BARA BRITH BISCUITS

Crisp, crumbly, buttery and shortbread-like, these biscuits have all the lovely flavours of Bara Brith - spices, tea-soaked dried fruit plus a touch of orange. The sheep are decorated with a simple icing - white for the fleece with black for heads and feet.

makes 24-26

FOR THE BISCUITS
2 strong tea bags
150ml boiling water
25g mixed dried fruit
1 teaspoon orange liqueur
finely grated zest of ½ medium
    orange
finely grated zest of ½ small
    unwaxed lemon

350g self-raising flour
¼ teaspoon ground mixed spice
¼ teaspoon ground ginger
¼ teaspoon ground cinnamon
¼ teaspoon fine sea salt
125g caster sugar
230g unsalted butter, chilled
    and diced
about 1½ tablespoons buttermilk

FOR THE ICING
500g icing sugar
about 6 tablespoons milk
few drops of almond extract
pearlescent-white edible food
    colouring paste (optional)
black edible food colouring
    (gel or paste)

you will need
1 sheep-shaped cutter,
7.5–9cm long; 2 baking
sheets, lined with baking
paper; squeezy icing piping
bottle; 2 small disposable
piping bags; a fine writer-
piping nozzle (no. 1.5 or 2)

1. Put the tea bags in a heatproof bowl and pour over the boiling water. Leave to steep until the tea is very strong, then remove the bags (give them a good squeeze). Stir in the dried fruit and orange liqueur, then set aside to soak until completely cold.

2. Drain the fruit very well (discard the tea). Put the fruit and the grated orange and lemon zests into the bowl of a food processor and blitz to make a thick paste (you can also do this by chopping the fruit and then grinding it with the zests using a mortar and pestle). Scrape out the paste into a bowl and set aside.

3. Sift the flour with the mixed spice, ginger, cinnamon and salt into a large mixing bowl. Stir in the sugar, then add the diced butter and rub in* until the mixture looks like fine crumbs. Add the fruit paste and rub in until thoroughly distributed. Add the buttermilk and mix everything together with a round-bladed knife. As soon as the mixture starts to clump together, use your hands to bring it all together into a dough (like making shortbread).

4. Turn out the dough on to a lightly floured worktop and roll out to about 4mm thick. Dip the cutter in flour, then stamp out shapes. Arrange on the lined baking sheets, setting the shapes slightly apart to allow for spreading during baking. Gather up the trimmings, re-roll and cut more shapes. Prick the shapes well with a fork, then chill while you heat the oven to 180°C/350°F/gas 4.

5. Bake the biscuits, in batches if necessary, for 13–15 minutes until lightly coloured – check after 10 minutes and rotate the baking sheets, if necessary, so all the biscuits colour evenly. Remove from the oven and leave the biscuits to cool and firm up on the sheets for 5 minutes before transferring to a wire rack to cool completely.

6. To decorate, sift the icing sugar into a mixing bowl. Add 4 tablespoons milk and the almond extract and mix with a wooden spoon to make a stiff but smooth icing (if necessary add a little more milk, a teaspoon at a time). Remove about 4 tablespoons of the icing and put into a small bowl; put another 4 tablespoons into a third bowl. Cover both small bowls. If using pearlescent-white food colouring, add a very little to the icing left in the mixing bowl and mix in along with enough milk, also adding this a few drops at a time, to make a smoothly flowing, coating consistency. Transfer this icing to the squeezy bottle and use to cover the biscuits – this is the fleecy white 'coat' on the sheep biscuits. Leave to set for about 1 hour.

7. Colour one of the small portions of icing with the black food colouring – you want a smooth piping consistency, so add a little more icing sugar or milk as needed. Transfer to a piping bag fitted with the writing nozzle and use to pipe the heads, legs/feet and features of the sheep.

8. Transfer the white icing from the last bowl to the other piping bag (wash the nozzle if necessary), then use to pipe the curly features of the fleece. Leave to set. Store the biscuits in an airtight container and eat within 4 days.

COCONUT MACAROON KISSES

Elegant, French-style coconut macaroons, these have the most perfect moist, sweet and chewy texture. Based on luscious crème pâtissière and desiccated coconut (with no flour, making them gluten-free), they are finished with a chocolate-glazed base. If you follow the recipe carefully you will find they are not at all difficult to make.

makes 20

| gluten free

FOR THE CRÈME PÂTISSIÈRE
5 tablespoons creamy milk
3 tablespoons caster sugar
1 tablespoon cornflour
1 medium egg yolk, at room temperature

FOR THE COCONUT MIXTURE
3 medium egg whites, at room temperature
½ teaspoon vanilla extract
100g caster sugar
200g desiccated coconut

FOR THE CHOCOLATE GLAZE
100g dark chocolate (about 70% cocoa solids)
2 tablespoons sunflower oil

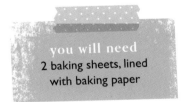

you will need
2 baking sheets, lined with baking paper

another idea: You'll have 2 egg yolks left, so why not use them to make a batch of lemon curd (see recipe on page 20)?

1. First make the crème pâtissière. Heat the milk in a small pan until steaming hot, then remove from the heat. Measure the caster sugar and cornflour into a small heatproof bowl (set on a damp cloth to prevent it from wobbling). Add the egg yolk and beat well with a wooden spoon for about a minute until very smooth and pale. Gradually stir in the hot milk, then tip the mixture back into the pan. Set over medium/low heat and whisk with a small hand wire whisk until the mixture boils and thickens. Scrape out on to a plate, press a piece of clingfilm on to the surface (to prevent a skin from forming) and leave to cool.

2. Meanwhile, make the coconut mixture. Heat the oven to 170°C/325°F/gas 3. Put the egg whites into a mixing bowl, add the vanilla extract and beat well with a fork until the whites are thoroughly broken up and the mixture is frothy. Add the caster sugar and beat with a wooden spoon for about a minute until the sugar has dissolved. Stir in the coconut. Add the crème pâtissière and mix in thoroughly so there are no streaks or lumps.

3. Scoop up some of the mixture using a teaspoon and pack into a tablespoon measure, then tap it out on to a lined baking sheet. If necessary, gently pat and mould the domed mound back into a fairly neat shape (don't worry if it looks slightly 'hairy' rather than smooth). Repeat with the rest of the mixture, setting the mounds slightly apart on the baking sheets.

4. Bake in the heated oven for 20 minutes until slightly golden with darker edges – the centre of each macaroon should still be moist, not firm and dry. Leave the macaroons to cool completely on the baking sheets.

5. When ready to finish, gently melt the chocolate*, then stir in the oil until thoroughly combined. Peel the macaroons off the lining paper and, one at a time, carefully dip the flat base of each into the chocolate glaze – the chocolate should evenly coat the base and extend 2–3mm up the sides. Place on a clean sheet of baking paper, chocolate base down. Leave to set.

6. When the chocolate is firm, gently peel the macaroons away from the paper. Store in an airtight container in a cool spot (not the fridge) and eat within 5 days. The macaroons will be moister and more chewy after 24 hours.

CARDAMOM LEMON BUNS

These gently spiced little buns are a lovely project for an afternoon bake. The sponge mixture is made from whisked eggs, just like a genoise sponge with extra whisked egg whites folded in, so it is wonderfully light. Melted butter adds a rich taste and soft texture. Prettily sandwiched with a lemony butter icing, these are perfect for teatime.

makes 12 pairs

FOR THE SPONGES

2 medium egg whites plus
  2 whole eggs, at room
  temperature
good pinch of fine sea salt
160g caster sugar
½ teaspoon finely grated
  lemon zest
seeds from 8 cardamom pods,
  finely ground
180g self-raising flour
115g unsalted butter, melted
  and cooled
150ml milk, at room temperature

FOR THE FILLING

60g unsalted butter, softened
200g icing sugar, plus extra for
  dusting
4 tablespoons lemon curd
  (for a recipe, see page 20)

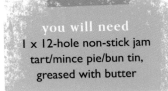

you will need
1 x 12-hole non-stick jam
tart/mince pie/bun tin,
greased with butter

1. Heat the oven to 180°C/350°F/gas 4. Put the 2 egg whites into a mixing bowl, or a free-standing electric mixer fitted with the whisk attachment. Break the 2 whole eggs into another, larger mixing bowl and set aside. Add the salt to the egg whites, then whisk*, using a hand-held electric whisk, or the whisk attachment, on high speed until stiff peaks form. Put to one side.

2. Add the sugar and lemon zest to the whole eggs. Whisk (there's no need to wash the whisk, but if you are using a stand mixer, transfer the whisked whites to a clean bowl) until the mixture becomes very pale and thick, and reaches the ribbon stage*. Add the cardamom and briefly whisk in.

3. Sift the flour on to the mixture, then drizzle the butter around the sides of the bowl. Start to fold* in the flour and butter gently using a large metal spoon or plastic spatula. When most of the flour has been incorporated, drizzle the milk into the bowl and continue folding until there are no streaks. Add the whisked egg whites and fold them in until completely amalgamated.

4. Spoon half the mixture into the greased holes of the tin – each hole should be about three-quarters full. Bake in the heated oven for 10–12 minutes until the little buns are pale golden with darker edges; they should be starting to shrink away from the sides of the moulds and feel springy when gently pressed in the centre*. Remove from the oven and allow the buns to cool in the tin for a minute, then gently flip out on to a wire rack so the domed tops are facing upwards. Leave to cool completely.

5. Wipe out the holes in the tin, then grease again with butter (if the tin is still very hot, leave it to cool first). Spoon the rest of the sponge mixture into the holes, dividing it equally. Bake as before, then leave to cool.

6. To make the lemon filling, beat the butter until creamy using a wooden spoon or electric whisk, then sift in the icing sugar and beat until very fluffy. Add 3 tablespoons of the lemon curd and beat in. Spoon in the last of the lemon curd and marble it through by swirling with a round-bladed knife.

7. When the buns are cold, spread the lemon filling over the flat sides of 12 buns, then sandwich with the other 12 (flat side to flat side). Dust with icing sugar before serving. Store in an airtight container and eat within 2 days.

VIENNESE WHIRLS

A classic: rich, crisp, beautifully piped biscuits sandwiched with home-made raspberry jam and a swirl of piped vanilla buttercream. Beating and piping skills are tested here as the biscuits should all be identical in colour and size.

makes 12

1. Start by making the jam. Put the raspberries into a small, deep-sided saucepan and crush them with a potato masher. Add the sugar and bring to the boil over a low heat, stirring occasionally until the sugar has dissolved. Increase the heat and boil for 4 minutes. Remove from the heat and carefully pour the jam into a shallow heatproof container. Leave to cool, then cover and chill until set.

2. To make the biscuits, heat the oven to 190°C/375°F/gas 5. Using the 4cm round cutter as a guide, draw 8 circles (spaced well apart) on each of the 3 sheets of lining paper cut to fit the baking sheets. Turn the paper over so the pencil marks are underneath and lay the paper on the baking sheets.

3. Measure the butter and icing sugar into a bowl and beat well until pale and fluffy. Sift the flour and cornflour on top and beat in well, slowly at first, to make a smooth mixture that can be piped.

4. Spoon the mixture into the piping bag fitted with the medium star nozzle. Pipe 24 whirls (not rosettes or stars) inside the circles drawn on the baking sheets – start the piping in the centre and move in a spiral, ending at the outer edge.

5. Bake in the centre of the heated oven for 13–15 minutes until a pale golden-brown colour – watch carefully to be sure the biscuits do not get too dark. Leave the delicate biscuits to firm up on the baking sheets for 5 minutes before transferring to a wire rack to cool completely and harden.

6. For the filling, measure the butter into a bowl and sift the icing sugar on top. Add the vanilla extract and beat with a wooden spoon or a hand-held electric whisk until very light and smooth. Spoon into the clean piping bag fitted with the large star nozzle.

7. Spoon a little jam on to the flat side of 12 of the biscuits and place jam-side up on a wire rack. Pipe the buttercream filling over the jam, in a whirl as you did when shaping the biscuits, and sandwich with the remaining biscuits, flat side to flat side. Turn the sandwiched biscuits over and dust with icing sugar to decorate.

FOR THE JAM
200g raspberries
250g jam sugar (sugar with added pectin)

FOR THE BISCUITS
250g unsalted butter, very soft
50g icing sugar, sifted
225g plain flour
25g cornflour

FOR THE FILLING
100g unsalted butter, softened
200g icing sugar, plus extra for dusting
½ teaspoon vanilla extract

you will need
3 baking sheets, lined with baking paper; a 4cm round cutter (see recipe); a piping bag; a medium star nozzle; a large star nozzle

BREADS

The great thing about baking bread (apart from eating it, of course) is that you need no special talent, ingredients or equipment to make a wonderful loaf. Hot or heavy hands? No problem here! No mixer or processor? A bowl and baking sheet are just fine. As long as you have the right flour, some yeast, salt and water, you'll be all set.

Not just for beginners, there are several simple recipes in this chapter to get you baking delicious loaves for the table: the Very Easy Boule Loaf (page 118) is just what it says it is, and is achieved without kneading. The deeply flavoured Crunchy Beer Bread (page 120) does require kneading plus an extended fermentation but the result is worth the wait.

Great-looking twists and shaped loaves are plentiful here. There's a skill to getting all the elements just right – the shape and appearance, the flavour of the dough, and the texture of the crumb and crust. Roasted Garlic Herb Twist (page 145) and Chocolate, Cardamom and Hazelnut Babka (page 159) illustrate two of the ways to make good-looking twisted loaves. There's more chocolate to enjoy in the pull-apart Cobbled Chocolate Loaf on page 137 and the Chocolate Orange Swirl Bread on page 150, which is made like Chelsea Buns.

A different sort of texture is found in Dampfnudeln (see page 139), a homely dessert from Alsace, in which dumplings made from a soft, light dough are poached and then served in a custard-style sauce along with one made from fresh plums. It's an unusual recipe that keen bread bakers will want to try.

Handling and working successfully with different doughs comes with practice; altering the flour or the liquid (or the proportions) means learning what does or doesn't work! Using soaked and chopped wheat grains to make a Sprouted Wheat Bread turns a simple recipe on its head – you'll enjoy the result (see page 133).

More experienced bakers looking for a weekend project, or a speciality for a particular occasion, will want to try making the pretty Cardamom Pear Plait (see page 162), which involves lamination (it's a yeasted rough puff pastry dough) and some intricate shaping. Similar is the laminated dough for the Danish pastries on page 170 and page 173, so irresistible with their deliciously crisp and flaky texture.

VERY EASY BOULE LOAF

Not just for novice bakers, this amazingly simple white loaf delivers an excellent crispy crust as well as a full-flavoured, open crumb - with hardly any effort. The damp, sticky dough is left to ferment overnight in the fridge. No kneading required! This is the ideal daily loaf - as good for toast as it is for sandwiches.

makes a medium loaf

| dairy free

450g strong white bread flour
5g fast-action dried yeast
 (from a 7g sachet)
7g fine sea salt
350ml water from the cold tap

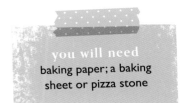

you will need
baking paper; a baking
sheet or pizza stone

another idea: Once you have perfected making your loaf you can try adding flavours, such as 1 tablespoon finely chopped fresh rosemary or poppyseeds, mixed in with the salt.

1. Put the flour and yeast into a large mixing bowl, or the bowl of a free-standing electric mixer fitted with the paddle-beater attachment. Mix thoroughly with your hand, then mix in the salt. Make a well in the centre and pour in the cold water. Using your hand, or the paddle-beater on the slowest speed, mix everything together to make a very soft, sticky dough. Once the dough has come together, continue mixing or stirring for 1 minute just to make sure the dough is even and lump-free. It won't look smooth and glossy like a conventional bread dough, or be as elastic, but don't worry!

2. Cover the bowl tightly with clingfilm or a snap-on lid (or transfer the dough to a plastic container with a snap-on lid) and put into the fridge. Leave for at least 6 hours, preferably overnight, but no longer than 24 hours. The dough will slowly rise until doubled, or a little more, in size and then slightly fall back.

3. Next day, flour your hands and the worktop, then scoop out the dough — it will feel cold and much firmer. Gently knead and shape the dough until it forms a ball — there's no need to spend a lot of time on this. Set the ball on a sheet of baking paper dusted with flour. Dust the top of the loaf with flour, then cover with a large, upturned bowl, or lay a large sheet of clingfilm loosely over the dough. Leave for about 2 hours to come back to room temperature and rise (or expand) until almost doubled in size.

4. Towards the end of the rising time, heat the oven to 230°C/450°F/gas 8. Put an empty roasting tin in the bottom of the oven to heat up, as well as the baking sheet or pizza stone on a shelf above.

5. When the dough is ready, make 5 deep slashes across the top of the ball with a very sharp knife. Carefully slide or lift the baking paper with the loaf on it on to the heated baking sheet or pizza stone. Pour a jug of cold water into the hot roasting tin to produce a burst of steam, then quickly close the oven door. Bake the loaf for 30–35 minutes until it is a rich golden brown and sounds hollow when tapped on the underside*. For best results check the loaf after 25 minutes and, if necessary, rotate the baking sheet to make sure the bread bakes evenly. Cool on a wire rack. This loaf is best eaten within 4 days, or toasted. The cooled loaf can also be tightly wrapped and frozen for up to a month.

CRUNCHY BEER BREAD

A deeply flavoured, great-smelling loaf, this is perfect with cheese or charcuterie. The dough is made with a mixture of wholemeal spelt and rye flours (you can buy a ready-made mix or create your own) plus malty beer instead of water. An extended rising time in the fridge develops the complex taste and helps give a good crust as well as preventing a too-crumbly texture.

makes a medium loaf | dairy free

600g wholemeal spelt and rye
    bread flour mix OR 400g
    wholemeal spelt bread flour
    plus 200g rye flour
½ teaspoon fast-action dried
    yeast
10g fine sea salt
1 tablespoon clear honey
1 tablespoon malt extract
400ml malt beer OR sweet/Irish
    stout

TO FINISH
2 tablespoons beer/stout, for
    brushing
2 tablespoons rye or spelt flakes
    OR cracked rye or spelt, for
    sprinkling

you will need
1 baking sheet, lined
with baking paper

1. Put the flour mix, or flours, into a large mixing bowl, or the bowl of a free-standing electric mixer fitted with the dough hook attachment. Using your hand, mix in the yeast and then the salt. Make a well in the centre.

2. Stir the honey and malt extract into the beer or stout, then pour into the well in the flour. Gradually work the flour into the liquid with your hand, or the dough hook on slowest speed, to make a soft, sticky dough. Leave the dough to sit in the bowl for 5 minutes to give the flour time to hydrate*. If, after this time, the dough feels a lot stiffer or dry, or there are dry crumbs, work in more beer a tablespoon at a time – the dough should feel slightly soft (and slightly tacky because of the rye).

3. Turn out the dough on to a lightly floured worktop and knead* thoroughly by hand for 10 minutes, or for 5 minutes with the dough hook on slow speed, until the dough feels firmer, elastic and less tacky.

4. Return the dough to the bowl, if necessary, and cover tightly with clingfilm or a snap-on lid (or transfer the dough to a plastic container with a snap-on lid). Leave in the fridge to slowly ferment and rise for at least 8 hours, preferably overnight, so the rich flavours can develop and deepen. The dough will double in size.

5. Turn out the dough on to a lightly floured worktop – the dough will feel very firm and cold – and gently knead for 2–3 minutes until it feels a little softer and more flexible. Shape into a neat ball and set on the lined baking sheet. Slip the sheet into a large plastic bag, slightly inflate so the plastic won't stick to the dough as it rises, and tie the ends. Leave to rise on the worktop until the dough has doubled in size: because it needs to come back to room temperature this will take 2–3 hours.

6. Towards the end of the rising time, heat the oven to 200°C/400°F/gas 6 and put a roasting tin into the bottom of the oven to heat up.

7. When the dough is ready, uncover it and brush it lightly with beer or stout. Sprinkle with the flaked or cracked spelt or rye, then cut a deep cross in the top of the ball with a sharp knife.

8. Put the baking sheet into the oven. Pour a jug of cold water into the hot roasting tin (to give a burst of steam), then quickly close the oven door. Bake the loaf for about 35 minutes until it is a rich chestnut brown and sounds hollow when tapped on the underside*.

9. Transfer the loaf to a wire rack and leave until completely cold before slicing. Best eaten within 5 days, or toasted. The cooled loaf can also be tightly wrapped and frozen for up to a month.

BLACK OLIVE FLATBREAD

Here's a simple yet delicious bread to start an Italian-style supper. It's made by working black olives and thyme into an extra-sticky dough, which is baked with a topping of goats' cheese. Use deeply flavoured Kalamata olives and your favourite goats' cheese - either soft and mild or stronger and more piquant. Serve with a fruity extra virgin olive oil and balsamic vinegar for dipping.

makes a large bread

1. To make the dough, combine the flour and yeast in a large bowl, then mix in the salt. Coarsely chop the olives with the thyme leaves, then add to the bowl. Mix in with your hand to distribute evenly. Make a well in the centre of the mixture. Pour the olive oil and lukewarm water into the well, then gradually draw the flour mixture into the liquid with your hand to make a very soft, very sticky dough.

2. This dough is too soft to knead* on a worktop so keep it in the bowl. Set the bowl on a damp cloth to prevent it from wobbling, then work the dough by vigorously slapping it against the sides of the bowl until it feels slightly firmer and is very stretchy indeed. This will take 8–10 minutes. Cover the bowl with clingfilm and leave to rise in a warm spot for 1½–2 hours until the dough is 2 to 2½ times its original size.

3. Scoop out the dough on to the cornmeal-dusted baking sheet. Oil your fingers and use to press out the dough to a rectangle about 30 x 25cm of even thickness. Leave to rise, uncovered, in a warm spot for 15 minutes.

4. Meanwhile, heat the oven to 200°C/400°F/gas 6.

5. Cut or crumble the goats' cheese into 1cm pieces and scatter over the dough. Sprinkle with black pepper (as much as you like), then drizzle the olive oil over the top. Leave for 10 minutes before placing the bread in the heated oven. Bake for 17–20 minutes until the bread is slightly puffed and golden around the edges.

6. Transfer the bread to a cutting board and scatter the thyme sprigs over the top. Eat warm, cut or torn into large pieces. This is best eaten soon after baking but you can reheat it later, the same day, in a 200°C/400°F/gas 6 oven for about 5 minutes.

255g strong white bread flour
1 x 7g sachet fast-action dried yeast
5g fine sea salt
100g pitted black olives
few sprigs of fresh thyme
1 tablespoon fruity olive oil
175ml lukewarm water

TO FINISH
75g log-style goats' cheese
coarsely ground black pepper
2 tablespoons olive oil
few sprigs of fresh thyme

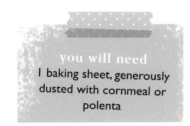
you will need
1 baking sheet, generously dusted with cornmeal or polenta

PAIN D'ÉPICES

This is a chocolate version of the classic French honey-spice loaf, and it couldn't be easier. Traditionally made with equal weights of flour and well-flavoured honey, it's enhanced with quatre épices (a ready-made mix of finely ground black pepper, cloves, ginger and nutmeg). If possible, use a food processor to grate or finely chop the chocolate quickly so it doesn't soften or melt before it goes into the mixture.

makes a medium loaf

210g plain flour
90g rye flour
2 teaspoons baking powder
¼ teaspoon fine sea salt
½ teaspoon ground cinnamon
½ teaspoon quatre épices
    OR ⅛ teaspoon each finely
    ground black pepper, cloves,
    ginger and nutmeg
100g dark chocolate (about 70%
    cocoa solids), grated or finely
    chopped
300g clear honey
2 medium egg yolks
5½ tablespoons milk

TO FINISH
2 tablespoons caster sugar
3 tablespoons milk

you will need
1 x 900g loaf tin, about
26 x 12.5 x 7.5cm, greased
and lined with a long strip
of baking paper*

1. Heat the oven to 180°C/350°F/gas 4. Sift both flours, the baking powder, salt and all the spices into a mixing bowl. Stir in the grated chocolate, then make a well in the centre. Spoon the honey into the well and add the egg yolks and milk. Mix everything together with a wooden spoon to make a thick, heavy, cake-like mixture.

2. Scrape the mixture into the prepared tin and spread evenly, making sure the corners are well filled. Bake in the heated oven for about 40 minutes until the top is a rich golden brown and a skewer inserted into the centre of the loaf comes out clean.

3. While the loaf is baking, measure the sugar and milk into a small pan. Set aside for now.

4. Remove the tin from the oven and run a round-bladed knife around the inside to loosen the loaf. Using the ends of the paper strip to help, lift out the loaf on to a wire rack. Peel off the lining paper strip.

5. Now heat the sugar and milk mixture, stirring, just until the sugar dissolves and the mixture is steaming hot. Remove from the heat and quickly brush over the top of the hot loaf. Leave to cool to room temperature before wrapping the loaf in baking paper or clingfilm. Store in an airtight container for 1–2 days before slicing (the complex flavours in the loaf will deepen and mature the longer it is kept).

STUFFED CHAPATIS WITH CORIANDER-TOMATO CHUTNEY

A great curry night accompaniment to impress your friends, these quickly made unleavened chapatis are filled with a spicy ginger-spinach mixture and then briefly cooked on top of the stove. Serve with a fresh chutney (see page 128).

makes 8 | dairy free

FOR THE CHAPATI DOUGH
300g atta/chapati flour OR 150g
    fine wholemeal plain flour
    plus 150g plain white flour
7g fine sea salt
1 tablespoon sunflower oil
about 200ml water, at room
    temperature
melted ghee or sunflower oil, for
    brushing (optional)

FOR THE FILLING
1 small onion, roughly chopped
4 garlic cloves, roughly chopped
35g piece fresh root ginger, peeled
    and roughly chopped
1 green chilli (or to taste), seeds
    removed, then roughly chopped
2 tablespoons sunflower oil
1 teaspoon ground cumin
½ teaspoon cumin seeds
125g split red lentils, rinsed
500ml water
200g baby leaf spinach
lemon juice, salt, black pepper and
    garam masala, all to taste

you will need
a tava/heavy cast-iron
frying pan/griddle

1. Make the chapati dough first as it needs time to rest. Put the flour(s) into a mixing bowl and stir in the salt. Trickle the oil over the top and briefly rub it into the flour. Pour about half of the water into the bowl and roughly mix in with your fingers until the flakes of dough start to come together. Gradually add enough additional water to make a sticky dough.

2. Using your knuckles, knead the dough thoroughly in the bowl until it doesn't stick to the sides of the bowl or your fingers, and feels firmer and elastic – this dough needs to be supple enough to roll out. Cover the bowl with clingfilm and leave to rest for at least an hour, and up to 3 hours.

3. Meanwhile, make the filling. Put the roughly chopped onion, garlic, ginger and chilli in a food processor and pulse to chop fairly finely. Heat half the oil in a non-stick frying pan, add the ground and whole cumin, and stir briefly. Add the finely chopped mixture and stir over medium heat until softened and golden. Remove from the heat and set aside.

4. Put the lentils in a large pan and add the water. Bring to the boil, then boil rapidly for 10 minutes, stirring frequently. Reduce the heat and simmer until the lentils are very soft. Add the spinach and cook, stirring, until wilted.

5. Add the lentil mixture to the onion mixture and cook over medium heat, stirring constantly, until the excess liquid evaporates, leaving a thick and fairly dry mixture (it should have the consistency of mashed potato). Add lemon juice, salt, pepper and garam masala to taste, then leave to cool.

6. To assemble the chapatis, divide the dough into 8 equal portions and roll out each one on a lightly floured worktop to a disc about 10cm across. Put a heaped tablespoon of the filling into the centre of each disc (you won't use all the filling), then draw up the edges of the dough (like a purse) to cover the filling and pinch to seal. Turn the 'purse' over and gently roll out as thinly as you possibly can without the filling breaking through the dough – the disc will now be 12–13cm in diameter.

7. To cook the chapatis, heat the tava (or frying pan or griddle) until very hot – avoid greasing it, if possible, or your kitchen will become very smoky. Place a chapati on the tava and cook for about 30 seconds, then flip it over and cook the second side for 30 seconds. Flip again and press down gently with a fish slice or large spatula. After 30 seconds flip and repeat – both sides should now be speckled with dark brown patches. Remove the chapati and quickly brush it with melted ghee or oil (if using). Keep warm wrapped in a clean dry cloth until all the chapatis are cooked, then eat immediately, with chutney. (You can reheat the remaining filling mixture in a small pan, adding enough water to make a slightly runny dhal side dish.)

CORIANDER-TOMATO CHUTNEY

Buy the ripest, juiciest tomatoes you can find for the best flavour, and add as much or as little heat as you like for this quick, fresh accompaniment for stuffed chapatis.

serves 4–6

2 tablespoons sunflower oil
1 large sweet onion, finely chopped
3 ripe, well-flavoured tomatoes (about 200g), roughly chopped
small handful of fresh coriander leaves
½ teaspoon brown mustard seeds
½ teaspoon coriander seeds, roughly cracked
large pinch of crushed red chilli flakes, or to taste
salt, to taste

1. Heat 1 tablespoon of the oil in a medium pan, add the onion and stir well, then cover and leave to cook very gently for 8–10 minutes until soft and golden. Add the tomatoes and coriander, and cook, stirring occasionally, for about 10 minutes until the tomatoes have softened. Tip the mixture into a food processor and pulse to make a coarse paste – the mixture should not be a smooth purée. Set aside.

2. Rinse out the pan and reheat with the remaining oil. Add the mustard and coriander seeds, and cook until they start to 'pop', then add the chilli flakes followed by the tomato mixture. Stir over medium heat for a minute or so until the chutney is thick. Remove from the heat and season with salt to taste. Leave to cool, then transfer to a serving bowl. Serve at room temperature the same or next day (keep tightly covered in the fridge).

GREEK COUNTRY BREAD

Ideal for picnics and summery meals, this walnut-filled loaf is perfect for dipping in good olive oil, and with ripe tomatoes and cheeses. The interesting method of construction - the dough is layered up with the filling - takes a bit of time and care but gives the loaf its unusual and appealing flaky texture.

makes a large loaf | dairy free

FOR THE DOUGH

325g strong white bread flour
100g stoneground wholemeal
   bread flour (wheat OR spelt)
1 x 7g sachet fast-action dried
   yeast
7g fine sea salt
2 tablespoons walnut oil OR olive
   oil, plus extra olive oil for
   kneading
275ml lukewarm water

FOR THE FILLING

250g walnut pieces
about 100ml olive oil, for brushing

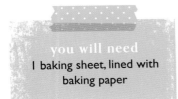
you will need
1 baking sheet, lined with
baking paper

1. To make the dough, put both flours and the yeast into a large mixing bowl, or the bowl of a free-standing electric mixer fitted with the dough hook attachment, and mix thoroughly with your hand. Mix in the salt, then make a well in the centre.

2. Spoon the oil into the well, then pour in the lukewarm water. Gradually draw the flour into the liquid with your hand, or the dough hook on slow speed, to make a soft but not sticky dough. Flours vary, so if the dough feels very sticky work in a little more white bread flour — you want to end up with a soft, but not sticky dough, as this will be the easiest to work later. As soon as the dough has come together, set aside so the flour can hydrate* for 5 minutes. If, after this time, the dough feels dry or slightly stiff and hard, or there are dry crumbs in the bottom of the bowl, work in a little more lukewarm water a tablespoon at a time.

3. If you are kneading by hand, lightly oil the worktop and your hands with a few drops of olive oil. Turn out the dough on to the oiled worktop and knead* it very thoroughly for 10 minutes (or knead for 5 minutes, without oil, using the dough hook on slow speed) until it feels very elastic and supple. Return the dough to the bowl, if necessary, then cover it tightly with clingfilm or a snap-on lid and leave on the worktop to rise for about 1 hour until the dough has doubled in size.

4. Meanwhile, heat the oven to 180°C/350°F/gas 4. Tip the walnuts into a large baking dish or tin and toast in the heated oven for 6–8 minutes just until they turn golden. Leave to cool, then cover the dish with a clean, dry tea towel and crush the nuts by gently bashing them with the base of a small pan into slightly smaller pieces — this crushing helps release their oils too. Set aside (you can turn off the oven for now).

5. Very lightly flour the worktop, then turn out the dough and divide it into 4 equal pieces (either by weight or by eye). Roll out one piece to a very thin 30cm square and carefully lift it on to a large sheet of baking paper lightly dusted with flour. Brush the square with olive oil, making sure the edges are not forgotten, then scatter a quarter of the nuts over the dough. Set this square to one side.

COBBLED CHOCOLATE LOAF

An attractive pull-apart bread made from two different doughs, each with a pure chocolate filling. The great thing is the chocolate that oozes out as the loaf is served! Perfect for brunch with jugs of hot chocolate.

makes a large loaf

FOR THE 'WHITE' DOUGH
100ml full-fat/whole milk
50g unsalted butter
seeds from 6 cardamom pods, finely crushed
250g strong white bread flour
5g fine sea salt
30g caster sugar
finely grated zest of 1 orange
1 x 7g sachet fast-action dried yeast
1 medium egg, at room temperature

FOR THE 'CHOCOLATE' DOUGH
120ml full-fat/whole milk
50g unsalted butter
½ teaspoon vanilla extract
250g strong white bread flour
15g cocoa powder, sifted
5g fine sea salt
30g caster sugar
1x 7g sachet fast-action dried yeast
1 medium egg, at room temperature

TO ASSEMBLE
1 x 120g bar dark chocolate (about 70% cocoa solids)
1 x 120g bar white chocolate (about 30% cocoa solids)

FOR THE GLAZE
40g caster sugar
40ml water
2 long strips pared orange peel
2 cardamom pods

you will need
1 x 25cm round springclip tin, greased with sunflower oil and sprinkled with fine semolina/polenta; a baking sheet, lined with baking paper

1. Start by making the cardamom and orange-flavoured 'white' dough. Put the milk, butter and crushed cardamom into a small pan and warm gently until the butter has completely melted. Leave to cool until lukewarm.

2. Put the flour, salt, sugar and orange zest into the bowl of a free-standing electric mixer fitted with the dough hook and combine with your hand. Add the yeast and mix in thoroughly. Beat the egg into the lukewarm milk, then pour this into the bowl. Mix everything together with the dough hook on low speed to make a very soft but not sticky dough; if necessary work in a little more flour.

3. Knead*, using the dough hook on slow speed, for about 5 minutes until the dough feels very smooth and stretchy. Transfer to an oiled bowl, cover with clingfilm and leave on the worktop to rise for about 1 hour until doubled in size.

4. Meanwhile, make the 'chocolate' dough in the same way (there's no need to wash the pan, bowl and dough hook): gently warm the milk and butter with the vanilla. Combine the flour, cocoa, salt and sugar, stir in the yeast and mix to a very soft dough with the milk mixture and egg. Now set aside, uncovered, to allow the flour to hydrate* for 5 minutes (the cocoa makes it harder for the flour to absorb the liquid quickly).

5. After this time, feel the dough and add a little more milk or flour as needed to make a soft but sticky texture. Knead with the dough hook on slow speed for 5 minutes until stretchy. Cover the bowl and leave to rise, alongside the white dough, for about 1 hour until doubled in size.

6. Break or chop up each bar of chocolate into 24 even-sized chunks, and divide into 12 pairs – each with 2 pieces of the same type.

7. Punch down the white dough to deflate it, then turn it out on to an unfloured worktop and knead into a ball. Weigh, then divide into 12 equal pieces. Roll each into a ball, then pat out to an 8cm disc. Set a pair of dark chocolate chunks in the centre. Gather up the edges of the disc like a purse or Chinese dumpling to enclose the chocolate and pinch to thoroughly seal. Gently roll the dough in your hand to make a neat ball again. Repeat with the chocolate dough, filling these balls with the white chocolate chunks.

8. Alternating the white dough and chocolate dough balls, arrange them, seam side down, in the prepared tin so they are closely packed together. Cover the top of the tin with clingfilm and leave on the worktop to rise for 50–60 minutes until doubled in size.

9. Towards the end of the rising time, heat the oven to 200°C/400°F/gas 6.

10. Uncover the tin and bake the loaf in the heated oven for 20 minutes until the tops of the balls are golden. Remove the tin from the oven and place the lined baking sheet, upside down, on top. Invert the whole lot, then unclip the tin and remove its side and base. Return the bread, upside down now on the lined baking sheet, to the oven and bake for a further 12–15 minutes until the top (what had been the base) is a good golden brown. Invert on to a wire rack and leave to cool for 5 minutes.

11. Meanwhile, make the glaze. Put the sugar, water and orange peel strips into a small pan. Lightly crush the cardamom pods and add. Heat gently, stirring, until the sugar dissolves, then bring to the boil and simmer for a minute. Remove the cardamom pods and orange peel, then lightly brush the glaze over the loaf.

12. Leave the loaf to cool until just warm, then transfer to a bread board. To serve, pull apart the balls and break them open to see the chocolate.

DAMPFNUDELN

Here is a traditional dessert from Alsace of light, sweet yeasted dumplings that are poached and then served with a custard-style vanilla sauce and a fresh plum sauce. If you enjoy custard, make double the amount of vanilla sauce to go with your dampfnudeln.

makes 12 to serve 4-6

1. To make the dampfnudeln, tip the flour into a large mixing bowl. Add the sugar to one side of the bowl and the yeast to the other. Make a well and pour in the warm milk, beaten eggs and cooled melted butter. Turn the milk mixture round with your fingers, picking up the flour from around the well, then continue mixing and working until the side of the bowl is clean and you have a rough, rather wet dough.

2. Tip the dough on to a lightly floured worktop. Knead* for 5–10 minutes: work through the initial wet stage until the dough starts to form a soft, smooth skin. Scatter the lemon zest on top of the dough and knead until the zest is evenly incorporated. Transfer the dough to a lightly oiled bowl, cover with clingfilm and leave to rise on the worktop for at least 1 hour until doubled in size.

3. Meanwhile, make the plum sauce. Roughly chop up the plums, discarding the stones, then tip into a pan. Add the orange juice and sprinkle over the sugar. Cook over a low heat until the sugar dissolves, stirring occasionally, then increase the heat and simmer for 10 minutes, mashing the plums with a wooden spoon as they soften. Remove from the heat and stir in the cinnamon. Leave to cool slightly before blending to a thick sauce using a hand blender or in a food processor. Set aside.

4. For the vanilla sauce, heat the milk with the cream in a heavy-based saucepan (preferably non-stick) over a medium heat to just below boiling point. Meanwhile, put the egg yolks, sugar, flour and vanilla paste in a large heatproof bowl set on a damp cloth (to prevent wobbling) and whisk together with a hand wire whisk until pale and fluffy. Gradually add the warmed creamy milk, whisking constantly.

5. Pour the mixture back into the pan and cook over a very low heat, stirring constantly with a wooden spoon, for 3–4 minutes until the sauce is smooth and thick enough to coat the back of the spoon. Remove from the heat. Cover the surface of the sauce with clingfilm, to prevent a skin from forming, and set aside.

6. Turn out the risen dough on to a lightly floured worktop. Fold the edges of the dough inwards repeatedly until all the air is knocked out. Divide the dough into 12 equal pieces and roll each into a neat ball.

FOR THE DAMPFNUDELN
500g strong white bread flour, plus extra for dusting
100g caster sugar
7g fast-action dried yeast
150ml full-fat/whole milk, warmed
2 large eggs, at room temperature, lightly beaten to mix
70g unsalted butter, melted
finely grated zest of 1 unwaxed lemon

FOR THE PLUM SAUCE
4 ripe plums
juice of 1 medium orange
50g demerara sugar
pinch of ground cinnamon

FOR THE VANILLA SAUCE
150ml full-fat/whole milk
150ml double cream
3 large egg yolks, at room temperature
50g caster sugar
2 teaspoons plain flour
½ teaspoon vanilla bean paste

FOR THE POACHING LIQUID
25g unsalted butter
150ml full-fat/whole milk
25g caster sugar

you will need
1 large, wide, heavy-based saucepan with a tight-fitting lid

7. For the poaching liquid, put the butter, milk and sugar in the large, wide saucepan and warm over a medium heat for 5 minutes until the sugar has completely dissolved, stirring occasionally. Remove the pan from the heat and add the dough balls, ensuring all are sitting on the base of the pan in a single layer. Leave to stand for 15 minutes until doubled in size.

8. Return the pan to a low-medium heat and cook, covered, for 25–30 minutes. Remove the lid and cook for a further 5–10 minutes until the base of each dumpling is golden and caramelised.

9. Just before the dumplings are ready, gently warm the plum and vanilla sauces in separate pans – take care not to let the vanilla sauce get too hot and start to steam.

10. Remove the dumpling pan from the heat. Carefully lift out the dumplings using a slotted spoon. Serve with the plum and vanilla sauces.

RAISIN KUGELHOPF

Traditionally baked for celebrations in Alsace, using a pretty fluted, deep ring mould, yeast-risen kugelhopf looks and tastes as much like a cake as a bread. It is made like brioche, with lots of butter squeezed into the kneaded dough, and as a result is very soft and sticky to work, although not really difficult if you take it step by step. The fine, rich, cake-like crumb is the result of several risings, including a spell in the fridge, so do allow plenty of time.

makes a medium loaf

1. First, prepare the mould (even if it has a non-stick coating): brush the inside, particularly the centre funnel and the rim, with plenty of soft butter. Chill for a few minutes until the butter is firm, then give the inside a second coat of butter. Set aside in a cool place.

2. To make the sponge, put the flour and sugar in a mixing bowl and combine with your hand. Sprinkle the yeast on top and mix in. Make a well in the centre and pour in the lukewarm milk. Using your hand, draw the flour into the milk to make a smooth, thick, sticky paste. Cover the bowl with clingfilm and leave on the worktop for an hour.

3. Meanwhile, put the raisins into a small pan and add enough water just to cover. Set over low heat and bring to the boil. Remove from the heat and drain the raisins thoroughly, then spread them out on kitchen paper and leave to dry.

4. Uncover the bowl – the sponge mixture will look slightly expanded. Set the bowl on a damp cloth to prevent it from wobbling. Put the whole eggs, the yolk and orange zest into a small bowl and beat with a fork just to combine. Add to the sponge and use your hand to squeeze and mix everything together until thoroughly combined. Using your hand like a paddle, gradually stir and beat in the 185g flour and the salt to make a very soft and sticky, wet, heavy dough.

5. This dough is too soft to knead* in the usual way, so to develop the gluten you need to beat the dough in the bowl by slapping it up and down with your hand. After 6–7 minutes of doing this, the dough will be smooth and feel firmer and very elastic.

6. Cut up the butter into small pieces and add them to the bowl. Squeeze the butter into the dough with your hand. Once all the butter has been incorporated – the dough will be slightly streaky – slap the dough up and down, as before, for 4–5 minutes to get rid of all the streaks.

FOR THE SPONGE
90g strong white bread flour
35g caster sugar
1 x 7g sachet fast-action dried yeast
90ml lukewarm full-fat/whole milk

TO FINISH THE DOUGH
85g raisins
2 medium eggs plus 1 yolk, at room temperature
finely grated zest of 1 medium orange
185g strong white bread flour
½ teaspoon fine sea salt
110g unsalted butter, softened

FOR THE GLAZE
4 tablespoons orange juice
4 tablespoons caster sugar
1 tablespoon orange-flavoured liqueur (optional)
2 tablespoons chopped brazil nuts OR almonds, for sprinkling

you will need
1 x 20cm fluted, deep ring mould/kugelhopf mould/bundt tin, very well greased with butter (see recipe)

7. Scatter the raisins over the dough, then gently squeeze to incorporate them – stop as soon as they are evenly distributed as you don't want the dough to become oily. Cover the bowl tightly with clingfilm and leave to rise on the worktop (not in the sun or close to heat as you don't want the butter to melt) for about 1 hour until the dough has almost doubled in size.

8. Lightly flour your hand and punch down the risen dough to deflate it. Re-cover the bowl and put it into the fridge. After 1 hour, uncover the dough and punch it down as before, then re-cover the bowl and chill the dough for another hour or so until it feels firm.

9. Turn out the dough on to a lightly floured worktop and gently knead it into a neat ball. Flour your thumb and first 2 fingers and press them together to make a beak shape. Push this into the centre of the ball to form it into a ring. Set the dough ring in the buttered mould – the ring should fit neatly over the funnel and fill the mould evenly. Cover the top of the mould with a damp tea towel and leave the dough on the worktop to rise for about 2 hours until doubled in size and risen to about 3cm below the rim of the mould.

10. Towards the end of the rising time, heat the oven to 190°C/375°F/gas 5.

11. Uncover the mould and bake the kugelhopf in the heated oven for about 30 minutes until the top is a rich golden brown and a skewer inserted halfway between the rim and the centre funnel comes out clean* – baking time will depend on your mould (kugelhopfs in traditional deep ceramic and earthenware moulds may take slightly longer than in metallic ones). Check after 20 minutes and, if the top seems to be browning too quickly, cover with foil or baking paper.

12. Remove the mould from the oven and set it on a wire rack. Leave the kugelhopf to cool and firm up for a couple of minutes while you make the orange glaze.

13. Put the orange juice and sugar in a small pan and stir over low heat until the sugar has completely dissolved, then bring to the boil. Remove from the heat and add the orange liqueur, if using.

14. Carefully unmould the kugelhopf on to the wire rack set over a plate (to catch the drips). Brush the hot syrup all over the top and sides, then scatter the nuts on top. Leave to cool completely.

15. To serve, transfer the kugelhopf to a serving plate or board. Carefully spoon any thickened syrup from the plate over the nuts to give them a glossy glaze. Best eaten the same or the next day – store in an airtight tin. After that, kugelhopf is delicious sliced for toast, French toast, or an extra-special bread and butter pudding.

ROASTED GARLIC HERB TWIST

Richly aromatic and appealing – who doesn't love garlic bread, warm from the oven? This is a loaf for a party, to serve with antipasti and salads, or with bowls of thick soup. The stripes of filling are made from mellow-roasted garlic cloves, well-flavoured blue cheese and fresh herbs.

makes a large loaf

1. To make the dough, put the flour and yeast into a large bowl, or the bowl of a free-standing electric mixer fitted with the dough hook attachment, and mix thoroughly with your hand. Mix in the salt. Make a well in the centre of the flour and pour in the oil and water. Gradually work the flour into the liquid with your hand, or the dough hook on slow speed, to make a very soft dough. If the dough sticks to the side of the bowl, work in a little more flour a tablespoon at a time; if there are dry crumbs in the bottom of the bowl, work in more water a tablespoon at a time.

2. Lightly rub your hands and the worktop with olive oil. Scoop out the dough on to the worktop and knead* thoroughly for about 10 minutes (or 5 minutes, without oil, using the dough hook on slow speed) until the dough feels firmer and slightly less sticky. Return it to the bowl, if necessary, then cover with a snap-on lid or clingfilm. Leave on the worktop to rise for about 1 hour until the dough has doubled in size.

3 Meanwhile, make the filling. Heat the oven to 200°C/400°F/gas 6. Cut the garlic bulb in half horizontally, then set both halves, cut-side up, in a small baking dish or tin (if some cloves become separated, just add them to the dish). Drizzle over the oil. Roast in the heated oven for 15–20 minutes until the garlic just starts to turn pale golden and soften. Don't let the garlic brown as this would add a bitter taste to the filling. Leave to cool (you can turn off the oven for now).

4. Put the herbs into the bowl of a food processor. Trim any rind from the cheese, then break up the cheese and add it to the processor bowl. Squeeze the garlic out of the papery skin into the bowl. Add several grinds of black pepper, then blitz everything together to make a smooth green paste, scraping down the sides of the processor once or twice. Set aside at room temperature until needed.

5. When the dough is ready, punch it down with your knuckles to deflate it, then scoop it out on to a floured worktop. Flour your fingers and pat out the dough to a 40cm square. Spread the garlic and herb paste over the dough, leaving a 1cm border clear all around. Roll up the dough tightly like a Swiss roll (as you roll, it will stretch and become a bit longer) and pinch the seam to seal it firmly.

FOR THE DOUGH
650g strong white bread flour
1 x 7g sachet fast-action dried
  yeast
10g fine sea salt
2 tablespoons olive oil, plus extra
  for kneading
425ml lukewarm water

FOR THE FILLING
1 large garlic bulb (or
  2 regular-sized)
1 tablespoon olive oil
large handful of fresh parsley sprigs
small bunch of fresh chives
additional fresh herbs: 3 sage
  leaves plus leaves from a few
  sprigs each of thyme, rosemary
  and oregano (all optional)
130g gorgonzola piccante
ground black pepper

TO FINISH
2 tablespoons olive oil, for
  brushing

you will need
1 large baking sheet/
roasting tin, lined with
baking paper

6. Flour a large, sharp knife and use to cut the roll in half lengthways. Twist the 2 halves together as neatly as possible, tucking the ends under. Lift on to the baking sheet, placing the twisted roll diagonally, and gently push it back into shape as needed.

7. Cover loosely with a large sheet of clingfilm and leave on the worktop to rise for about 45 minutes until almost doubled in size – make sure the dough isn't left in a sunny or warm spot: if it rises too quickly, or too much, the twist will lose its definition.

8. Towards the end of the rising time, heat the oven to 220°C/425°F/gas 7.

another idea: If it's the right time of year and you can find them, replace the chives with a handful of fresh, young wild garlic leaves.

9. Uncover the loaf and brush with the olive oil, then bake in the heated oven for 30–35 minutes until the loaf is a good golden brown. Transfer to a wire rack and leave to cool until barely warm before slicing to eat. The loaf reheats well: put it straight on to the oven shelf in a preheated 200°C/400°F/gas 6 oven and bake for 12–15 minutes until crisp and hot.

FRESH HERB FOUGASSE

Packed with aromatic fresh herbs - rosemary, thyme and sage - and fruity olive oil, and finished with crushed sea salt, this golden, crisp bread is redolent of the sunny Mediterranean. Enjoy it warm.

dairy free | _____ makes 2

1. Put the flour, fine salt and yeast into the bowl of a free-standing electric mixer fitted with the dough hook – take great care not to put the salt directly on top of the yeast. Add the olive oil and three-quarters of the warm water, then start mixing on a low speed. As the dough begins to come together, add the remaining water very slowly, trickling it into the bowl, then mix/knead* for a further 6–8 minutes on a medium speed to make a soft, smooth, pliable dough.

2. Add the rosemary, thyme and sage and mix for 1 minute until the herbs are evenly distributed in the dough. When the dough is thoroughly kneaded it will be very elastic – you should be able to stretch it away from the sides and base of the bowl. Transfer the dough to the oiled container, cover with a snap-on lid or clingfilm and leave to rise for about 1 hour until at least doubled in size, and bouncy and shiny.

3. Mix together equal quantities of white flour and semolina, and use to heavily dust the worktop. Carefully tip the dough on to this: it will be quite loose and flowing but don't worry! Divide in half. Lift each piece of dough on to a prepared baking sheet and gently spread out to a flat oval.

4. Using a pizza wheel-cutter, make 2 cuts down the middle of one oval, starting and stopping 2cm from each end, then make 6 diagonal cuts in the dough on both sides of this central cut, to form a leaf design. Stretch the dough out to emphasise the holes you've cut, to ensure they don't close up during rising. Repeat with the second dough oval.

5. Place each baking sheet in a large plastic bag, slightly inflate it to prevent the dough from sticking to the plastic as it rises and secure the ends. Leave to rise for 20 minutes. Towards the end of this time heat the oven to 220°C/425°F/gas 7.

6. Uncover the loaves, then either spray them with a little olive oil using a water-spray bottle, or drizzle the oil over them. Sprinkle the dried oregano over the loaves. Bake for 15–20 minutes until the fougasses are nicely golden and sound hollow when tapped on the underside*. Remove from the oven and, while still hot, brush with more olive oil, then sprinkle with crushed sea salt. Serve warm, as soon as possible.

500g strong white bread flour, plus extra for dusting
10g fine sea salt
10g fast-action dried yeast (from 2 x 7g sachets)
2 tablespoons olive oil, plus extra for brushing/spraying
350ml warm water
2 teaspoons chopped fresh rosemary, plus extra to finish
2 teaspoons chopped fresh thyme
2 teaspoons chopped fresh sage
fine semolina, for dusting
½ teaspoon dried oregano
crushed sea salt, to finish

you will need
1 square plastic container, about 3 litre capacity, oiled; 2 baking sheets, lined with baking paper; a water-spray bottle (optional)

CHOCOLATE ORANGE SWIRL BREAD

Made in the same way as Chelsea buns, with a sweet, rich orange and cardamom-flavoured dough, and a warmly spiced, fragrant chocolate-nut filling (there's a red-hot chilli in there!), this bread is sure to impress.

makes a large loaf

FOR THE DOUGH
330ml full-fat/whole milk
6 tablespoons fat-free natural yoghurt
115g unsalted butter, softened, plus extra for the bowl
145g caster sugar
finely grated zest of 1 large (or 1½ medium) oranges
seeds from 4 cardamom pods, finely ground

7g fine sea salt
680g strong white bread flour, plus extra for dusting
12g fast-action dried yeast (from 2 x 7g sachets)

FOR THE FILLING
110g dark chocolate (about 80% cocoa solids), broken up
75g ground almonds
75g flaked almonds

¾ teaspoon cocoa powder
¾ teaspoon ground ginger
¾ teaspoon ground cinnamon
large pinch of grated nutmeg
¼ bird's-eye chilli, or to taste, seeds and ribs removed then finely chopped

FOR THE GLAZE
1 medium egg, beaten to mix
1 tablespoon cacao nibs

you will need
1 rectangular baking tin/cake tin/roasting tin, 20 x 30 x 6cm, greased with butter and base-lined*

1. Gently warm the milk with the yoghurt, then leave to cool until it feels very comfy when you dip in your little finger. Meanwhile, put the softened butter, sugar, orange zest, ground cardamom and salt into the bowl of a free-standing electric mixer fitted with the whisk attachment. Beat until the mixture is light and creamy. Scrape down the sides of the bowl, and replace the whisk with the dough hook attachment.

2. Pour the lukewarm milk mixture into the bowl. Mix the flour with the yeast, then tip into the bowl. Using the dough hook on slow speed, mix together all the ingredients to form a soft but not sticky dough. If the dough seems dry or there are dry crumbs in the base of the bowl, work in more lukewarm milk a tablespoon at a time.

3. Using the dough hook on slow speed, knead* the dough for 5 minutes until it is very smooth and pliable. Transfer to a large mixing bowl that has been lightly greased with butter, cover tightly with clingfilm and leave to rise on the worktop for about 1 hour until doubled in size.

4. Meanwhile, make the filling. Put the dark chocolate pieces, the ground and flaked almonds, cocoa powder, ginger, cinnamon, nutmeg and chilli into the bowl of a food processor. 'Pulse' several times, scraping down the sides of the bowl, until the mixture looks like fine breadcrumbs. Weigh the mixture and transfer one-third to another bowl (this will be used for the smaller roll).

5. Punch down the risen dough to deflate it, then scoop out on to a lightly floured worktop and shape into a ball. Weigh the dough and cut off one-third; cover this with the upturned bowl and set aside (this will be used for the smaller roll.)

6. Roll out or pat out the remaining dough to a 20 × 40cm rectangle, placing it horizontally in front of you so the long sides are top and bottom. Scatter the two-thirds portion of filling over the dough, spreading it evenly – leave a 1cm border along the long edge closest to you. Gently press the filling on to the dough. Starting from the long edge farthest away from you, roll up the dough fairly tightly (like a Swiss roll) until you reach the 1cm border of dough. Gently stretch and pull out this border until it is 2cm wide, then finish rolling up the dough. Carefully pinch the dough seam to seal the roll.

7. Turn the roll over so it is seam-side down on the worktop. Trim off the ends to make a neat 36cm roll. Using a ruler and a sharp knife, cut the roll across into 12 cylinders, each 3cm thick. Arrange them, cut-side up and widely spaced, in the prepared tin in 4 rows of 3.

8. Now make the small roll in the same way: roll out the reserved dough to a 20 × 30cm rectangle and cover with the reserved filling, leaving a 1cm border on the long edge nearest to you. Roll up the dough and seal as before, then cut across into 6 cylinders, each 4cm thick. Arrange them cut-side up in the gaps between the groups of the larger rolls. Cover lightly with a large sheet of clingfilm, or slip the tin into a large plastic bag and secure the ends. Leave on the worktop to rise for about 45 minutes until the rolls are doubled in size and have joined up.

9. Towards the end of the rising time heat the oven to 200°C/400°F/gas 6. When the bread is ready, uncover and brush it carefully with the beaten egg, then sprinkle with the cacao nibs. Bake in the heated oven for about 35 minutes until a rich golden brown and firm – check after 25 minutes and rotate the tin, if necessary, so the bread bakes evenly.

10. Remove from the oven and run a round-bladed knife around the inside of the tin to loosen the bread. Gently turn it out on to a wire rack and leave to cool before pulling apart to serve. Eat the same or the next day (keep in an airtight tin).

PARMESAN PROSCIUTTO CIABATTA

One of the trickiest breads to bake at home, ciabatta is made in stages, starting with a 'biga' - an Italian version of a sourdough starter - that is slowly fermented to add flavour and liveliness. A dough scraper is invaluable here as the dough (best made by hand) is fairly tricky to work, being more like a thick batter. Large bubbles of air, the enemy of most other bread doughs, are encouraged in ciabatta so a really warm kitchen is ideal. In this recipe the dough is flavoured with small nuggets of cheese and air-dried ham. If possible buy your prosciutto from the supermarket deli counter and ask for it to be cut fairly thick (about 2mm), rather than the usual paper-thin slices, to make chopping easier.

makes 3 medium loaves

1. First make the 'biga'. Put both of the flours, the yeast and sugar into a very large mixing bowl (the sugar will help feed the yeast and keep it going). Mix well with your hand, then pour in the lukewarm water and mix it in to make a fairly sticky dough. Beat this dough with your hand, slapping it against the sides of the bowl, for 2 minutes. Cover the bowl tightly with clingfilm and leave to ferment at normal room temperature for 8–12 hours — the dough will rise enormously and then collapse.

2. Next day, to finish the dough, uncover the bowl and pour in the lukewarm water and olive oil. Work the liquids into the dough with your hand by squeezing it through your fingers and beating with your hand until you have a smooth batter.

3. In another bowl, mix the bread flour with the plain flour, then tip half into a third bowl. Add the yeast to the flour in one bowl, and the salt to the flour in the other bowl.

4. Add the flour with the yeast to the bowl containing the biga and mix in with your hand to make a thick, sticky, batter-like dough. Beat this dough in the bowl with your hand, slapping it up and down, for about 5 minutes until it has been thoroughly stretched and becomes very elastic. Cover the bowl tightly with clingfilm and leave in a warm spot to rise for 1½–2 hours until the dough is about 2½ times its original size (this is why you need an extra large bowl to start with).

5. Meanwhile, cut away any rind from the prosciutto, then chop in a food processor to make small gravel-like chunks. Repeat with the cheese. Set the prosciutto and cheese aside on the worktop to come to room temperature.

6. Uncover the dough and add the flour/salt mixture. Work in with your hand to make a soft, sticky dough. Work the dough in the bowl for a couple of minutes until you can turn it out on to the unfloured worktop.

FOR THE 'BIGA'
200g strong white bread flour
50g plain white flour
1 teaspoon fast-action dried yeast (from a 7g sachet)
1 teaspoon caster sugar
200ml lukewarm water

TO FINISH THE DOUGH
350ml lukewarm water
3 tablespoons extra virgin olive oil
400g strong white bread flour
100g plain white flour
1 x 7g sachet fast-action dried yeast
8g fine sea salt
85g prosciutto, in a thick slice
60g Parmesan cheese, in a piece
fine cornmeal or polenta, for dusting

you will need
2 baking sheets;
baking paper

7. Knead* the dough thoroughly by gathering it up (with the help of a dough scraper) and slapping or throwing it back down on to the worktop. Do this energetically for a good 10 minutes until the dough feels silky smooth and is extremely elastic. It will still be soft and sticky, though firmer than before.

8. Scatter the chopped prosciutto and cheese over the dough and work in until evenly distributed. Shape into a ball. Return the dough to the bowl, cover again and leave to rise in a warm place for about 1 hour until doubled in size. Towards the end of this time gently warm the baking sheets, then line them with baking paper and dust generously with cornmeal or polenta.

9. Using a dough scraper, carefully ease the risen dough out on to the lightly floured worktop – don't punch down or deflate the dough, but treat it very delicately. Using the well-floured dough scraper or a knife, divide the mass of dough into 3 roughly equal strips – they won't be neat. With the help of the scraper, carefully transfer the strips of dough to the warmed lined baking sheets (2 on one sheet, spaced well apart). Use your fingers to gently stretch, not press, each strip of dough into the characteristic slipper-like shape – very roughly 30cm long and 8cm wide; try not to disturb all the big bubbles. Don't worry about the loaves having an uneven, rustic look – here the texture and appearance of the crumb is what matters.

10. Sprinkle lightly with flour, then slip the sheets into a large plastic bag, inflate it so the plastic won't stick to the rising dough, and close the ends tightly. Leave in a warm place for 30 minutes until almost doubled in size.

11. Towards the end of the rising time, heat the oven to 230°C/450°F/gas 8.

12. Uncover the loaves and bake in the heated oven for about 20 minutes until puffed and golden brown. Cool on a wire rack. Eat warm or the same day. The breads can also be split and toasted or grilled the next day.

SWEET LITTLE BRIOCHE DOUGHNUTS

Here are the lightest, most divine doughnuts you can make. A challenge for any baker, the sweet, egg-rich brioche dough needs a good deal of kneading - before and after working in plenty of soft butter - to become silky-smooth and elastic. Thorough chilling is essential too as the dough is rolled out like pastry. Once quickly fried, they're rolled in sugar and filled with a sharp-sweet lemon curd. A real treat for a special brunch.

makes about 16

FOR THE SWEET BRIOCHE
225g strong white bread flour
½ teaspoon fine sea salt
2 tablespoons caster sugar
1½ teaspoons fast-action dried
   yeast (from a 7g sachet)
3 tablespoons cold milk
2 medium eggs plus 1 yolk,
   chilled
½ teaspoon vanilla extract
150g unsalted butter, at room
   temperature, diced

TO FINISH
sunflower oil, for deep-frying
caster sugar, for sprinkling
5–6 tablespoons lemon curd
   (for a recipe, see page 20)

you will need
1 baking sheet, lined with
baking paper; a small piping
bag fitted with a small
round nozzle (3–4mm)

1. Put the flour, salt and sugar into a mixing bowl, or the bowl of a free-standing electric mixer fitted with the dough hook attachment. Mix together, then sprinkle the yeast over the top and mix in. Make a well in the centre.

2. Combine the milk, whole eggs and yolk, and vanilla in a small bowl or jug and beat with a fork just until combined. Pour into the well in the flour mixture. Using your hand, or the dough hook on slow speed, gradually mix the flour into the eggs to make a very heavy, very sticky dough (it will stick to the sides of the bowl and your fingers).

3. Knead* the dough thoroughly in the bowl by slapping it up and down with your hand, or using the dough hook on slow speed, until the dough becomes very smooth, slightly paler and firmer, and very elastic. This will take 10–15 minutes by hand, or 6–8 minutes in the mixer.

4. Gradually work in the butter, a few pieces at a time, by squeezing it in through your fingers (or using the dough hook) to make a smooth, streak-free dough that feels softer and stickier; use a dough scraper to scrape down the sides of the bowl regularly. Now, repeat the slapping/kneading for another 10 minutes (or 5 minutes with the dough hook) so the dough feels silky and elastic again.

5. Cover the bowl with a snap-on lid or clingfilm. Leave the dough to rise, at normal room temperature, for about 1½ hours until doubled in size.

6. Flour your hand and punch down the risen dough to deflate it, then cover the bowl again and put it in the fridge. Chill the dough for at least 6 hours, or preferably overnight.

7. Next day, scoop out the cold, firm brioche dough on to a lightly floured worktop. Knead once or twice – you don't want the dough to soften – then roll it out to a square with 21cm sides and about 1.5cm thick (it will feel like shortcrust pastry). Using a pizza wheel-cutter or a sharp knife, trim the sides to make a 20cm square, then cut this into 16 squares (you can re-roll the trimmings and cut more squares).

another idea: While the unfilled doughnuts are still warm, dust them with cinnamon sugar and serve with Hot Bitter Chocolate Sauce (see page 20) for dessert. OR Fill the doughnuts with a rich custard (see Vanilla Crème Mousseline on page 19) instead of lemon curd.

8. Arrange the dough squares on the lined baking sheet, well apart to allow for expansion, and cover lightly with a sheet of clingfilm. Leave to rise on the worktop, at room temperature, for 1–1½ hours until just doubled in size.

9. Heat the oil in a large deep pan to 180°C/350°F. Deep-fry the doughnuts a few at a time so the pan is not crowded: uncover 3 or 4 of the risen squares and gently lower them, one at a time, into the hot oil. Fry for about 4 minutes, turning them frequently with a slotted spoon, until they are a good dark golden brown. Lift them out and drain thoroughly on kitchen paper, then immediately roll in caster sugar. Before adding the next batch of doughnuts to the oil, check that it has returned to the correct temperature.

10. Leave the doughnuts to cool until you can handle them comfortably. Spoon the lemon curd into the piping bag. Using the tip of a small, sharp knife, make a small hole in the centre of one side of each doughnut, then push the end of the piping nozzle into the hole and squeeze the bag so a little of the lemon curd fills the centre. Dust the doughnuts again with sugar and eat as soon as possible.

CHOCOLATE, CARDAMOM AND HAZELNUT BABKA

A handsome, great-tasting loaf made in the traditional way by twisting together two cut-open ropes of sweet soft dough filled with dark and white chocolate and hazelnuts. The glossy finish is a result of two glazes - an egg wash applied before baking, and a sweet glaze brushed on after the loaf comes out of the oven.

makes a large loaf

FOR THE DOUGH
280g strong white bread flour, plus extra for dusting
½ teaspoon fine sea salt
50g caster sugar
seeds from 8 cardamom pods, finely ground
5g fast-action dried yeast (from a 7g sachet)
1 medium egg, at room temperature

125ml full-fat/whole milk, lukewarm
30g unsalted butter, softened, plus extra for the bowl

FOR THE FILLING
45g dark chocolate (about 70% cocoa solids)
15g white chocolate (about 30% cocoa solids)

30g blanched hazelnuts
30g unsalted butter, softened

FOR THE EGG GLAZE
1 medium egg yolk, mixed with 2 teaspoons water

FOR THE SWEET GLAZE
70g caster sugar
60ml water

1. Put the flour, salt, sugar and ground cardamom into a large mixing bowl and mix well together with your hand. Sprinkle the yeast into the bowl and mix in. Make a well in the centre. Beat the egg into the lukewarm milk, then pour the mixture into the well. Using your hand, mix everything together to make a very soft dough — if there are dry crumbs or the dough feels stiff, work in lukewarm water a tablespoon at a time.

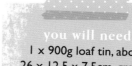

you will need
1 x 900g loaf tin, about 26 x 12.5 x 7.5cm, greased with butter and lined with a long strip of baking paper*

2. Rub the worktop with about 10g of the soft butter so it is lightly greased, then turn out the dough on to it (the worktop is not dusted with flour at this stage). Knead* the dough thoroughly for about 10 minutes until it is smooth and pliable and feels slightly firmer. Cut the rest of the butter (20g) into pieces, add to the dough and continue kneading for a couple of minutes until thoroughly combined and the dough is streak-free. Gather into a ball and put into a mixing bowl that has been lightly greased with butter. Cover tightly with clingfilm and leave to rise on the worktop for about 1 hour until doubled in size.

3. Meanwhile, make the filling. Chop up the dark and white chocolate and put into the bowl of a food processor. Add the hazelnuts and run the machine to chop fairly finely (you can also chop the chocolate and nuts by hand using a large sharp knife). Set aside.

4. When the dough has risen, punch it down to deflate, then turn it out on to a lightly floured worktop. Lightly flour a rolling pin and roll out the dough to a neat 26 x 35cm rectangle. The dough should be lying horizontally, with the long sides top and bottom. Using an offset palette knife, spread the soft butter over the dough, then scatter the choc-nut filling over the top in an even layer. Starting from the long edge nearest to you, carefully roll up the dough (like a Swiss roll). When you reach the far edge, pinch the dough seam to seal firmly.

5. Turn the roll over so it is seam-side down, then cut it in half down its length. Turn the 2 pieces so the cut surfaces are facing up. Pinch the pieces together at one end, then carefully and evenly twist the pieces together (the twist shouldn't be loose but don't stretch the dough either). Lift into the prepared tin, neatly tucking the ends underneath. Slip the tin into a large plastic bag, slightly inflate to prevent the dough from sticking to the plastic as it rises, and secure the ends. Leave on the worktop to rise for about 1 hour until doubled in size.

6. Towards the end of the rising time, heat the oven to 190°C/375°F/gas 5. When the loaf is ready, uncover it and brush the top neatly with the egg glaze. Bake in the heated oven for 30–40 minutes until a good golden brown and firm.

7. Near the end of the baking time make the sweet glaze. Put the sugar and water into a small pan and heat gently, stirring until the sugar has dissolved. Bring to the boil and simmer for a minute to make a light syrup. Remove from the heat.

8. Set the baked loaf, still in the tin, on a wire rack. Leave to cool for 2–3 minutes, then brush with the hot sugar syrup. Run a round-bladed knife around the inside of the tin to loosen the loaf, then very carefully lift it out on to the wire rack and peel off the lining paper. Brush the exposed sides with the sugar syrup so the whole loaf has a shiny, sticky glaze. Leave until cold before slicing. Eat the same or the next day (keep in an airtight tin).

CARDAMOM PEAR PLAIT

The dough for this beautiful bread is a yeasted version of rough puff pastry: cold
butter is grated into the flour/yeast mixture, then egg and cold milk are quickly mixed in.
There's no kneading as you don't want the gluten developed - that would make the dough
elastic (and the 'rolling and folding' stages more tricky) and the crumb would be less tender.
Filled with a rich mixture of cardamom-scented pears, dried cranberries and almonds,
the plait is finished with an icing glaze and flaked almonds - the perfect glamorous
centrepiece for an autumn supper party.

makes a large bread; cuts into 8

FOR THE DOUGH
200g slightly salted butter in one
   piece, well chilled (see recipe)
225g strong white bread flour
1 x 7g sachet fast-action dried
   yeast
25g caster sugar
¼ teaspoon fine sea salt
seeds from 4 green cardamom
   pods, finely ground
1 medium egg
6 tablespoons cold milk

FOR THE FILLING
2 large, just-ripe Comice pears
   (or similar short, fat pears)
55g slightly salted butter, softened
3 tablespoons caster sugar
seeds from 2 green cardamom
   pods, finely ground
50g soft-dried cranberries
50g ground almonds
1 medium egg yolk

TO FINISH
1 medium egg, beaten, to glaze
85g icing sugar
1 teaspoon lemon juice
2 tablespoons milk
2 tablespoons toasted flaked
   almonds, for sprinkling

you will need
1 baking sheet, lined
with baking paper

1. Before you start to make the dough be sure the butter is very hard: if
necessary give it a few minutes in the freezer. Combine the flour and yeast
in a mixing bowl and stir in the sugar, salt and ground cardamom. Wrap
one end of the piece of butter in foil (to make it easier to hold), then grate
into the bowl of flour using the coarse side of a cheese grater. Stop every
now and then, and toss the strands of butter in the flour to coat – this will
prevent them from clumping together. When all the butter has been grated
into the bowl, gently mix and toss it with the flour using a round-bladed
knife so all the butter strands are coated, as well as evenly distributed.

2. Make a well in the centre of the mixture. Beat the egg with the cold milk
just until combined, then pour into the well. Using the round-bladed knife,
quickly work everything together to make a shaggy-looking dough that just
comes together (if there are dry crumbs and the dough seems hard and
dry, work in more milk a tablespoon at a time – do this slowly as the dough
should not become wet or sticky). Shape the dough into a ball (don't knead
or work it), then cover the bowl and put it into the fridge. Chill for 2 hours
so the dough can rest and firm up.

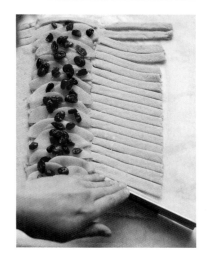

3. Turn out the chilled dough on to a lightly floured worktop and gently pat to a brick shape. Flour a rolling pin and use it to gently press the dough until the rectangle is about 1cm thick – it will look very streaky.

4. Now, using short brisk strokes (rather than one long rolling movement), roll out the dough away from you to a 45 × 15cm rectangle. Fold the dough in 3 like an envelope, brushing off excess flour as you go: fold the top third down to cover the middle third, then fold the bottom third up to cover the other 2 layers. Gently but firmly seal the edges (not the folded edge nearest to you) by pressing with the rolling pin. Set the dough on a plate, cover with clingfilm and chill for 30 minutes. This is the first 'turn' or 'roll and fold'.

5. Unwrap the dough on to the worktop, placing it so the rounded folded edge is now by your left hand. Repeat the rolling, folding and chilling as before (second 'turn'). Repeat 2 more times, each time placing the dough so the rounded folded edge is on the left side, to make a total of 4 'turns'. Wrap and chill the dough for 1 hour.

6. Meanwhile make the filling. Peel, quarter and core the pears, then cut each quarter lengthways into 4 slices. Melt 15g of the butter in a non-stick frying pan. Add the pears and sprinkle over 1 tablespoon of the sugar, the ground cardamom and cranberries. Cook over medium heat, shaking the pan and stirring frequently, for about 5 minutes until the pears turn golden and translucent. Remove the pan from the heat and leave to cool.

7. Put the remaining 40g soft butter and 2 tablespoons sugar into a bowl. Add the ground almonds and egg yolk and beat everything together with a wooden spoon to make a thick, spreadable paste. Set aside.

8. Unwrap the dough on to a lightly floured worktop and roll out away from you to make a 31 × 36cm rectangle. Using a pizza wheel-cutter or a large sharp knife, trim the sides to make a neat 30 × 35cm rectangle (the short sides should be top and bottom). Spread the almond paste in an 8cm-wide strip lengthways down the centre of the rectangle, leaving a 2cm clear border at the top and bottom. Starting at the top end, arrange the pear slices on the paste, slightly overlapping, in a neat row. Scatter the cranberries over the pears.

9. At both the top and bottom, fold the 2cm 'flap' of dough over the filling, then cut off the doubled dough rectangles on either side of the filling.

10. Brush the 2 folded-over flaps of dough with beaten egg, then brush egg over the exposed dough on the long sides. Make diagonal cuts, 1.25cm apart, in the dough, from the edge to the filling, all the way down the sides. Starting at the end nearest to you bring one strip over from the left side, then one over from the right side, so the strips cross over the filling. Continue folding the strips, alternating sides, over the filling to cover it.

11. Lift the plait on to the lined baking sheet and cover lightly with a sheet of clingfilm. Leave on the worktop, at normal room temperature, to rise for about 1 hour until the plaited strips have almost doubled in size.

12. Towards the end of the rising time, heat the oven to 200°C/400°F/gas 6. Uncover the plait and brush lightly with beaten egg, then bake in the heated oven for 25–30 minutes until well risen, crisp and golden – check after 20 minutes and rotate the sheet, if necessary, so the plait bakes evenly.

13. Meanwhile, make the icing glaze. Sift the icing sugar into a bowl, then mix in the lemon juice and milk until smooth and runny. As soon as the plait is ready, transfer it to a wire rack and brush immediately with the glaze. Sprinkle the flaked almonds over the top. Leave to cool and serve warm, or at room temperature.

MALLORCAS

These are the lovely sweet and soft, spiral-shaped breakfast buns from Majorca, perfect warm from the oven with preserves and coffee. The dough is very rich with butter and eggs, so needs to be chilled overnight to enable it to be rolled out, cut into long strips and carefully shaped.

makes 12

1. To make the dough, put the flour and yeast into a mixing bowl, or the bowl of a free-standing electric mixer fitted with the dough hook attachment, and combine with your hand. Add the sugar and salt, and thoroughly mix in. Make a well in the centre of the mixture.

2. In a small bowl beat the eggs with the water just to mix, then add to the well. Gradually work the flour into the liquid with your hand, or the dough hook attachment on slow speed, to make a rather firm, slightly heavy dough. Cut up the butter into small pieces and gradually add to the bowl, squeezing the butter into the dough between your fingers, or using the dough hook on slow speed.

3. Once all the butter has been added, the dough will look streaky and a bit lumpy and uneven but don't worry! Knead* the dough in the bowl by scooping it up and slapping it down with your hand for 6–7 minutes (or about 5 minutes using the dough hook on slow speed) until it becomes very smooth, soft and elastic (if using a mixer, don't forget to keep scraping down the sides of the bowl).

4. Cover the bowl tightly with clingfilm or a snap-on lid and place in the fridge. Leave to rise and firm up for at least 6 hours, preferably overnight. This long chilling is important as it makes the dough easier to handle and shape into neat spirals.

5. Next day, scoop out the dough on to a lightly floured worktop and roll it out to a 30cm square. Using a ruler and a pizza wheel-cutter or a large sharp knife, cut the dough into 12 long strips. Brush the strips lightly with melted butter (you won't need it all – save the rest for later), then roll up each one fairly tightly to make a neat spiral. Set the spirals on the lined baking sheets, well apart to allow for expansion (you don't want them to join up when they have risen). Use the tip of a small, sharp knife to gently poke the inside end of the dough strip down into the centre of the spiral (so it doesn't pop out during baking), and tuck the outside end of the strip under the bun. Cover loosely with a large sheet of clingfilm and leave to rise on the worktop for 1½–2 hours until doubled in size.

FOR THE DOUGH
350g strong white bread flour
1 x 7g sachet fast-action dried yeast
40g caster sugar
5g fine sea salt
3 medium eggs, at room temperature
5 tablespoons cold water
150g unsalted butter, softened

TO FINISH
40g unsalted butter, melted
icing sugar, for dusting

you will need
1–2 baking sheets, lined with baking paper

6. Towards the end of the rising time, heat the oven to 190°C/375°F/gas 5.

7. Uncover the spirals and gently flatten them slightly with the flat of your hand. Brush with the rest of the melted butter, then bake in the heated oven for 15–17 minutes until golden. For best results check after 10 minutes and, if necessary, rotate the sheets so the buns bake evenly.

8. Remove from the oven and immediately dust the buns with plenty of icing sugar, then transfer them to a wire rack. Leave to cool slightly before eating warm (or at room temperature). Best eaten the same day, or the next day split and toasted, or used for toasted sandwiches.

---

another idea Mallorcas make great toasties for an indulgent brunch. Split day-old buns, dusting off the sugar, fill with slices of ham and cheese, and brush the outsides with butter (melted with a good pinch of cayenne pepper), then cook briefly in a non-stick frying pan until golden brown on both sides.

ORANGE PAIN AUX RAISINS

These great-looking flaky spirals have a tangy filling of orange crème pâtissière and raisins - just perfect with coffee! They are made from a tricky laminated yeast dough that is crisp yet tender and melt-in-the-mouth.

makes 18

FOR THE DOUGH

500g strong white bread flour
finely grated zest of 2 oranges
5g fine sea salt
50g caster sugar
1 x 7g sachet fast-action dried
   yeast
50g slightly salted butter, at room
   temperature, diced
2 medium eggs, at room
   temperature
200ml lukewarm water
200g slightly salted butter, chilled

FOR THE FILLING

70g caster sugar
20g plain flour
20g cornflour
2 medium egg yolks, at room
   temperature
300ml full-fat/whole milk
finely grated zest of 2 oranges
1½ teaspoons vanilla extract
30g unsalted butter, at room
   temperature
200g raisins

TO FINISH

1 medium egg, beaten, to glaze
3 tablespoons sieved apricot jam
   OR apricot glaze
1½ tablespoons water
200g icing sugar, sifted
2–3 tablespoons fresh orange juice

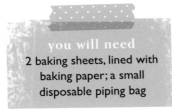

you will need
2 baking sheets, lined with
baking paper; a small
disposable piping bag

1. To make the dough, put the flour into a large mixing bowl, add the orange zest, salt and sugar, and mix in with your hand. Work in the yeast. Add the diced butter and rub in* until the mixture looks like fine crumbs. Lightly beat the eggs with the lukewarm water using a fork, then add to the bowl. Mix everything together with your hand to make a soft but not sticky dough, adding a little more flour or water as necessary. Turn out on to a lightly floured worktop and knead* gently for about 2 minutes just until smooth. Return to the bowl, cover with clingfilm and leave to rise in a slightly warm spot for about 1 hour until doubled in size.

2. Punch down the risen dough in the bowl, then turn out on to the lightly floured worktop again. Roll out away from you to a 20 x 50cm rectangle (short sides top and bottom). Place the chilled butter between 2 sheets of floured baking paper and bash with a rolling pin to a 40 x 18cm rectangle. Cut this in half to make two 18 x 20cm rectangles. Set one of these on the short side of the dough nearest to you, positioning the butter so one 18cm edge is right in the middle of the dough's short side. Fold up this portion of dough, with the butter, so it covers the middle portion of the dough rectangle. Repeat at the top of the dough with the second piece of butter, then fold this down over the centre to make 3 layers of dough sandwiched with 2 layers of butter. Use the rolling pin to seal the edges, then wrap in clingfilm and chill for 20 minutes.

3. Meanwhile make the crème pâtissière for the filling. Put the sugar, flour, cornflour and egg yolks into a heatproof bowl set on a damp cloth (to prevent wobbling), add 2 tablespoons of the measured milk and beat well with a wooden spoon until smooth and creamy. Heat the rest of the milk with the orange zest and vanilla in a medium pan until just boiling. Add the milk to the bowl in a thin, steady stream, stirring constantly. Tip back into the pan and stir over medium heat until the mixture boils and thickens. Remove from the heat and stir in the butter. Transfer to a clean heatproof bowl, press clingfilm on the surface (to prevent a skin from forming) and leave to cool, then keep in the fridge until needed.

4. Unwrap the dough and place it on the floured worktop so the rounded folded edges are on the sides. Roll out to a 20 x 50cm rectangle, then fold in 3, seal the edges, wrap and chill for 20 minutes – this is your first 'turn' (see Pecan and Maple Pinwheels, opposite, for more information about how to roll and fold). Repeat 2 more times to make a total of 3 turns, then chill for 50 minutes.

5. To shape the dough spirals, roll out the dough away from you to a rectangle about 48 x 36cm and 5mm thick (short sides top and bottom). Trim to a 46 x 34cm rectangle. Stir the crème pâtissière until smooth, then spread over the dough, leaving a 5cm-wide border clear along the short side nearest to you. Scatter the raisins evenly over the crème pâtissière. Roll up the dough, Swiss-roll style, starting from the short side farthest away from you. When you reach the edge near you, firmly pinch the dough together to seal. The roll will have stretched. If it feels very soft at this point, wrap it and chill for 20 minutes.

6. Cut the roll across into 18 equal, thick slices and place these cut-side down on the lined baking sheets, well apart to allow for expansion. Cover lightly with clingfilm and leave on the worktop to rise for about 20 minutes until doubled in size. Meanwhile, heat the oven to 190°C/375°F/gas 5.

7. Lightly brush the dough with beaten egg to glaze, then bake in the heated oven for 18–21 minutes until a rich golden brown and crisp – check after 15 minutes and rotate the sheets, if necessary, so the dough bakes evenly.

8. Transfer the pastries to a wire rack. Heat the apricot jam with the water (or heat the glaze) until boiling and smooth, then quickly brush over the hot pastries to glaze. Leave to cool.

9. Mix the icing sugar with enough strained orange juice to make a smooth piping consistency. Transfer to the piping bag, snip off the tip and pipe thin zigzags of icing across each pastry (you could also drizzle the icing from a spoon). Leave for a few minutes to set before serving.

PECAN AND MAPLE PINWHEELS

Pecans and maple syrup flavour these pretty pinwheel-shaped pastries. The pastry used is a butter-rich yeasted dough, which is laminated, or layered, like puff pastry. The chilling times are vital to prevent the butter from oozing out

makes 12

FOR THE DOUGH
500g strong white bread flour
10g fine sea salt
50g caster sugar
1 x 7g sachet fast-action dried
 yeast
1 medium egg plus 1 yolk, at
 room temperature
100ml lukewarm water
150ml lukewarm full-fat/whole milk
320g unsalted butter, chilled

FOR THE FILLING
100g pecan halves
40g light muscovado sugar
1½ tablespoons maple syrup
20g unsalted butter, softened

TO FINISH
1 medium egg
1 tablespoon milk
3 tablespoons sieved apricot jam
 OR apricot glaze

1½ tablespoons water
½ teaspoon lemon juice

FOR THE ICING (OPTIONAL)
125g icing sugar, sifted
1½–2 tablespoons boiling water
few drops of vanilla extract

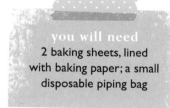

you will need
2 baking sheets, lined
with baking paper; a small
disposable piping bag

1. To make the dough, put the flour, salt and sugar into a mixing bowl and stir until combined, then mix in the yeast. Lightly beat the whole egg and yolk with the water and milk using a fork, then add to the bowl. Mix to a soft but not sticky dough with your hand, adding more flour or water as necessary. Turn out on to a lightly floured worktop and knead* for about 5 minutes until very smooth. Return to the bowl, cover and leave to rise on the worktop for about 1 hour until doubled in size.

2. Punch down the risen dough in the bowl, then tip it out on to the lightly floured worktop again. Roll it out away from you to a 20 x 40cm rectangle (short sides top and bottom).

3. Place the butter between 2 lightly floured sheets of baking paper and bash out with a rolling pin to a 20cm square. Set the piece of butter in the middle of the dough rectangle. Fold the top of the dough down over the butter square and the bottom of the dough up, so both short sides meet in the centre to cover the butter. Lightly press down on the edges to seal. Using the rolling pin, gently press the dough on to the butter, working down from the centre and then upwards from the centre.

4. Gently roll out the dough away from you to a 25 x 45cm rectangle (short sides top and bottom). Fold the dough in 3 like a business letter: fold the top third down over the centre third, then fold the bottom third up over the other 2 layers. Seal the edges with the rolling pin. Wrap and

chill for 15 minutes – this is your first 'turn'. Repeat 2 more times, each time placing the dough so the folded edges are on the sides before you roll out, to make a total of 3 turns, then chill for 40 minutes.

5. Meanwhile, make the filling. Roughly chop 25g of the pecans and set aside. Put the rest into a food processor and blitz until fairly fine. Tip into a bowl, add the sugar, maple syrup and soft butter, and mix to a thick paste. Cover and set aside on the worktop until needed.

6. When ready to shape the pinwheels, roll out the dough on the lightly floured worktop to a 35 × 46cm rectangle. Trim to a neat 33 × 44cm. Using a pizza wheel-cutter or large knife, cut into 12 squares. Press a finger into the centre of each square to form a small hollow and add a rounded teaspoon of the filling. With a small floured knife make a 4cm cut from each corner into the centre.

7. Beat the egg with the milk to make a glaze and lightly brush over the edges of the squares. Fold alternate corners into the centre of each square and press them firmly together to make pinwheel shapes. Arrange the pinwheels, well apart, on the lined baking sheets. Sprinkle with the chopped pecans. Cover lightly with clingfilm and leave to rise on the worktop for about 20 minutes. Meanwhile, heat the oven to 200°C/400°F/gas 6.

8. Uncover the pastries and brush lightly with the egg glaze. Bake in the heated oven for 15–20 minutes until a good golden brown and crisp – check after 12 minutes and rotate the baking sheets, if necessary, so the pastries bake evenly.

9. Transfer the pastries to a wire rack. Quickly heat the sieved apricot jam with the water and lemon juice (or heat the glaze) until boiling and smooth, then brush over the hot pastries. Leave to cool.

10. If you want to add an icing drizzle, mix the icing sugar with enough boiling water to make a smooth piping consistency. Stir in the vanilla extract. Transfer to the piping bag, snip off the tip and pipe zigzags of icing over the pinwheels (or drizzle the icing from a spoon). Leave to set before serving.

It's a well-known fact that however good the meal, there's always room for dessert. Luckily, we've got ideas for when prep time is short as well as when you want to plan ahead for a special occasion.

As always, fresh fruit and berries are the dessert stars, from the simply delicious Gingered Plum Kuchen on page 187 (a great year-round bake) to Grand Strawberry Mousse Cake (page 214), a true summertime showstopper, featuring a joconde sponge base, a piped sponge band and strawberry mousse filling, all finished with dipped strawberries.

Batters make many a traditional dessert, notably pancakes. On page 184 you'll find a recipe for delicate, exquisitely lacy, piped pancakes, which sound so simple – but perfection takes practice. Everyone's favourite snack on Spanish holidays, churros are made from a paste-like dough that is piped and deep-fried, then served with a sauce for dipping. Two deliciously crisp and light churros recipes (one features a light, tropical, egg-free dough, the other a filling) are on pages 188 and 203.

Family feasts are well provided for with the desserts in this chapter. A fantastic bake to get young helpers involved is the Banana Split Ice-Cream Cake: layers of chocolate sponge, vanilla and banana ice cream, and a gooey banana caramel layer complemented with a thick chocolate sauce. The recipe for all this fabulousness is on page 199. The Caffe Latte Gingerbread Cheesecake (page 196) gets better and better as it matures, which makes it the perfect dessert to store hidden away at the back of the fridge, ready for an invasion of guests. Its base is made from thin, crisp spicy biscuits – the recipe for these makes enough for a tin of biscuits to hand around with coffee too.

If you're hoping for some classic comforting desserts, there's a crème caramel, but with a twist: it's made with maple syrup, not sugar, which adds a unique flavour to the silky, slow-baked custard and topping sauce (see page 192). The Mulled Wine, Cranberry and Apple Crumble (page 191) is best enjoyed in deepest winter, with plenty of custard (or even a scoop of ice cream) – just the smell from the oven of the wine-infused fruit is intoxicating.

UPSIDE-DOWN FRESH CHERRY SPONGE PUDDING

When fresh, sweet cherries are in season, make this simple and pretty pudding. The cherries are baked underneath a very rich, almond-flavoured creamed sponge mixture, and turned out so the cherries form the topping. Serve warm from the oven with custard or cream.

serves 6–8

FOR THE BASE
about 550g fresh cherries
25g chopped/nibbed almonds

FOR THE SPONGE
135g unsalted butter, softened
135g caster sugar
3 medium eggs, at room
   temperature
2 teaspoons cherry brandy or
   kirsch OR ¼ teaspoon
   almond extract
65g self-raising flour
good pinch of fine sea salt
100g ground almonds
25g chopped/nibbed almonds

TO DECORATE
2 tablespoons toasted flaked
   almonds

TO SERVE
Vanilla Egg Custard (see page 18)
   OR pouring cream

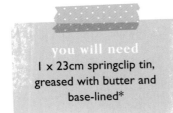

you will need
1 x 23cm springclip tin,
greased with butter and
base-lined*

1. Heat the oven to 180°C/350°F/gas 4. Rinse the cherries, then dry on kitchen paper. Pull off the stems and stone the cherries. Arrange them in neat concentric circles in a single layer on the base of the tin, packing them in tightly. Scatter the almonds in between, then set the tin aside.

2. Put the butter into a large mixing bowl, or the bowl of a free-standing electric mixer fitted with the whisk attachment. Beat with a hand-held electric whisk, or the whisk attachment, until creamy and mayonnaise-like. Gradually beat in the sugar. Scrape down the sides of the bowl, then keep on beating for another minute or so until the mixture is light and fluffy.

3. Break the eggs into a smaller bowl or jug, add the cherry brandy and beat with a fork until well mixed. Gradually add the eggs to the butter mixture, a tablespoon at a time, beating well after each addition and adding a tablespoon of the weighed flour with each of the last couple of additions of egg (to prevent the rich mixture from curdling). Scrape down the sides of the bowl from time to time to make sure all the mixture is beaten in.

4. Sift the rest of the flour plus the salt into the bowl, then add the ground almonds and the chopped/nibbed almonds. Gently but thoroughly fold* into the beaten mixture using a large metal spoon or plastic spatula.

5. Spoon the mixture on top of the cherries in the tin and spread evenly. Gently bang the tin on the worktop to settle the contents, then bake in the heated oven for 50–60 minutes until the sponge is a good golden brown and starting to shrink away from the sides of the tin; a skewer inserted into the centre should come out clean*.

6. Run a round-bladed knife around the inside of the tin to loosen the sponge, then unclip the tin, lift off the sides and invert the pudding on to a warmed serving platter. Remove the base of the tin and the lining paper. Scatter the flaked almonds over the cherries. Serve hot with custard or pouring cream. Enjoy any leftovers the next day, in wedges as cake – nice with whipped cream.

BLACKBERRY AND APPLE BUCKLE

An old-fashioned buckle, where fruit is combined with a very light, egg-rich, buttery sponge and topped with a crunchy crumble, is a good, simple way to use up a windfall of delicious summer and autumn fruit. You can adapt this recipe to whatever fruit is available – here it's tangy cooking blackberries and tart eating apples, but do try blueberries, pears, large firm raspberries, and firm nectarines or peaches. The name of the dish comes from the way the topping buckles or dimples over the very soft, just-set filling.

serves 6

FOR THE TOPPING
90g plain flour
finely grated zest of ½ medium
   unwaxed lemon
70g light muscovado sugar
70g unsalted butter, chilled
   and diced

FOR THE BASE
150g tangy blackberries
1 medium Braeburn or other
   tart eating apple
115g unsalted butter, softened
100g caster sugar
finely grated zest of ½ medium
   unwaxed lemon
2 medium eggs, at room
   temperature, beaten to mix
75g plain flour
1 teaspoon baking powder

TO SERVE
icing sugar, for dusting
yoghurt OR cream

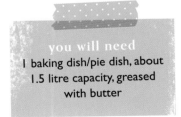

you will need
1 baking dish/pie dish, about
1.5 litre capacity, greased
with butter

1. Heat the oven to 180°C/350°F/gas 4. Make the topping first so it can firm up in the fridge while you make the filling. Mix the flour, lemon zest and sugar (press out any lumps) in a mixing bowl. Add the pieces of butter and rub in* until the mixture looks like very coarse crumbs. Cover the bowl and keep in the fridge until needed.

2. Rinse the berries, then tip on to a plate lined with kitchen paper and leave to dry. Peel, quarter and core the apple, then chop into chunks about 1cm. Transfer to a bowl and gently mix in the blackberries.

3. Put the softened butter into a mixing bowl, or the bowl of a free-standing electric mixer fitted with the whisk attachment. Beat with a wooden spoon or hand-held electric whisk, or the whisk attachment, until creamy and mayonnaise-like. Add the sugar and lemon zest and beat thoroughly until the mixture is very light and fluffy. Gradually add the eggs, a tablespoon at a time, beating well after each addition.

4. Scrape down the sides of the bowl. Sift the flour and baking powder into the bowl and fold* in with a plastic spatula or large metal spoon until just combined. Add the blackberries and chopped apple to the bowl and gently fold in until evenly distributed.

5. Spoon the mixture into the buttered dish and spread evenly. Scatter the topping mixture over the filling in an even layer. Bake in the heated oven for 35–40 minutes until golden brown and crisp. Remove from the oven, dust with icing sugar and eat warm with yoghurt or cream.

LACE PANCAKES

Not just for Shrove Tuesday, these pancakes are small works of art and great fun to make!
It's all done with a squeezy bottle and a hot frying pan.

makes 12

175g plain flour
1 large egg plus 1 yolk, at
   room temperature
300ml milk
25g unsalted butter, melted

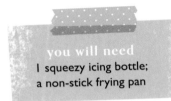

you will need
1 squeezy icing bottle;
a non-stick frying pan

1. Sift the flour into a bowl and make a well in the centre. Put the whole egg, yolk and a little of the milk into another bowl, or wide-necked jug, and whisk with a hand wire whisk until thoroughly combined. Pour into the well in the flour.

2. Whisk together gently, gradually mixing in half of the remaining milk and drawing in the flour a little at a time, to make a smooth batter. Stir in the remaining milk. Cover and leave to stand for about 15 minutes, at room temperature.

3. Stir the batter gently, then pour into the plastic squeezy bottle.

4. Heat a frying pan over a medium heat and brush with a little melted butter. Tilt the squeezy bottle and drizzle the batter into the pan to create a lacy pattern like the one in the photograph, or to your own design.

5. Cook the pancake over a medium-high heat for 45–60 seconds until small holes appear on the surface and the underside is lightly browned. Carefully loosen the pancake with a palette knife or fish slice, then turn it over by flipping it. Cook the other side for about 30 seconds until golden.

6. Slide the pancake out of the pan on to a warmed plate. Reheat the pan and lightly grease it again before making the next pancake in the same way. Refill the squeezy bottle as necessary.

7. Serve the pancakes hot, as they are made, or stack them on a plate and reheat before serving – cover with foil and warm through in a 170°C/325°F/gas 3 oven for 10–15 minutes. (If the pancakes are hot when you stack them they will not stick together, so there is no need to interleave them with greaseproof paper.)

GINGERED PLUM KUCHEN

A German-style fruit-topped dessert cake you can make all year round: as good with custard in winter, as it is with whipped cream in summer. The base, which is deeply flavoured with a combination of honey and glacé ginger, is firm enough to absorb the sweet juices from the topping of fresh plums. After baking the kuchen is bathed in a honey syrup and served hot, or just warm.

cuts into 8

1. Heat the oven to 170°C/325°F/gas 3. Put the butter into a mixing bowl, or the bowl of a free-standing electric mixer fitted with the whisk attachment, and beat with a wooden spoon or hand-held electric whisk, or the whisk attachment, until creamy and mayonnaise-like. Add the sugar (make sure it is lump-free) and beat thoroughly until the mixture is very light and fluffy.

2. Add the lemon zest and honey and beat in. Scrape down the sides of the bowl, then gradually add the eggs, a tablespoon at a time, beating well after each addition and adding a tablespoon of the weighed flour with the last addition of egg. Remember to scrape down the sides of the bowl from time to time so all the mixture is amalgamated.

3. Add the chopped glacé ginger to the bowl and fold* in with a plastic spatula or large metal spoon until thoroughly combined. Sift the remaining flour, the baking powder and ground ginger into the bowl and carefully fold in. Spoon into the prepared tin and spread evenly.

4. Rinse the plums, then cut each in half vertically, twist and gently pull apart. Remove the stones. Arrange the halves, cut side up, on top of the ginger sponge mixture, setting them closely together – the number of plums needed depends on their size.

5. Bake in the heated oven for 50–60 minutes until a good golden brown and a skewer inserted into the centre of the cake comes out clean*. Remove from the oven and run a round-bladed knife around the inside of the tin to loosen the kuchen. Unclip the tin and set the kuchen on a large, rimmed heatproof platter.

6. Combine the lemon juice, honey and sugar in a small pan and stir over low heat until the sugar has dissolved. Turn up the heat and bring to the boil. Let the syrup foam up, then remove the pan from the heat. Quickly spoon the syrup over the hot kuchen. Serve hot or warm, with custard or ice cream. Eat any leftovers at room temperature – like a cake – the next day.

125g unsalted butter, softened
90g light muscovado sugar
grated zest of 1 medium unwaxed lemon
80g clear honey
3 medium eggs, at room temperature, beaten to mix
200g white spelt flour
65g ready-chopped glacé ginger
2 teaspoons baking powder
2 teaspoons ground ginger
6–8 just-ripe plums

TO FINISH
3 tablespoons lemon juice
3 tablespoons clear honey
3 tablespoons caster sugar

TO SERVE
Vanilla Egg Custard (see page 18) OR vanilla ice cream

you will need
1 x 23cm springclip tin, greased with butter and base-lined*

TROPICAL CHURROS

A fabulous combination of light, crisp coconut churros and a vibrant tropical fruit-curd dipping sauce made from passionfruit and mango. The dough is made in the same way as choux but without the eggs, then the piped teardrop shapes are quickly fried.

makes 36

FOR THE DIPPING SAUCE
4 ripe passionfruits
1 small (or ½ large) ripe mango
1 tablespoon lemon juice
1 medium egg plus 1 yolk, at
   room temperature
75g caster sugar
60g unsalted butter, at room
   temperature, diced
2 tablespoons double cream,
   well chilled

FOR THE CHURROS
135g desiccated coconut
240g plain flour
400ml water
240ml full-fat/whole milk
¼ teaspoon fine sea salt
30g unsalted butter
1 teaspoon vanilla bean paste
2–3 drops coconut extract
3 tablespoons extra virgin coconut oil
sunflower oil, for deep-frying

TO FINISH
30g desiccated coconut
50g caster sugar
30g coconut flakes, for sprinkling

you will need
1 large piping bag fitted
with an open star nozzle;
3 baking sheets, lined with
baking paper

1. First make the passionfruit and mango dipping sauce. Halve the passionfruits and scoop out the seeds and pulp into a sieve set over a medium-sized heatproof bowl. Press the pulp through the sieve; discard the seeds. Peel the mango and cut the flesh into chunks (discard the stone). Put the mango chunks into a food processor with the lemon juice and blitz to make a smooth purée. Transfer the purée to the bowl containing the sieved passionfruit pulp.

2. Add the whole egg, yolk and sugar and mix well with a wooden spoon. Set the bowl over a pan of simmering water (the base of the bowl shouldn't touch the water) and cook, stirring constantly, until the mixture has thickened enough to coat the back of the spoon – don't let the mixture get hot (and certainly not anywhere near boiling) as it will scramble.

3. Lift the bowl off the pan and stir in the butter, a few pieces at a time. As soon as all the butter has been amalgamated, transfer the fruit curd to a clean heatproof bowl. Press a piece of clingfilm on to the surface of the curd to prevent a skin from forming. Leave to cool, then chill thoroughly for about 2 hours.

4. Using a hand wire whisk, whip the cream* in a small bowl to soft peaks, then gently fold* into the chilled fruit curd. Transfer to a serving bowl, cover and keep in the fridge until needed.

5. Make the churros while the sauce is chilling. Grind the desiccated coconut, in batches, to a fine powder – a spice or coffee grinder works better than a blender or food processor. Tip into a dry heavy-based frying pan and stir over low heat for a minute or so until very lightly coloured. Cool, then combine with the flour and set aside for now.

6. Put the water, milk, salt, butter, vanilla paste, coconut extract and coconut oil into a large pan. Set over low heat and stir gently with a wooden spoon until the fats have completely melted. Bring to the boil, then tip in the coconut/flour mixture, all in one go. Beat vigorously with a wooden spoon over low heat for a couple of minutes until the mixture has formed a very smooth, glossy and thick dough that leaves the sides of the pan clean. Remove the pan from the heat and leave the dough until it is cool enough to handle comfortably.

7. Transfer the dough to the piping bag fitted with the star nozzle. Pipe on to the lined baking sheets in ropes about 14cm long, curled to make teardrop shapes about 8cm long from the tip to the rounded edge. Chill for 10–15 minutes until just firm.

8. Meanwhile, heat the sunflower oil in a deep-fat fryer to 190°C/375°F, and combine the desiccated coconut and caster sugar on a large plate. Line another large plate with sheets of kitchen paper.

9. Carefully peel a churro off the baking paper and gently lower into the hot oil using a fish slice. Fry, turning frequently, for 3–4 minutes until a rich golden brown, crisp and cooked through. Remove from the fryer with a slotted spoon, draining off as much oil as possible, then drain well on the kitchen paper. Quickly transfer to the plate of coconut and sugar and toss until lightly coated – this is your 'test run', so adjust the frying time and/or temperature of the oil if necessary before you fry the rest of the churros, in batches of 3 or 4.

10. Arrange the churros on a large serving platter and scatter the coconut flakes over them. Serve as soon as possible, with the passionfruit and mango dipping sauce.

MULLED WINE, CRANBERRY AND APPLE CRUMBLE

This is the perfect Boxing Day dessert - a spiced wine-infused fruity crumble to follow the cold meats and salad. Cranberries work well with cooking apples (a variety that keeps a bit of texture during cooking such as Howgate Wonder is best here) and, along with the mulled wine, tint the fruit filling a ruby-red colour. Serve with plenty of real egg custard.

serves 4-6

1. Start by making the mulled wine, which can be done up to a day ahead – the longer it can be left to infuse, the better (you could also use up any ready-made mulled wine for this bake). Put the wine, sugar, cinnamon stick, clove-stuck clementine, a few gratings of nutmeg and the cardamom pods into a small pan. Heat gently, stirring occasionally, until the sugar has completely dissolved and the wine is steaming hot. Don't let the mixture boil. Remove from the heat, cover the pan and leave to infuse for at least 1 hour and up to a day.

2. Meanwhile, make the crumble mixture. Weigh the flour, ground almonds and ground toasted hazelnuts into a mixing bowl and mix well with your hand. Add the pieces of cold butter and rub in* until the mixture looks like fine crumbs. Stir in the sugar. Cover the bowl with clingfilm and keep in the fridge until needed (the mixture can be kept chilled for up to 48 hours).

3. When ready to assemble the crumble, peel, quarter and core the apples. Cut into thick slices straight into a large pan. Add the cranberries (no need to thaw if frozen). Strain the mulled wine into the pan (discard the flavourings), then set over medium heat. Cook gently, stirring frequently, for about 10 minutes until the cranberries burst and the apples start to soften. Remove from the heat. Taste the mixture: depending on the apple variety you may need to add a little more sugar. Transfer the mixture to the baking dish and leave until cool.

4. Heat the oven to 180°C/350°F/gas 4. Scatter the crumble topping evenly over the fruit mixture. Bake in the heated oven for 30–35 minutes until the crumble is golden brown and the filling is starting to bubble up around the edges. Serve hot from the oven with custard or ice cream.

FOR THE MULLED WINE
150ml red wine
4 tablespoons demerara sugar
1 cinnamon stick
1 clementine, stuck with 2 cloves
grated nutmeg
2 cardamom pods

FOR THE CRUMBLE
50g plain flour
50g ground almonds
50g ground toasted hazelnuts
50g unsalted butter, chilled and diced
50g demerara sugar

FOR THE FRUIT MIXTURE
1kg cooking apples (Howgate Wonders or Bramleys)
75g fresh/frozen cranberries

TO SERVE
Vanilla Egg Custard (see page 18) OR vanilla ice cream

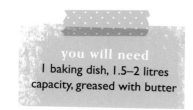
you will need
1 baking dish, 1.5–2 litres capacity, greased with butter

MAPLE SYRUP CRÈME CARAMEL

Here the ever-popular rich, creamy custard dessert is flavoured and topped with maple syrup, rather than caster sugar. Pure maple syrup - avoid the 'maple-flavour' types - is carefully boiled until reduced to a thick, strongly flavoured caramel sauce to form the base for the custard cream. You can add a sophisticated finishing touch with maple pecan pralines.

makes 4 | gluten free

FOR THE BASE
150g pure maple syrup

FOR THE CUSTARD
3 medium eggs, at room
   temperature
60g pure maple syrup
125ml milk
225ml single cream

TO SERVE (OPTIONAL)
Maple Pecan Pralines (see page 21)

you will need
4 x 150ml (size 1) ramekins;
a roasting tin/bain-marie

1. Start by making the maple caramel for the base. Weigh the maple syrup into a medium pan (or a small deep pan – the mixture will foam up) and bring to the boil. Quickly turn down the heat so the syrup just simmers. Leave to simmer gently, shaking the pan from time to time, for 20 minutes until the syrup looks darker and thick, resembling a traditional caramel.

2. Divide the maple caramel among the 4 ramekins, tilting them gently and carefully (the syrup will be very hot indeed) to swirl the caramel to cover the base and a little way up the sides. Set aside to cool and harden.

3. Meanwhile, make the custard. Heat the oven to 150°C/300°F/gas 2. Whisk the eggs with the maple syrup in a heatproof bowl until thoroughly combined. Gently warm the milk with the cream in a pan over low heat; don't let it get too hot – you should be able to dip your finger in for a moment. Pour the milk/cream on to the egg mixture in a thin, steady stream, whisking constantly. Strain the egg mixture into a jug – this will remove the chalazae (egg cords) as well as the air bubbles.

4. Set the ramekins in the roasting tin and carefully pour the custard into them. Now pour enough almost-boiling water into the tin to come halfway up the sides of the ramekins. Bake in the heated oven for 40–50 minutes until the custard is set – check with the tip of a knife inserted into the middle. The top of the custard should have an even colour, not a darker/damp-looking centre, and should only just wobble if gently jiggled. (Ramekins come in different qualities/thicknesses so the baking time can vary.) Take care not to overcook – watch out for tiny bubbles appearing around the edge of the dishes – which would make the custards grainy.

5. Remove from the oven and lift the dishes from the roasting tin on to a wire rack. Leave to cool, then cover and chill overnight, to allow time for the caramel to soften and form a sauce.

6. When ready to serve, gently loosen each custard by running a thin, round-bladed knife around the inside of the ramekin. Place a small rimmed plate, upturned, on top of the ramekin, then turn it over and give it a little shake to release the custard and the caramel sauce. Lift off the ramekin. Garnish with pecan pralines, if you like.

DESSERTS & PUDDINGS

CHOCOLATE-HAZELNUT ROCHERS

This recipe will extend your baking skills beyond simple meringues: the classic combo of hazelnuts and chocolate is mixed into a glossy stiff meringue to make craggy streaked mounds called 'rochers' (the French word for rocks). Sandwiched with whipped cream, they make a rich yet light dessert.

makes 6 pairs

gluten free

100g blanched hazelnuts
100g dark chocolate (about 70% cocoa solids)
3 medium egg whites, at room temperature
good pinch of cream of tartar
175g caster sugar

FOR THE FILLING

200ml double cream, well chilled
1 teaspoon hazelnut liqueur
OR vanilla extract

you will need
2 baking sheets, lined with baking paper

another idea: For sheer indulgence, use vanilla ice cream instead of cream and serve with Hot Bitter Chocolate Sauce (see page 20).

1. Heat the oven to 180°C/350°F/gas 4. Tip the hazelnuts into a small baking dish or tin and toast in the heated oven for 7–10 minutes until golden brown. Leave to cool. Turn down the oven to 120°C/250°F/gas ½.

2. Gently melt the chocolate*, then leave to cool until needed. Meanwhile, use a large sharp knife to chop each hazelnut roughly into 2 or 3 pieces.

3. Put the egg whites and cream of tartar into a large bowl, or the bowl of a free-standing electric mixer fitted with the whisk attachment. Whisk the whites* with a hand-held electric whisk, or the whisk attachment, to the soft peak stage. Whisk in the sugar a heaped tablespoon at a time to make a very stiff, glossy meringue.

4. Scatter the chopped nuts over the meringue, then drizzle the chocolate over the top. Using a large metal spoon or plastic spatula, gently fold* the nuts and chocolate into the meringue using just 2 or 3 strokes to give a distinct, streaked/marbled effect.

5. Using a soup spoon or kitchen spoon, scoop up a heaped spoonful of the meringue mixture, then use a second spoon to gently push the mixture off and on to the lined baking sheet to make a craggy, rough-looking mound. Repeat to make 12 mounds, spacing them well apart to allow for expansion.

6. Bake in the heated oven for 2 hours until firm. Turn off the oven and leave the meringues inside the cooling oven until they are completely cold before carefully peeling them off the lining paper (they can be stored in an airtight container for up to 3 days).

7. Shortly before you want to assemble the rochers, chill a bowl for whipping the cream. Pour the well-chilled cream and the hazelnut liqueur or vanilla into the chilled bowl and whip the cream* until it is very thick and just past soft peak stage – it needs to hold a shape.

8. Using an offset palette knife, swirl whipped cream over the flat base of a meringue, then sandwich with another (flat base to flat base). Repeat until they are all sandwiched. Eat immediately or cover lightly and keep in the fridge until ready to serve (best eaten the same day).

CAFFE LATTE GINGERBREAD CHEESECAKE

Inspired by the wonderful old-style Flemish coffee shops (now very much back in fashion), this cheesecake has a base made from those ultra-thin, very crisp, spicy biscuits traditionally served with coffee, and a rich, velvety, coffee-flavoured filling spiked with glacé ginger. It looks really impressive but is not a difficult bake.

serves 12

FOR THE BASE

190g Crisp Spiced Wafers (see page 96; this is about half the quantity) OR store-bought thin, crisp ginger or spice biscuits
70g unsalted butter, melted

FOR THE FILLING

800g full-fat cream cheese
150ml soured cream
4 medium eggs, at room temperature
300g caster sugar
1 teaspoon vanilla extract
1 slightly rounded tablespoon instant coffee (granules or powder)
1 tablespoon boiling water
1 tablespoon coffee liqueur
40g ready-chopped glacé ginger

TO FINISH

cocoa powder, for dusting

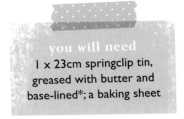

you will need
1 x 23cm springclip tin, greased with butter and base-lined*; a baking sheet

1. To make the cheesecake base, heat the oven to 150°C/300°F/gas 2. Crush the spiced wafers in a food processor, or by putting them into a plastic bag and bashing with a rolling pin. Tip the crumbs into a bowl and stir in the melted butter until thoroughly combined. Transfer the mixture to the prepared tin and press on to the base with the back of a spoon to make an even layer. Bake in the heated oven for 10 minutes. Leave to cool while you make the filling.

2. Put the cream cheese, soured cream, eggs, sugar and vanilla extract into a food processor and blitz until the mixture is very smooth and creamy. Transfer 200ml to a measuring jug and set aside for the topping. Dissolve the coffee in the boiling water, then stir in the coffee liqueur. Add to the mixture remaining in the processor along with the glacé ginger, then 'pulse' a few times until thoroughly combined.

3. Set the springclip tin on a baking sheet. Pour the coffee filling on top of the biscuit base. Place the tin, on the baking sheet, in the heated oven and bake for 1 hour – the cheesecake filling will still 'wobble' if you gently jiggle the tin but the top should be just set. Remove the cheesecake, on its baking sheet, from the oven. Starting in the centre, carefully pour the reserved creamy white filling mixture on top, if possible leaving a 1cm border of coffee-coloured filling showing all round the edge.

4. Return the cheesecake to the oven and bake for a further 20–30 minutes until the filling has just a slight wobble. Turn off the oven and leave the cheesecake inside, with the door slightly ajar, to cool for 1 hour. After this time, remove the cheesecake from the oven and run a round-bladed knife around inside the tin to loosen the cheesecake, then leave to cool completely. Once cold, cover with clingfilm and chill overnight.

5. Unclip the side of the tin and set the cheesecake on a serving platter. Dust with cocoa powder just before serving – for extra effect use a stencil. Keep any leftovers in the fridge.

BANANA SPLIT ICE-CREAM CAKE

Party treat time! There are lots of elements here, just as in an old-fashioned banana split: bananas (of course), vanilla ice cream (home-made or ready-made), a gooey thick caramel sauce and a rich chocolate sauce, plus a whisked chocolate sponge for sandwiching it all together. It's a lot of fun to make and will really wow your family.

serves 10–12

FOR THE SPONGE
4 medium eggs, at room temperature
100g caster sugar
65g self-raising flour
35g cocoa powder

FOR THE BANANA CARAMEL
150g caster sugar
4 tablespoons water
250g peeled ripe bananas (about 3–4 medium), thickly sliced

4 tablespoons whipping cream
good pinch of sea salt flakes

FOR THE ICE CREAM
350ml milk
1 vanilla pod, split open lengthways
4 medium egg yolks, at room temperature
90g caster sugar
1 ripe medium banana
250ml whipping cream, well chilled

FOR THE CHOCOLATE TOPPING
200g dark chocolate (about 70% cocoa solids)
5 tablespoons whipping cream

TO FINISH
fresh or maraschino cherries
2 tablespoons chopped pistachios
paper cocktail umbrellas (optional)

you will need
1 x 23cm springclip tin, greased with butter and base-lined*; a 23cm disc of thin card or thin cake board

1. Start by making the sponge. Heat the oven to 180°C/350°F/gas 4. Break the eggs into a large mixing bowl, or the bowl of a free-standing electric mixer fitted with the whisk attachment, and add the sugar. Whisk with a hand-held electric whisk, or the whisk attachment, until the mixture is very pale and has reached the ribbon stage*. Sift the flour and cocoa on top of the mixture and carefully fold* in with a large metal spoon or plastic spatula.

2. Transfer the mixture to the prepared tin and gently level the surface. Bake in the heated oven for about 25 minutes until the sponge is well risen and starting to shrink away from the sides of the tin, and will pass the fingertip test*. Run a round-bladed knife around the inside of the tin to loosen the sponge, then turn it out on to a wire rack and leave to cool. (Once cold, the sponge can be stored in an airtight container for up to 24 hours before assembling the dessert.) Wash and dry the tin to use later.

3. To make the banana caramel, tip the sugar into a medium pan and add the water. Heat gently, stirring frequently with a wooden spoon, until the sugar has completely dissolved. Turn up the heat and let the syrup boil, without stirring, until it turns to a rich golden-brown caramel. Remove from the heat and carefully add the banana slices (take care: splashes will burn). Stir well, then stir in the cream and salt. Set the pan back over low heat and stir gently for a minute or so to make a thick caramel sauce with distinct slices of banana. Tip into a heatproof bowl and set aside to cool.

4. For the ice cream, heat the milk with the split vanilla pod until steaming hot, then remove from the heat, cover and leave to infuse for 30 minutes. Meanwhile, put the egg yolks and sugar into a large heatproof bowl and whisk for 4–5 minutes, using a hand wire whisk or a hand-held electric whisk, until very thick and pale. Fish the vanilla pod out of the milk and, with the tip of a small knife, gently scrape out the vanilla seeds. Add these to the milk. Reheat the milk until very hot but not quite boiling, then pour on to the yolk mixture in a thin, steady stream while whisking constantly.

5. Tip the mixture back into the pan and set over low heat. Cook, stirring constantly with the wooden spoon, until the custard thickens enough to coat the back of the spoon and you can draw a clear line through with your finger. If you want to check with a thermometer, the custard will be about 85°C/185°F. Immediately pour the custard into a clean heatproof bowl and leave to cool, then cover and chill for at least 3 hours, preferably overnight.

6. Peel and thinly slice the banana, then wrap tightly in clingfilm and keep in the freezer until needed.

7. When you are ready to assemble the ice-cream cake, clear a space in the freezer. Set the card disc in the bottom of the springclip tin. Cut the chocolate sponge cake into 2 layers* and place the bottom layer in the tin, cut-side uppermost. Cover the tin with clingfilm and put it into the freezer.

8. Put the bowl of banana caramel into the fridge to chill for 15–20 minutes – it needs to be spreadable but not hard. Meanwhile, stir the custard well, then stir in the chilled cream. Pour into an ice-cream machine and churn until softly frozen but not solid.

9. As soon as the ice cream is ready, you will need to work quickly. Remove the tin from the freezer and spoon half of the ice cream on top of the sponge in an even layer. Cover and return to the freezer. Add the frozen banana to the remaining ice cream, then churn it again for a few minutes.

10. Remove the tin from the freezer and spoon the chilled banana caramel over the ice cream layer on the sponge. Set the second sponge layer on top, crust-side uppermost. Spoon the banana ice cream over the top to make an even layer. Quickly cover the tin and return it to the freezer. Leave until the dessert is frozen and firm – at least 4 hours, preferably overnight.

11. Near serving time, gently melt the chocolate* with the cream, then leave to cool for 5 minutes. Have the cherries, chopped nuts and cocktail umbrellas at hand. Run a round-bladed knife around the inside of the tin to loosen the ice-cream cake, then unclip the tin and set the cake on a serving platter. Spoon and swirl the chocolate sauce quickly over the cake so it covers the top and drips down the sides. Before it completely sets hard, arrange the decoration on the top. Serve immediately, using a large sharp knife dipped in hot water to cut thick wedges.

PISTACHIO AND WHITE CHOCOLATE CHURROS

A very pretty Spanish-style dessert made from deep-fried sweet choux dough filled with a rich pistachio and white chocolate custard. The light, crisp, finger-like churros are decorated with melted white chocolate and chopped pistachios, and served with a dark chocolate dipping sauce.

makes 26

FOR THE PISTACHIO CUSTARD FILLING
250g unsalted pistachio nuts (shelled)
60g icing sugar, sifted
125ml full-fat/whole milk
5 medium egg yolks, at room temperature
30g salted butter, at room temperature, diced
50g white chocolate (about 30% cocoa solids), finely chopped

few drops of almond extract
few drops of edible green food colouring (paste or gel – optional)

FOR THE CHURROS
25g granulated sugar
165g salted butter
375ml water
¼ teaspoon fine sea salt
225g plain flour, sifted
4 medium eggs, at room temperature

1 teaspoon vanilla extract
100g vanilla caster sugar
sunflower oil, for deep frying
60g white chocolate, chopped

FOR THE CHOCOLATE SAUCE
150g dark chocolate (about 70% cocoa solids), chopped
150ml single cream
2 tablespoons amaretto, or to taste

you will need
3 baking sheets, lined with baking paper; a large piping bag fitted with a large star nozzle; a medium piping bag fitted with a 3mm plain round nozzle

1. Make the custard filling first so it has time to firm up. Heat the oven to 180°C/350°F/gas 4. Weigh the pistachios into a medium pan, add cold water to cover and bring to the boil, then simmer for 10 seconds. Drain in a sieve, then tip on to several sheets of kitchen paper. Pat dry and rub the nuts with the paper to slip off the papery brown skins. Transfer the skinned nuts to a baking dish or tin, spread out and toast in the heated oven for 5 minutes to dry them and add a little colour. Leave to cool (you can turn off the oven).

2. Set aside 100g of the pistachios for the decoration. Tip the remaining nuts into a food processor, add the icing sugar and blitz (scraping down the sides of the bowl occasionally) to make a fine powder. Warm the milk in a non-stick medium pan. Add the egg yolks to the processor bowl and run the machine until thoroughly combined with the nut powder. Then, with the machine running, slowly pour in the warm milk through the feed tube. Scrape down the sides of the bowl, then run for a few more seconds.

3. Scrape the mixture back into the medium pan and set over low heat. Stir constantly with a wooden spoon until the mixture thickens to a custard that will just coat the back of the spoon – don't let the custard get too hot or the eggs will scramble. Remove from the heat and stir in the butter and

then the chopped chocolate. When both have melted, add almond extract to taste. If necessary, add a tiny bit of green food colouring. Set a fine sieve over a heatproof bowl and push the custard through it. Discard the larger nut pieces left in the sieve (you need a smooth mixture that will pipe easily). Press a piece of clingfilm on to the surface to prevent a skin from forming. Leave to cool, then chill thoroughly – at least 2 hours but preferably 4.

4. To make the churros dough, put the sugar, butter, water and salt into a large pan and heat gently, stirring frequently, until the sugar has dissolved and the butter has melted. Bring to the boil, then tip in the flour, all in one go. Beat vigorously over low heat until the mixture forms a smooth, glossy ball of thick dough. Remove from the heat and transfer to a large heatproof bowl. Leave to cool until lukewarm, then, one at a time, add the eggs, beating well after each addition – you can do this with a wooden spoon but it is easier with a hand-held electric whisk. Whisk in the vanilla extract.

5. Transfer to the large piping bag fitted with the star nozzle. Pipe the churros dough on to 2 of the lined baking sheets: pipe into straight fingers exactly 10cm long, cutting off the dough with kitchen scissors to give a neat rounded end. Dust the third lined baking sheet with some of the vanilla sugar.

6. Heat the oil in a deep-fat fryer or large, deep pan to 190°C/375°F. Carefully remove one piped finger from the baking sheet (the best way to do it is to set a large palette knife parallel to the finger and slide it underneath) and gently lower it into the hot oil. Fry, turning it frequently so it colours evenly, for about 6 minutes until a rich golden brown and cooked through. Lift out and drain on kitchen paper, then roll in the vanilla sugar to coat all over. Leave to cool on the baking sheet. This is your 'test run' – adjust the heat of the oil and frying time as necessary, then continue to fry the rest of the churros, in small batches so the fryer doesn't become crowded. Drain each batch and roll in sugar; add more sugar to the baking sheet as needed.

7. When all the churros have been fried, make a small hole in one rounded end of each and gently push a bamboo skewer right down the length of the finger to make a tunnel (remove the skewer). Spoon the pistachio custard into the piping bag fitted with the small round nozzle and pipe into the churros through the small hole to fill the tunnel.

8. Finely chop the reserved pistachios and put into a small dish. Gently melt the white chocolate*. To decorate the churros, dip one end first into the melted chocolate and then into the nuts. Arrange on a large platter and leave to set in a cool spot (not the fridge).

9. Meanwhile, make the sauce. Put the chocolate into a heatproof bowl. Heat the cream in a small pan until almost boiling, then pour over the chocolate and stir until melted and smooth. Stir in amaretto to taste. Transfer to a serving bowl and serve immediately with the churros.

SUMMER PICNIC ROULADE

Just perfect for a sunny day: a very light genoise sponge lusciously filled with whipped cream, a sweet-sharp lemon curd and juicy berries, then decorated with some beautiful piping and more berries.

serves 8–10

1. Heat the oven to 200°C/400°F/gas 6. To make the genoise sponge, put the sugar and eggs into a large heatproof bowl and whisk for a few seconds with a hand-held electric whisk, just until combined. Set the bowl over a pan of gently simmering water (the base of the bowl shouldn't touch the water) and whisk on full speed until the mixture is very thick, pale and mousse-like and has reached the ribbon stage* – take care not to let the mixture get too hot or it will scramble. Remove the bowl from the pan and whisk until the mixture returns to room temperature.

2. Sift (for the second time) about a third of the flour into the bowl and gently fold* in. Repeat to add the remaining flour in 2 batches, then drizzle the cooled melted butter around the side of the bowl and carefully fold into the mixture. Transfer to the lined tin and spread evenly with an offset spatula, taking great care that the corners are well filled. Bake in the heated oven for 10–12 minutes until the sponge is golden and feels springy when lightly pressed in the centre with a fingertip*.

3. While the sponge is baking, cut a sheet of baking paper larger than the tin, lay it on the worktop and lightly dust it with icing sugar. When the sponge is baked, invert the tin on to the baking paper, then lift off the tin and peel away the lining paper. Fold the edge of the sugar-dusted baking paper over one short end of the sponge. Starting at this end, roll up the sponge fairly tightly with the paper inside. Transfer the roll to a wire rack and leave until completely cold.

4. Meanwhile, make the lemon curd. Combine the cornflour and lemon zest and juice in a bowl, mixing well together. Put the butter and sugar into a medium pan and heat very gently, stirring. As soon as the butter starts to melt, add the lemon mixture and stir well. Keep stirring until the butter has completely melted, then remove the pan from the heat and stir in the beaten eggs and yolk. Return the pan to the heat and stir constantly until the mixture thickens and comes to the boil. Pour the curd into a heatproof bowl and press a piece of clingfilm on the surface to prevent a skin from forming. Leave to cool, then keep in the fridge until needed.

5. Whip the chilled cream* with the icing sugar until it stands in soft peaks when the whisk is lifted. Cover and keep in the fridge until needed. Hull the 200g strawberries and slice thinly. Cover and set aside.

FOR THE SPONGE
120g caster sugar
4 medium eggs, at room
  temperature
100g plain flour, sifted
20g unsalted butter, melted
  and cooled
icing sugar, for dusting

FOR THE LEMON CURD
1 tablespoon cornflour
finely grated zest and juice of
  4 medium unwaxed lemons
130g unsalted butter, at room
  temperature, diced
190g caster sugar
3 medium eggs plus 1 yolk, at
  room temperature, beaten

FOR THE CREAM
600ml double cream, well chilled
30g icing sugar, sifted
200g ripe strawberries

TO DECORATE
30g white chocolate, finely grated
3 large, even-sized strawberries
25g finely chopped pistachios

you will need
1 Swiss roll tin, 24 x 30cm,
greased with butter and
base-lined*; baking paper;
a large piping bag fitted with
a medium star nozzle

6. To assemble the roulade, gently unroll the sponge on the worktop. Transfer two-thirds of the whipped cream to the piping bag and set this aside. Spread about half of the rest of the cream over the sponge, leaving a 1cm border clear at the short edge at the end of the roll. Then spread a thick layer of lemon curd over the cream, leaving a border as before (any leftover lemon curd can be kept in the fridge for up to a week). Cover evenly with sliced strawberries. Carefully re-roll the sponge (without the paper) and transfer it to a serving board or plate.

7. Spread the remaining whipped cream in the bowl over the top and sides of the roll (not the ends) to make a very thin 'crumb-catcher' layer. Decorate with neatly piped lines of cream and finish with 3 rosettes on the top. Scatter grated chocolate over the roulade, then set a whole strawberry on each rosette. Sprinkle the chopped pistachios all over the roulade. Keep in the fridge until ready to serve. Best eaten the same day.

CHOCOLATE AND RASPBERRY TERRINE

This beautiful terrine is perfect for a special meal. Chocolate sponge fingers surround a thick mousse of melted dark chocolate, raspberry purée and whipped cream. There's a hidden layer of raspberries inside, and the terrine is served with a fresh raspberry sauce whose acidity works well with the rich filling. Once assembled the terrine will benefit from a night in the fridge, and there is very little last-minute work.

serves 8-10

FOR THE CHOCOLATE SPONGE FINGERS

3 medium eggs, at room
   temperature, separated
good pinch of fine sea salt
80g caster sugar
½ teaspoon vanilla extract
60g plain flour
15g cocoa powder

FOR THE MOUSSE FILLING

325g fresh raspberries
60g icing sugar, sifted
1 tablespoon raspberry liqueur
   OR kirsch (optional)
300ml double cream, chilled
185g dark chocolate (about 70%
   cocoa solids)

TO FINISH

icing sugar, for dusting
100ml double cream, whipped
raspberries, to decorate
Fresh Raspberry Sauce (see page
   19), to serve

you will need
2 baking sheets, lined
with baking paper; a large
disposable piping bag OR
a large piping bag fitted with
a 1cm plain nozzle; a 900g
loaf tin, about 26 x 12.5 x
7.5cm; a small piping bag
fitted with a star nozzle

1. Heat the oven to 180°C/350°F/gas 4. The mixture for the sponge fingers will be piped on to the baking sheets in 10cm fingers, so draw 'tramlines' 10cm apart on the baking paper you have cut to line the baking sheets, then flip the paper over so the lines are on the underside but still visible.

2. Put the egg whites and salt into a large mixing bowl, or the bowl of a free-standing electric mixer fitted with the whisk attachment. Whisk the whites* with a hand-held electric whisk, or the whisk attachment, until they will stand in stiff peaks. Sprinkle half of the caster sugar over the top and whisk for a few more seconds until the whites are stiff and glossy. Set aside (transfer to another bowl if you want to whisk the yolks in the stand mixer).

3. Put the egg yolks into another large bowl and add the rest of the caster sugar and the vanilla. Whisk (there's no need to wash the beaters) at high speed until the mixture is very thick and pale and has reached the ribbon stage*. Add a third of the whisked whites to the bowl and fold* in with a large metal spoon or plastic spatula. Add half of the remaining whisked whites and fold in quickly but gently using as few movements as you can. Fold in the last of the whites in the same way. Sift the flour and cocoa on top of the mixture and gently but thoroughly fold in: you want the mixture to be fairly stiff so resist the urge to overmix as it will quickly turn runny.

4. Spoon the mixture into the piping bag fitted with the plain nozzle (if you are using a disposable bag, snip off the tip to make a 1cm opening). Pipe 10cm-long fingers crossways between the tramlines drawn on the lined baking sheets, spacing the fingers slightly apart to allow for spreading. You should be able to make about 34 fingers.

5. Dust with icing sugar, then bake in the heated oven for 11–12 minutes until just firm. Remove from the oven and leave to firm up on the baking sheets for a minute, then transfer the fingers to a wire rack to cool. (The sponge fingers can be stored in an airtight container for up to 4 days.)

6. When you are ready to assemble the terrine, completely line the loaf tin with clingfilm (you may need to use overlapping sheets), leaving the ends of the clingfilm hanging over the rim. Set aside 100g raspberries and put the remaining 225g berries plus the icing sugar and liqueur (if using) into a food processor. Blitz to make a thick purée. Press through a fine sieve into a bowl (to remove the seeds), then set aside on the worktop until needed.

7. Whip the cream* until thick and floppy – the stage before soft peak. Leave on the worktop to come up to room temperature: when it is time to assemble the mousse all the elements need to be roughly the same temperature for a smooth result. Gently melt the chocolate*, then leave to cool until barely warm (you don't want it to start to set and go lumpy).

8. Meanwhile, remove 1 tablespoon of the raspberry purée and use to brush over the clingfilm lining the loaf tin, just to moisten. Now line the sides of the tin with sponge fingers: stand them vertically, pressing the rounded top side of each against the damp clingfilm, and close together. They will stand above the rim of the tin. Line the base of the tin with a layer of sponge fingers, rounded side down and close together (this will be the top of the dessert when it is unmoulded, so arrange the sponge fingers as neatly as possible).

9. Stir the room-temperature raspberry purée into the melted chocolate, then fold this mixture into the room-temperature whipped cream. Working as quickly as possible (before the mixture becomes too firm), spoon half into the loaf tin and spread evenly. Arrange the saved whole raspberries over the top, then cover with the remaining chocolate mixture, spreading it evenly. Bang the tin on the worktop a couple of times to settle the mixture. Using a small sharp knife, trim the sponge fingers so they are the same height as the filling. Fold over the ends of the clingfilm to cover the terrine and chill for 6 hours, or overnight, until firm.

10. When ready to serve, invert the terrine on to a serving platter and lift off the tin. Carefully peel off the clingfilm. Dust the terrine with icing sugar. Decorate with swirls of whipped cream piped with the star nozzle and a few extra raspberries. Serve cut in thick slices, with the raspberry sauce.

MARJOLAINE

This wonderfully spectacular dessert is built from four layers of nut meringue, called *dacquoise*, filled with a praline buttercream plus ganache and finished with more piped ganache and toasted nuts.

serves 10-12

FOR THE DACQUOISE
125g blanched almonds
125g blanched hazelnuts
300g caster sugar
25g cornflour
6 large egg whites, at room
    temperature

FOR THE GANACHE
360g dark chocolate (about 46%
    cocoa solids)

270ml double cream

FOR THE PRALINE
100g blanched almonds
300g caster sugar
100ml water

FOR THE FRENCH BUTTERCREAM
225g caster sugar
75ml water
pinch of cream of tartar

8 large egg yolks, at room
    temperature
350g unsalted butter, at room
    temperature, diced

TO ASSEMBLE
150g flaked almonds
50g toasted, chopped hazelnuts
50g slivered pistachios

you will need
2 Swiss roll tins, each
20 x 30cm, brushed
with vegetable oil and
base-lined*; baking paper;
a baking sheet; a medium
piping bag fitted with a
small star nozzle (no. 33)

1. Start with the dacquoise. Heat the oven to 180°C/350°F/gas 4. Tip the almonds and hazelnuts into the bowl of a food processor and 'pulse' until finely ground. Transfer the nuts to a roasting tin and spread evenly, then toast in the heated oven for 10–12 minutes, stirring every 3 minutes, until lightly golden. Tip into a large heatproof bowl and leave to cool before stirring in 100g of the caster sugar and the cornflour.

2. Reduce the oven temperature to 150°C/300°F/gas 2. Put the egg whites into the bowl of a free-standing electric mixer fitted with the whisk attachment and whisk the whites* on medium speed for about 2 minutes until white and frothy. Increase the whisking speed and gradually add the remaining 200g caster sugar, a tablespoon at a time. Whisk to a stiff, glossy meringue. Scatter the toasted nut mixture on top and gently fold* into the meringue.

3. Divide the meringue equally between the 2 prepared Swiss roll tins and spread evenly with an offset palette knife. Bake for 45–60 minutes until lightly golden and firm to the touch. Turn off the oven, open the oven door so it is just ajar and leave the meringues inside until completely cooled.

4. Remove the tins from the oven and gently invert each on to a sheet of baking paper. Lift off the tins and carefully peel off the lining paper from the bottom of the meringues. Cover lightly and set aside until needed (if made in advance, keep in an airtight tin).

5. For the chocolate ganache, break the chocolate into pieces and put into a heatproof bowl. Heat the cream in a pan until just simmering, then pour over the chocolate and stir until the mixture is smooth. Leave to cool, then cover and chill, stirring occasionally, until thick enough to spread and pipe.

6. For the praline, have the baking sheet, lined with baking paper, ready. Toast the blanched almonds in a dry frying pan, stirring constantly, until they turn golden. Tip the nuts on to a piece of kitchen paper and set aside. (Don't wash the frying pan – you'll need it later.) Put the sugar and water in a pan and heat gently until the sugar has completely dissolved, then turn up the heat and boil the syrup until it turns a rich golden colour (170°C/338°F/caramel stage on a sugar thermometer). Remove the pan from the heat, quickly add the toasted almonds and stir well. Pour on to the lined baking sheet and spread out evenly (work quickly). Leave to cool. Once set, tip the praline into the bowl of a food processor and blitz to a fine powder.

7. To make the French buttercream, combine the sugar, water and cream of tartar in a heavy-based pan and heat gently until the sugar has completely dissolved, stirring occasionally. Bring to the boil and boil rapidly until the syrup reaches 115°C/240°F/soft-ball stage on a sugar thermometer.

8. Meanwhile, put the egg yolks into the (washed) bowl of the mixer fitted with the (washed) whisk attachment. Whisk briefly to combine the yolks. Once the sugar syrup has come to temperature, gradually whisk it into the yolks, adding it in a thin, steady stream. Continue whisking for 5–10 minutes until the mixture is very thick and completely cooled. Now slowly add the butter bit by bit, whisking until completely amalgamated and very smooth. Fold* in the praline powder. Cover and keep in the fridge until needed.

9. Toast the flaked almonds in the dry frying pan, stirring constantly, until golden brown. Tip on to a piece of kitchen paper.

10. Carefully cut the dacquoise sheets in half lengthways so you have 4 strips of meringue each measuring 30 x 10cm. Place one strip on a serving plate and spread a quarter of the praline buttercream over the surface. Top with a second strip of dacquoise and cover with a third of the chocolate ganache. Add a third layer of dacquoise and spread another quarter of the praline buttercream over it. Set the final strip of dacquoise on top.

11. Spread the remaining praline buttercream over the top and sides of the assembled gâteau. Press the toasted flaked almonds on to all 4 sides. Spoon the remaining ganache into the piping bag and pipe around the top edge of the gâteau and then across the top in 7 diagonal lines. Fill the gaps between the diagonal piped lines with alternating toasted chopped hazelnuts and slivered pistachios. Keep the Marjolaine in the fridge until ready to serve – remove from the fridge 10–15 minutes before serving.

GRAND STRAWBERRY MOUSSE CAKE

A glorious, extravagantly pretty dessert to make when strawberries are at their very best, this has to be the ultimate summer showstopper. A light, creamy mousse is set on top of an almond sponge, and finished with a band of sponge fingers. Strawberries dipped in white chocolate decorate the patterned strawberry top of the cake.

serves 8-10

FOR THE SPONGE BASE
100g unsalted butter, softened
150g caster sugar
3 medium eggs, at room
   temperature, beaten to mix
90g ground almonds
40g self-raising flour, sifted
1 tablespoon kirsch OR milk

FOR THE SPONGE FINGERS
3 medium eggs, at room
   temperature, separated

large pinch of fine sea salt
75g caster sugar
½ teaspoon vanilla extract
75g plain flour
icing sugar, for dusting

FOR THE BRUSHING SYRUP
75g caster sugar
4 tablespoons water
1 tablespoon kirsch

FOR THE STRAWBERRY MOUSSE
1.5kg ripe strawberries
100g caster sugar
4 sheets leaf gelatine (from
   a 13g/8-sheet pack)
1–2 teaspoons kirsch OR
   lemon juice, to taste
250ml whipping cream, well
   chilled

FOR THE DECORATION
100g white chocolate, chopped

you will need
1 x 20cm springclip tin,
greased with butter and
base-lined*; 2 baking sheets,
lined with baking paper;
a large piping bag fitted
with a 1cm plain nozzle; a
20cm thin card cake board;
a ribbon

1. Start by making the sponge base for the mousse cake. Heat the oven to 180°C/350°F/gas 4. Put the soft butter, sugar, eggs, ground almonds, flour and kirsch or milk into a large mixing bowl, or the bowl of a free-standing electric mixer fitted with the whisk attachment. Beat with a hand-held electric whisk, or the whisk attachment, until the mixture is smooth, light and creamy.

2. Transfer the mixture to the prepared tin and spread it evenly. Bake in the heated oven for about 30 minutes until the sponge is golden and starting to shrink away from the sides of the tin; it should pass the fingertip test*. Run a round-bladed knife around the inside of the tin to loosen the sponge, then turn it out on to a wire rack and leave to cool completely. (Once cold, the sponge can be stored in an airtight container for up to 24 hours.) Wash the tin, ready to use later for assembling the cake.

3. To make the sponge-finger 'band' for the side of the cake, first draw 2 sets of 'tramlines' 7.25cm apart on each sheet of baking paper you have cut to line the baking sheets – these lines will help you make all the sponge fingers the same length as you pipe them. Turn the papers over and place on the baking sheets; the drawn lines on the underside should still be visible.

FOREST FRUITS STRAWBERRY MOUSSE CAKES

A delightfully summery dessert made from light sponge cake, a creamy mixed berry fruit mousse, fresh strawberries and a raspberry jelly topping. There's even a tempered chocolate log to complete the fruits of the forest theme.

makes 12

FOR THE VANILLA SPONGE
155g self-raising flour
½ teaspoon baking powder
170g caster sugar
170g unsalted butter, softened,
 OR baking margarine
3 medium eggs, at room
 temperature, beaten to mix
1 teaspoon vanilla extract
1½ tablespoons semi-skimmed
 milk

FOR THE FRUIT MOUSSE
4 leaves gelatine (from
 a 13g/8-leaf pack)
145ml whipping cream
125g each blackberries, raspberries
 and hulled strawberries
1 tablespoon icing sugar
100g golden caster sugar
finely grated zest of 1 medium
 orange
250ml double cream, chilled

FOR THE MOULDS
200g hulled strawberries, thinly
 sliced

FOR THE RASPBERRY TOPPING
3 leaves gelatine (from
 a 13g/8-leaf pack)
200g raspberries
50g caster sugar
100ml water

you will need
Several sheets/strips acetate
(see recipe); a 7cm food
ring; a baking sheet, lined
with baking paper; a 24 x
30cm Swiss roll tin, greased
with butter and base-lined*;
a 7cm plain round cutter

1. Start by preparing the moulds to shape the tiny mousse cakes: cut 12 strips of acetate to fit inside the food ring (each about 8 x 23cm). One at a time, fit the strips inside the food ring to form a cylinder and secure with masking tape, then remove from the ring. Set the small cylinders upright on the lined baking sheet.

2. To make the sponge, heat the oven to 190°C/375°F/gas 5. Sift the flour, baking powder and sugar into the bowl of a free-standing electric mixer fitted with the whisk or paddle attachment. Mix briefly, then add the softened butter (or margarine) and eggs and mix, starting slowly and gradually increasing the speed, just until smoothly combined. Scrape down the sides of the bowl, then add the vanilla and milk and mix on high speed for 20 seconds.

3. Transfer the mixture to the prepared Swiss roll tin – take great care to spread it perfectly flat and of even thickness as you will be cutting the baked sponge into even discs. Bake in the heated oven for 10–13 minutes until the sponge is golden and feels springy when lightly pressed in the centre with a fingertip*. Invert on to a wire rack, peel off the lining paper and leave to cool.

4. Once cold, transfer the sponge to a board and stamp out 12 discs using the round cutter. Press a disc (crust-side down) into each acetate cylinder to make a flat base. (Save the sponge trimmings for a trifle.)

5. For the fruit mousse, put the leaves of gelatine into a bowl of cold water and leave to soak and soften for 5 minutes. Meanwhile, heat the whipping cream in a small pan until steaming hot; remove from the heat. Squeeze the gelatine leaves to remove the excess water, then add to the hot cream and whisk, using a wire hand whisk, until completely melted and smooth. Set aside.

6. Put the blackberries, raspberries and hulled strawberries into the bowl of a food processor, add the icing sugar and blitz to form a thick purée. Set a fine sieve over a large bowl and press the purée through it to remove the seeds. Add the caster sugar, orange zest and warm gelatine/cream mixture and stir gently until the sugar has completely dissolved. Leave on the worktop, stirring frequently, until the mixture has cooled to room temperature and is starting to thicken. Whip the double cream* until it is floppy – just before soft peak. Fold* the whipped cream into the fruit mixture until smooth and even; it will be thick but pourable. Transfer it to a large jug.

7. Arrange 4 or 5 strawberry slices around the inside of each acetate ring, resting them on the top edge of the vanilla sponge and pressing them firmly against the acetate so they stand upright. Carefully pour the mousse mixture into the moulds so they are equally filled. Chill for about 1 hour until set and firm.

8. When the mousses have set, prepare the raspberry jelly topping. Soak the leaves of gelatine in cold water as before. Purée and sieve the raspberries as before, then weigh the purée into a pan – you need 115g. Add the sugar and water and heat gently, stirring, until the sugar has dissolved and the mixture is steaming hot. Remove from the heat. Squeeze the excess water from the gelatine and add to the pan. Whisk until melted and smooth using a wire hand whisk, then transfer to a clean jug. Leave until cool and starting to thicken, stirring frequently.

9. Carefully pour a little of the raspberry jelly liquid (about 1½ tablespoons) on top of each set mousse, then return them to the fridge to firm up for about 1 hour.

10. Meanwhile, melt the dark chocolate*, then temper* it. Pour the chocolate over a marble slab and spread it thinly. Leave to cool until it feels tacky and a bit leathery to the touch. Using a metal bench scraper, make short sharp cuts under the chocolate on a diagonal so the chocolate shavings will roll and curl. Use a skewer or cocktail stick to transfer the chocolate curls to a flat plate. (Left-over chocolate scrapings can be saved and re-melted for another use.)

11. Once the mousse cakes are firmly set, carefully peel away the acetate collars with the help of an offset palette knife (if in doubt, first pop them in the freezer for 10 minutes). If necessary, gently smooth and neaten the side of the mousse layer and sponge edge with the palette knife. Add a chocolate curl to the top of each little mousse cake and serve immediately.

SWEET PASTRY

&

PÂTISSERIE

Pastry covers a seemingly endless range of techniques, textures and uses, so whatever your skill level there's always so much to learn. The most basic and multi-purpose pastry is shortcrust, which can be flavoured and enriched with ground nuts, cocoa, egg yolks or sugar. Then there are the richer, flakier pastries, made by layering the dough with butter, as well as paste-like choux, made in a pan and baked to an airy puff.

If you have never made pastry before, give the Torte de Ricotta on page 226 a try: shortcrust pastry rolled and stamped out (just like jam tarts) with a quickly put-together filling. Or buy filo pastry – it needs some careful handling to prevent the delicate sheets from drying, but is easy enough to assemble into an impressive Pistachio Chocolate Baklava (page 233).

'Baking blind' is a key pastry-making skill, and one to master if you are to avoid the dreaded 'soggy bottom'! Try the Bakewell Tart on page 228 to test yourself. Other recipes that give you a chance to practise lining a flan tin and baking blind, using different kinds of pastry, are the Lemon and Lemon Confit Tart on page 238, Five Nut Caramel Tart (page 241) and Armagnac, Prune and Almond Tart (page 244).

Every cook wants to have a really wonderful apple pie recipe to turn to – it's what completes a proper Sunday lunch after all. There are two in this chapter to add to your repertoire. The Roasted Apple Brown Sugar Pie on page 230 is a traditional deep, double-crust pie jam-packed with fruit – a perfect way to use windfalls – while the Swiss Apple-Almond Slice (page 261) is an elegant shortbread-based fruit and nut confection finished with a piped lattice topping.

The most complex pastry-making technique involves lamination, the skilled rolling and folding of dough with butter that results in that most ethereal of pastries – puff. In Gâteau St-Honoré (page 268), the crisp, buttery shards of puff pastry are served under the creamy layers of filling, but with Mil Hojas (page 267), there's no hiding place. This – the Spanish millefeuille – is the way to demonstrate your light touch and rolling-pin skills.

TORTE DE RICOTTA

Pretty little tarts filled with soft Italian cheese and chocolate, these are finished with pine nuts – found on all the best-looking Italian pastries. The shortcrust pastry is easy to make in a processor or by hand and the tartlet cases don't need to be baked blind, so this is a great recipe for whipping up in a hurry.

makes 12

FOR THE SHORTCRUST PASTRY
180g plain flour
good pinch of fine sea salt
2 teaspoons caster sugar
finely grated zest of 1 medium
    unwaxed lemon
100g unsalted butter, chilled
    and diced
about 2 tablespoons icy cold water

FOR THE FILLING
125g ricotta (with about 13% fat)
1 tablespoon clear honey
½ teaspoon dark rum OR vanilla
    extract
25g dark chocolate chips (about
    70% cocoa solids)
45g pine nuts

TO FINISH (OPTIONAL)
36 blueberries
12 raspberries
3 tablespoons sieved apricot
    jam OR apricot glaze

you will need
1 round, fluted cutter, about
7.5cm diameter; a 12-hole
jam tart/mince pie/bun tin

1. To make the shortcrust pastry in a food processor, put the flour, salt, sugar and zest into the processor bowl and 'pulse' a couple of times to combine. Add the pieces of butter and blitz until the mixture looks like fine crumbs. With the machine running, add the cold water through the feed tube, then stop the machine as soon as the mixture comes together to form a ball of soft but not sticky dough. If the dough feels hard and stiff, or won't come together, work in more cold water a teaspoon at a time. Remove the dough from the machine and flatten into a thick disc. Wrap and chill for 10 minutes.

2. To make the pastry by hand, sift the flour, salt and sugar into a mixing bowl, then stir in the zest. Rub in* the butter, then stir in the water with a round-bladed knife. Wrap and chill.

3. While the dough is chilling, heat the oven to 180°C/350°F/gas 4, and make the filling. Put the ricotta, honey and rum (or vanilla) into a bowl and beat well with a wooden spoon until smooth and creamy. Mix in the chocolate chips.

4. Roll out the pastry dough on a lightly floured worktop to a rectangle about 3mm thick and roughly the size of your tin. Dip the round cutter in flour, then stamp out discs of pastry. Gather up the trimmings, re-roll and cut more discs until you have 12. Gently press a pastry disc into each hole in the tin to line the bottom and sides neatly.

5. Spoon the ricotta mixture into the pastry cases, dividing it equally. Scatter the pine nuts on top. Bake in the heated oven for 16–20 minutes until the pastry is lightly coloured, the filling is puffed and the nuts are golden. Remove from the oven and leave to cool for 5 minutes before carefully removing the tarts from the tin on to a wire rack. Leave to cool completely before eating.

6. For a glamorous tea party, finish the cooled tarts with a fruit topping. Place 3 blueberries and a raspberry on the top of each tart. Gently melt the sieved apricot jam or glaze, then bring it to the boil. Carefully brush the hot glaze over the top of the fruit to completely cover it with a shiny, even finish. Cool before serving.

BAKEWELL TART

For this classic, you want to achieve perfectly cooked pastry and
a delicious, spongy frangipane filling with a level, nicely golden
surface plus some beautifully feathered icing.

serves 12

FOR THE JAM
200g raspberries
250g jam sugar (sugar with
   added pectin)

FOR THE SWEET SHORTCRUST
PASTRY
225g plain flour
150g unsalted butter, chilled
   and diced
25g icing sugar, sifted
1 large egg, beaten to mix
2 tablespoons icy cold water

FOR THE FILLING
150g unsalted butter, softened
150g caster sugar
150g ground almonds
1 large egg, at room temperature,
   beaten to mix
1 teaspoon almond extract

FOR THE ICING
300g icing sugar, sifted
1 teaspoon almond extract
3 tablespoons water
pink edible food colouring
   (gel or paste)

you will need
1 x 23cm fluted, deep, loose-
based flan tin; a baking sheet;
a small piping bag fitted with
a no. 2 plain writing nozzle

1. To make the jam, put the raspberries in a small deep-sided pan and crush them with a potato masher. Add the sugar and dissolve over a low heat. Increase the heat and bring to the boil, then boil for 4 minutes. Remove from the heat and pour into a shallow container. Cool, then cover and chill until set.

2. To make the pastry, weigh the flour into a bowl. Add the pieces of butter and rub* into the flour until the mixture resembles fine breadcrumbs. Stir in the icing sugar with a round-bladed knife. Make a well in the centre of the mixture, pour in the beaten egg and water, and mix to form a soft but not sticky dough.

3. Turn out the dough on to a lightly floured worktop and roll out to a large disc. Use to line the flan tin*. Prick the base of the pastry case well, then chill for 30 minutes. Meanwhile, heat the oven to 200°C/400°F/gas 6.

4. Line the pastry case with baking paper and fill with baking beans, then bake blind* for 15 minutes. Remove the beans and paper and bake for a further 5 minutes to dry out the base. Set aside to cool. Reduce the oven to 180°C/350°F/gas 4 and put the baking sheet into the oven to heat up.

5. For the filling, put the butter and sugar in a bowl and cream together until pale and fluffy using a hand-held electric whisk or wooden spoon. Add the ground almonds, egg and almond extract and mix in with a plastic spatula.

6. Spoon 4 tablespoons of the raspberry jam into the pastry case and spread evenly over the base. Spoon the filling mixture on top and spread out gently until level using an offset palette knife. Set the flan tin on the heated baking sheet in the oven and bake for 25–35 minutes until the filling is golden and a skewer inserted into the centre comes out clean. Transfer the tin to a wire rack and leave to cool completely.

7. For the icing, mix the icing sugar with the almond extract and cold water to make a smooth, fairly thick but still fluid consistency. Transfer 3 tablespoons of the icing to a separate bowl. Tint with a little pink food colouring to make a raspberry-coloured icing. Spoon this icing into the small piping bag.

8. Spoon the white icing on top of the tart and spread out evenly with an offset palette knife. Pipe the pink icing in parallel lines over the white icing, then drag a cocktail stick through the lines to create a feathered effect. Leave to set.

ROASTED APPLE BROWN SUGAR PIE

This pie is sure to be a real family favourite. Cooking the apples with brown sugar and cinnamon in the oven first gives them a deeper flavour; using tart dessert apples (Braeburns are a good choice) means they keep their shape and texture, and the filling needs less sugar. The rich, buttery shortcrust pastry is easily and speedily made in a food processor.

serves 12

FOR THE APPLE FILLING
1.5kg Braeburn or other tart eating apples
35g dark muscovado sugar, or to taste
1 teaspoon ground cinnamon
2 tablespoons cornflour
50g unsalted butter, diced

FOR THE RICH SHORTCRUST PASTRY
300g plain flour
good pinch of fine sea salt
3 tablespoons caster sugar
200g unsalted butter, chilled and diced
1 medium egg yolk
3½ tablespoons cold milk

TO FINISH
1 medium egg white
2 tablespoons caster sugar

TO SERVE
Vanilla Egg Custard (see page 18) or vanilla ice cream

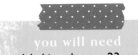

you will need
1 baking sheet; a 23cm fluted, deep, loose-based flan tin

1. Start with the filling – it needs to be cold when the pie is assembled. Heat the oven to 190°C/375°F/gas 5. Peel, quarter and core the apples, then cut into thick slices, straight into a roasting tin (if you are using windfalls aim for about 1.15kg prepared apples). Sprinkle the sugar, cinnamon and cornflour over the apples, add the butter and gently toss everything together.

2. Roast in the heated oven, stirring occasionally, for 30–35 minutes until starting to colour and soften. Remove from the oven (you can turn it off for now) and transfer the apples and any juice in the roasting tin to a heatproof bowl. Taste and add a little more sugar or cinnamon as needed. Leave to cool, then cover and chill for about 1 hour.

3. Meanwhile, make the pastry. Tip the flour into a food processor, add the salt and sugar, and 'pulse' until combined. Add the pieces of butter and blitz until the mixture looks like fine crumbs. Combine the egg yolk and milk and pour into the processor through the feed tube while the machine is running. As soon as the mixture comes together to form a ball of soft but not sticky dough, stop the machine. Carefully remove the dough, flatten it into a thick disc and wrap in clingfilm. Chill for 15–20 minutes until firm but not hard.

4. You can also make the pastry by hand: sift the flour, salt and sugar into a mixing bowl, add the pieces of butter and rub in* until the mixture looks like fine crumbs, then mix in the yolk/milk mixture using a round-bladed knife.

5. When ready to assemble, heat the oven to 200°C/400°F/gas 6, and put the baking sheet into the oven to heat up.

6. Unwrap the pastry. Cut off a third and wrap up this portion again, then set it aside. Roll out the larger portion of pastry on a lightly floured worktop to a 30cm disc and use to line the flan tin*. Leave the excess pastry hanging over the rim of the tin for now. Roll out the reserved pastry to a disc about 2cm larger than the top of the flan tin (this will be the lid of the pie).

7. Gently stir the cold filling, then spoon it into the pastry case and level the surface. Brush the pastry rim with water just to dampen it. Loosely roll the pastry lid around the rolling pin and unroll over the tin to cover the filling. Press and pinch the pastry edges together quite firmly to seal them. Trim off the excess pastry with a small sharp knife.

8. Beat the egg white with a fork until frothy, then brush lightly over the top of the pie. Sprinkle evenly with the sugar. Cut 6 slits in the pastry lid with the tip of a sharp knife. Set the flan tin on the heated baking sheet in the oven and bake for 20 minutes. Reduce the oven to 180°C/350°F/gas 4 and bake for a further 15–20 minutes until the pastry is golden brown and crisp.

9. Remove the pie from the oven and leave to cool for 10 minutes before carefully unmoulding. Serve warm with custard or ice cream.

PISTACHIO CHOCOLATE BAKLAVA

Tiny diamonds or squares of sheer delight: layer upon layer of pastry, both crisp and honey-syrup soaked, filled with plenty of crunchy pistachios and bittersweet chocolate. The rich flavours develop as the baklava cools and becomes sticky, so be patient and plan ahead. Enjoy as a dessert or with cups of espresso after dinner.

cuts into 30 pieces

1. The filo pastry will become hard and unusable if it dries out, so don't unwrap until you need it. Once opened, keep the sheets covered with a damp cloth/tea towel or clingfilm while you are working with them, and remove just one sheet at a time.

2. To make the filling, tip the pistachios into a food processor and chop them until they look like coarse breadcrumbs with a few large gravel-like pieces – they should not become a fine powder. Transfer to a large, heavy-based, dry frying pan and stir over low to medium heat for about 4 minutes until lightly coloured with a good nutty aroma (take care as the nuts can quickly scorch). Remove from the heat and stir in the sugar. Leave until completely cold.

3. Put the chocolate into the processor and chop into small pieces about the same size as the nuts. Stir into the cold nut mixture.

4. Heat the oven to 180°C/350°F/gas 4. Lightly brush the inside of your roasting/baking tin with a little of the melted butter. Now unwrap the filo and unfold/unroll the pastry sheets to form a stack. Remove one sheet – keep the rest of the stack covered with a damp cloth or clingfilm – and lay it on the base of your tin (depending on their size, you may need 2 sheets, slightly overlapping, to cover the base). Leave excess pastry hanging over the sides of the tin for now. Brush the filo layer lightly with butter, then lay another sheet (or 2) on top. Continue layering the pastry, brushing each sheet with butter, until you have 6 layers of pastry in the tin.

5. Sprinkle a third of the nut/choc filling evenly over the pastry. Cover with 2 more layers of buttered filo. Sprinkle half the remaining filling on top, then cover with 2 more layers of buttered filo. Sprinkle the rest of the filling evenly over the top layer.

6. Fold in any overhanging pastry, brushing lightly with melted butter as you work (use kitchen scissors to trim away any thick pastry edges and overlaps at the corners). Lay the remaining sheets of pastry on top, buttering them as you go. Finally, use the scissors to trim and neaten up the pastry edges so the baklava doesn't look untidy.

300g filo pastry (about 16 sheets), thawed if frozen

FOR THE FILLING
350g unsalted pistachio nuts (shelled)
3 tablespoons caster sugar
100g dark chocolate (about 70% cocoa solids), broken up
150g unsalted butter, melted

FOR THE SYRUP
275g caster sugar
225ml water
1 cinnamon stick
1 tablespoon lemon juice
2 tablespoons Greek honey

you will need
1 roasting/baking tin (not loose-based), about 20.5 x 30 x 3cm

7. Using a sharp knife, cut the baklava right through (not just the top pastry layers) into diamonds or squares – it's much easier to do this before baking than afterwards. Sprinkle the top lightly with water, then bake in the heated oven for 15 minutes. Increase the oven temperature to 190°C/375°F/gas 5 and bake for a further 15 minutes until the pastry is crisp and a good golden colour.

8. Towards the end of the baklava baking time, make the honey soaking syrup. Put the sugar, water and cinnamon stick into a medium pan and heat gently, stirring frequently, until the sugar has completely dissolved. Bring to the boil, then stir in the lemon juice and honey. Simmer gently for about 10 minutes to make a light syrup. Remove from the heat and cool the syrup for 5 minutes or so.

9. As soon as the baklava is ready, take it out of the oven and pour the hot honey syrup evenly over it. Leave to cool and absorb the syrup. Once cold, cover the tin and leave the baklava at room temperature overnight to allow the flavours to deepen before eating. Store in an airtight container and eat within 5 days.

BITTER CHOCOLATE AND PEAR TARTLETS

Perfect for an elegant tea party: these small but very rich tartlets combine chocolate biscuit pastry, bitter chocolate custard and thinly sliced pears. Chocolate pastry needs to be handled with care as touching it with floury hands (or a rolling pin) can leave highly visible white fingerprints! It's easiest to roll it out between sheets of clingfilm. It's also a good idea to mix a couple of teaspoons each of flour and cocoa ready for when you need to handle the dough.

makes 12

1. Start by making the pastry. Put the flour, salt, cocoa and icing sugar into a food processor and 'pulse' a few times until thoroughly combined. Add the butter and blitz until the mixture looks like fine crumbs. Add the egg yolks, water and vanilla bean paste and run the machine until the mixture comes together to make a heavy, slightly sticky dough.

2. Cut 2 large sheets of clingfilm and spread one on the worktop. Turn out the dough on to the centre of the clingfilm and press down to a thick disc. Cover with the other sheet of clingfilm. Chill the dough for 20–30 minutes until firm but not hard.

3. Place the dough, still between the 2 layers of clingfilm, on the worktop and roll out to a rectangle that is slightly larger than your tin. Peel off the top layer of clingfilm, then stamp out 12 rounds with the cutter – if necessary, gather up the dough trimmings, re-roll and cut out more rounds until you have 12. Peel each round off the clingfilm and gently press into a hole in the tin to line evenly. Chill for about 20 minutes.

4. Meanwhile, heat the oven to 180°C/350°F/gas 4. Line each pastry case with a small square of baking paper, fill with baking beans and bake blind* in the heated oven for 7 minutes until the pastry is just set. Carefully remove the paper and beans and bake the pastry cases for a further 5 minutes (take care not to let the pastry overcook and darken as it will be baked again and you don't want it to scorch and taste bitter). Leave to cool while you make the filling. Put the baking sheet into the oven to heat up.

5. Peel and halve the pears, then scoop out the cores with a melon baller or teaspoon. Cut across into 3mm-thick slices to fit across the very top of the pastry cases. Cover with clingfilm.

6. Gently melt the chocolate*, then cool until lukewarm. Put the eggs, cream, caster sugar and vanilla into a mixing bowl and mix with a hand wire whisk until thoroughly combined. Scrape the melted chocolate into the bowl and whisk for a minute until the mixture is very smooth, glossy and thick.

FOR THE CHOCOLATE PASTRY
150g plain flour
¼ teaspoon fine sea salt
75g cocoa powder
100g icing sugar
150g unsalted butter, chilled and diced
2 medium egg yolks
2 tablespoons icy cold water
¼ teaspoon vanilla bean paste

FOR THE FILLING
2 medium just-ripe pears
150g dark chocolate (about 70% cocoa solids), broken up
2 medium eggs, at room temperature
150ml double cream, at room temperature
60g caster sugar
½ teaspoon vanilla bean paste
1½ tablespoons cacao nibs, for sprinkling
icing sugar, for dusting

you will need
1 x 7.5cm fluted or plain round cutter; a 12-hole jam tart/mince pie/bun tin; a baking sheet

7. To assemble the tartlets, spoon 1½–2 tablespoons of the chocolate custard into each tartlet case to almost but not quite fill it. Gently set 3 overlapping slices of pear on top. Sprinkle with cacao nibs. Set the tin on the heated baking sheet in the oven and bake for 17–19 minutes until the custard is just set – the filling will firm up as it cools so take care not to over-bake the tartlets.

8. Set the tin on a wire rack and leave the tartlets to cool completely and firm up before gently unmoulding (use a small palette knife to help ease them out of the tin). Dust with icing sugar. Best eaten the same or the next day (keep in an airtight tin).

LEMON AND LEMON CONFIT TART

Everyone loves a lemon tart and this version is even more lusciously lemony - a combination of an almond-rich shortcrust pastry case, a buttery lemon filling and an intensely flavoured bittersweet topping of tender sliced lemons. Chill thoroughly and serve with fluffy crème Chantilly for the perfect summery dessert.

serves 10-12

FOR THE ALMOND PASTRY

175g plain flour
good pinch of fine sea salt
25g ground almonds
30g icing sugar
finely grated zest of ½ medium
    unwaxed lemon
100g unsalted butter, chilled
    and diced
1 medium egg yolk
2 tablespoons icy cold milk

FOR THE LEMON FILLING

2 medium eggs, at room
    temperature
100g caster sugar
finely grated zest and juice of
    1½ medium unwaxed lemons
60g ground almonds
115g unsalted butter, melted
    and cooled

FOR THE LEMON CONFIT

4 medium unwaxed lemons
100g caster sugar

TO SERVE

Crème Chantilly (see page 18)

you will need
1 x 23cm fluted, deep,
loose-based flan tin;
a baking sheet

1. Begin by making the almond pastry. Put the flour, salt, ground almonds, icing sugar and lemon zest into a food processor and 'pulse' a few times until combined. Add the pieces of butter and blitz until the mixture looks like fine crumbs. Add the egg yolk and milk and run the machine again until the mixture comes together to form a ball of soft but not sticky dough. Shape the dough into a thick disc, wrap in clingfilm and chill for 15–20 minutes until firm but not hard.

2. Turn out the dough on to a lightly floured worktop. Roll out to a disc about 29cm across and use to line the flan tin*. Prick the base well, then chill for 15 minutes. Meanwhile, heat the oven to 180°C/350°F/gas 4.

3. Line the pastry case with baking paper, fill with baking beans and bake blind* in the heated oven for 12–14 minutes until the pastry is set. Carefully remove the paper and beans and bake for a further 10–12 minutes until the pastry base is completely dry and slightly coloured. Leave to cool. Put the baking sheet into the oven to heat up.

4. While the pastry case is baking start on the filling. Put the eggs, sugar and lemon zest into a mixing bowl, or the bowl of a free-standing electric mixer fitted with the whisk attachment. Whisk with a hand-held electric whisk, or the whisk attachment, until the mixture is thick and mousse-like and has reached the ribbon stage*. Gradually whisk in the lemon juice (the mixture will become thinner). Stir in the ground almonds using a plastic spatula or a large metal spoon, and then the cooled melted butter. Leave to stand for 5–10 minutes until the mixture looks curdled and rather like yellowish cottage cheese.

5. Spoon the mixture into the cooled pastry case and spread it evenly. Set the flan tin on the heated baking sheet and bake for 20–25 minutes until the filling is a light gold colour, slightly puffed and just set when lightly touched in the centre. Remove from the oven and leave to cool.

6. To make the lemon confit, trim the ends from the lemons, then cut the fruit in half lengthways. Slice the halves across as thinly as possible, discarding any pips. Bring a large pan of water to the boil, then remove from the heat. Add the lemon slices and leave to soak until the water is cold.

7. Drain the slices in a colander, then return them to the saucepan. Pour over just enough cold water to cover the slices and bring to the boil. Reduce the heat and simmer gently for about 5 minutes until the peel on the lemon slices feels tender when pierced with a fingernail. Gently stir in the sugar and leave to dissolve over low heat. Turn up the heat and simmer for about 5 minutes until the slices look translucent.

8. Set the colander over a smaller pan and tip the lemon slices into it to drain. When they are thoroughly drained, arrange them on top of the lemon filling in the tart – try to give them a bit of height, rather than packing them down neatly.

9. Put the pan of drained-off lemon syrup on to the heat and boil rapidly for 4–5 minutes until reduced by about half to a sticky glaze. Brush or spoon the glaze over the lemon slices to give them a glossy finish (you may not need all of it).

10. Leave until cold, then chill for at least 2 hours before serving (the tart can be kept in the fridge for up to 2 days). Serve with crème Chantilly.

FIVE NUT CARAMEL TART

Orange zest and sea salt flakes flavour the dark and sticky caramel sauce gluing together the scores of crunchy nuts that fill this tart. The pastry is a crumbly orange shortcrust - perfect with the rich, creamy filling. Serve in thin slices - good for a pudding with vanilla ice cream.

serves 12

1. To make the orange shortcrust pastry in a food processor, put the flour, salt, sugar and orange zest into the processor bowl and 'pulse' a few times until combined. Add the diced butter and blitz until the mixture looks sandy. With the machine running, add the yolk and water through the feed tube and run the machine until the mixture comes together to make a ball of firm dough. Flatten the dough into a thick disc, wrap in clingfilm and chill for about 15 minutes until firm.

2. To make the pastry by hand, sift the flour, salt and sugar into a mixing bowl, then stir in the orange zest. Add the butter and rub in*. Mix in the egg yolk and water with a round-bladed knife, then wrap and chill.

3. Roll out the dough on a lightly floured worktop to a disc about 29cm across and use to line the flan tin*. Roll the rolling pin across the top of the tin to cut off the excess pastry, then neaten the rim with your fingers. Prick the base with a fork. Chill the pastry case for 15 minutes.

4. Meanwhile, heat the oven to 190°C/375°F/gas 5. Line the pastry case with baking paper and fill with baking beans, then bake blind* in the heated oven for 12–15 minutes until lightly golden and just firm. Carefully remove the paper and beans and bake the pastry case for a further 7–10 minutes until crisp and golden. Set aside to cool while you make the filling. Leave the oven on.

5. Tip each type of nut into a separate baking dish or tin and toast in the oven until lightly coloured (or toast each type of nut, in succession, using the same baking dish or tin). They will colour at different rates: the walnuts will take 8–10 minutes, pistachios 7–9 minutes, flaked almonds about 8 minutes, pecans about 10 minutes and hazelnuts 9–12 minutes. Watch them carefully – you don't want them to colour too deeply as they will be baked again later. Remove from the oven and leave to cool. Put a baking sheet into the oven to heat up.

6. Now make the caramel. Put the caster sugar and water into a medium pan and heat gently, stirring frequently with a wooden spoon, until the sugar has completely dissolved (it's a good idea to have a small bowl of cold water and a pastry brush at hand so you can use the wet brush to dislodge any stuck-on sugar crystals from the side of the pan).

FOR THE ORANGE SHORTCRUST PASTRY
175g plain flour
pinch of fine sea salt
1 tablespoon caster sugar
finely grated zest of ½ medium orange
100g unsalted butter, chilled and diced
1 medium egg yolk
1½ tablespoons icy cold water

FOR THE NUT MIX
75g walnut pieces
75g unsalted pistachio nuts (shelled)
75g flaked almonds
75g pecan halves
75g blanched hazelnuts

FOR THE CARAMEL
300g caster sugar
90ml cold water
325ml crème fraîche
finely grated zest of ½ medium orange
½ teaspoon sea salt flakes, or to taste

you will need
1 x 23cm fluted, deep, loose-based flan tin; a baking sheet

7. Turn up the heat and bring the sugar syrup to the boil. Once it starts boiling, leave it to boil rapidly, without stirring, for 5–8 minutes until it turns to a rich chestnut-coloured caramel – you can gently rotate and tip the pan from time to time to check the colour.

8. Carefully draw the pan off the heat. Wearing an oven glove to hold the pan handle (or with your hand covered with a dry towel), add the crème fraîche – the mixture will splutter and bubble up, so take care. The caramel will harden to a lump in the base of the pan.

9. Return to a low heat and stir with a wooden spoon for several minutes until the caramel has completely melted and is very smooth. Bring to the boil, then remove from the heat. Carefully stir in the toasted nuts to coat them all completely. Mix in the orange zest and sea salt flakes.

10. Set the flan tin on the heated baking sheet and carefully pour in the hot caramel-nut filling, making sure the pastry case is evenly filled. Bake for about 15 minutes until the filling is bubbling. Leave to cool before unmoulding. Serve at room temperature, cut in thin slices.

ARMAGNAC, PRUNE AND ALMOND TART

A true French classic - a tart case made from pâte sucrée, a crisp biscuit-like pastry containing plenty of egg yolks, and a simple but luxuriously rich filling of large, Armagnac-soaked French prunes, almonds and crème fraîche. This pastry is made by hand, straight on the worktop, not in a mixing bowl or processor, and is worked (*fraisage* is the term pâtissiers use) with the heel of the hand to make it supple enough to line a flan tin.

serves 12

300g pitted soft-dried Agen prunes
5 tablespoons Armagnac
   OR brandy

FOR THE PÂTE SUCRÉE
200g plain flour
¼ teaspoon fine sea salt
100g unsalted butter, chilled
4 medium egg yolks
100g caster sugar
¼ teaspoon vanilla bean paste

FOR THE CRÈME
200ml full-fat crème fraîche
1 medium egg
35g ground almonds
50g caster sugar
2 tablespoons flaked almonds
icing sugar, for dusting

you will need
1 x 23cm fluted, deep,
loose-based flan tin;
a baking sheet

1. Put the prunes and Armagnac or brandy into a bowl and stir well, then cover and leave to macerate for at least 4 hours – overnight is best.

2. Next day make the pâte sucrée. Sift the flour and salt on to a clean worktop and make a large well in the centre. Put the chilled butter between sheets of clingfilm and pound it with a rolling pin until it is pliable but still cold. Cut the butter into flakes or small pieces and put into the well along with the egg yolks, caster sugar and vanilla bean paste. Put the fingertips of one hand together to form a beak shape and use to mash together the ingredients in the well. Once they are thoroughly combined, gradually work in the flour with your fingers, using a plastic dough scraper or metal spatula to help you draw the flour in. When the mixture looks shaggy with coarse crumbs, gather the whole lot together to make a rough ball of dough.

3. Now start to work the dough – this is known as *fraisage* – to make it supple: press down on the ball of dough with the heel of your hand and push it away from you, then gather up the dough into a ball again using the dough scraper and repeat. Continue working the dough like this for a minute until it is silky-smooth and pliable. Shape into a thick disc, wrap in clingfilm and chill for 20–30 minutes until firm but not hard.

4. Roll out the pastry on a lightly floured worktop to a disc about 29cm across and use to line the flan tin*. Prick the base well and chill for about 20 minutes. Meanwhile, heat the oven to 180°C/350°F/gas 4.

5. Line the pastry case with baking paper and fill with baking beans, then bake blind* for 13–15 minutes until firm. Carefully remove the lining paper and beans, then return the pastry case to the oven and bake for 10 more minutes until dry and lightly coloured. Leave to cool while you make the filling. Put the baking sheet into the oven to heat up.

6. Set a sieve over a wide-necked jug or bowl and pour the soaked prunes and Armagnac into it. When the prunes are thoroughly drained, arrange them in the base of the pastry case. Add the crème fraîche, egg, ground

almonds and sugar to the Armagnac in the jug or bowl and whisk, using a hand wire whisk, until thoroughly combined. Pour the crème mixture over the prunes and scatter the flaked almonds evenly on top.

7. Set the flan tin on the heated baking sheet in the oven and bake for 30–35 minutes until the filling is puffed, light golden and just firm to a light touch. Leave to cool for 10 minutes before unmoulding. Dust with icing sugar and eat while still warm, or at room temperature.

PASTEIS DE NATA

Unlike British custard tarts, which are cooked 'low and slow' until the custard just sets, these Portuguese favourites are baked 'hot and quick' so the custard boils. The very thin pastry cases are made from spirals of flaky pastry dusted with cinnamon - a lovely crisp contrast to the soft, shiny custard filling. The tarts would take a bit of practice to look like those from the pastry shops of Lisbon but they will taste just as delicious.

makes 24

1. To make the pastry, sift the flour and salt into a mixing bowl. Cut off 10g of the weighed butter and rub* into the flour until the mixture looks like fine crumbs. Stir in the icy water with a round-bladed knife to make a very soft and slightly sticky dough. Cover the bowl with clingfilm and leave to rest on the worktop (in hot weather put the bowl in the fridge).

2. Meanwhile, put the remaining 100g butter between 2 sheets of clingfilm or baking paper and beat it with a rolling pin until it is supple but still cool. Divide it into small, flake-like pieces.

3. Turn out the dough on to a floured worktop and roll out with a floured rolling pin to a 24cm square. Dot the top two-thirds of the square with a third of the butter pieces. Fold the bottom (unbuttered) third up to cover the middle third of the square, then fold the top (buttered) third down to make a 3-layer sandwich. Gently press the open edges to seal. Wrap in clingfilm and chill for 15 minutes.

4. Unwrap the dough and set it on your worktop so the folded edges are now at the sides. Repeat the dotting with butter, using half of the remainder, and folding, then wrap and chill as before. Meanwhile, mash the last of the butter until it is spreadable but still cool.

5. Lightly flour the worktop with flour and add a light dusting of ground cinnamon. Roll out the dough away from you to a 15 x 45cm rectangle. Spread with the remaining butter so the dough is evenly covered from end to end. Starting at the short side nearest to you, roll up the dough like a Swiss roll. Wrap in clingfilm and chill for about 3 hours until very firm.

6. Dust the worktop with flour and cinnamon again and place the unwrapped roll of dough on it. Roll the dough back and forth with your hands to stretch it out to a neat, even cylinder 24cm long. Cut across into 24 equal slices. Set one slice, cut side down, in each hole of the mini-muffin tray. Using your thumbs, gently press the slice of dough on to the base and up the sides of the hole to make a very thin pastry case that extends slightly above the rim of the mould. When all the cases have been formed, keep in the fridge until ready to fill.

FOR THE FLAKY PASTRY

135g plain flour
2 good pinches of fine sea salt
110g unsalted butter, chilled
100ml icy cold water
ground cinnamon, for dusting

FOR THE FILLING

150ml single cream
1 cinnamon stick
15g cornflour
½ teaspoon vanilla bean paste
125g caster sugar
5 tablespoons cold water
4 medium egg yolks, at room temperature
icing sugar, for dusting

you will need
1 x 24-hole mini-muffin tray (each hole about 4.5cm across and 2cm deep), ungreased; a baking sheet

7. Heat the oven to 240°C/450°F/gas 8 and put the baking sheet into the oven to heat up.

8. To make the custard filling, pour 125ml of the cream into a small pan, add the cinnamon stick and bring to the boil. Remove from the heat and leave to infuse for 10 minutes. Put the cornflour and vanilla bean paste into a medium heatproof bowl, or wide-necked jug, add the remaining 25ml cream and stir until smooth. Pour the hot cream (discard the cinnamon stick) into the cornflour mixture and stir until smoothly amalgamated.

9. Put the sugar and water into a small pan and heat gently until the sugar has completely dissolved. Bring to the boil and cook for about 2 minutes until the syrup reaches 104°C/220°F on a sugar thermometer. Remove from the heat and pour on to the cream mixture in a thin, steady stream, whisking constantly with a hand wire whisk. When all the sugar syrup has been incorporated, whisk in the egg yolks.

10. Remove the muffin tray from the fridge and set it on the heated baking sheet. Working quickly, pour the warm custard into the pastry cases so they are almost full, then put the tray (on the baking sheet) into the heated oven. Bake for 8–10 minutes until the pastry is golden brown.

11. Set the tray on a wire rack. Dust the tartlets with plenty of icing sugar and then a light dusting of ground cinnamon. Leave to firm up for 5 minutes before transferring to the rack to cool completely. Eat the same day.

COFFEE ÉCLAIRS

Cream-filled éclairs are a true teatime classic, but adding coffee to the choux pastry recipe gives these a fantastic smell as well as extra flavour. The fingers are filled with a very rich coffee crème pâtissière and topped with a coffee fondant icing, but the decoration is pure chocolate - a beautiful dark, glossy tile for that extra 'wow' factor.

makes 10

FOR THE COFFEE CHOUX PASTRY
150g plain flour
115g unsalted butter
1 tablespoon caster sugar
½ teaspoon fine sea salt
2 teaspoons instant coffee
   (granules or powder)
225ml cold water
4 medium eggs, at room
   temperature

FOR THE COFFEE CRÈME PÂTISSIÈRE
250ml creamy milk
1½ tablespoons instant coffee
   (granules or powder)
3 medium egg yolks
50g caster sugar
20g cornflour
½ teaspoon vanilla bean paste
   or extract
30g unsalted butter, at room
   temperature
125ml double cream, well chilled

FOR THE COFFEE FONDANT
200g fondant icing sugar
1 tablespoon instant coffee
   (granules or powder)
2 tablespoons boiling water

TO FINISH (OPTIONAL)
chocolate coffee beans, to
   decorate
50g dark chocolate (about 70%
   cocoa solids), broken up

you will need
1 large piping bag fitted
with a 2cm plain nozzle;
2 baking sheets, lined with
baking paper; a large piping
bag fitted with a large star
nozzle; an acetate strip OR
chocolate transfer sheet
cut to 30 x 12cm

1. Heat the oven to 200°C/400°F/gas 6. To make the choux pastry, sift the flour on to a large sheet of baking or greaseproof paper. Weigh the butter into a medium pan. Add the sugar, salt, instant coffee and cold water. Set the pan over medium/low heat and gently melt the butter, stirring frequently. Once the butter has completely melted, turn up the heat. As soon as the water starts to boil, tip in the sifted flour and pull the pan off the heat. Beat everything together vigorously with a wooden spoon – it will look a complete mess at first, but gradually, as you beat, it will come together to form a ball of heavy, sticky dough. Return the pan to low heat and beat the dough well for 1–2 minutes until it looks glossy and comes cleanly away from the sides of the pan.

2. Tip the dough into a heatproof mixing bowl, or the bowl of a free-standing electric mixer fitted with the whisk attachment. Leave to cool for a couple of minutes, then beat the dough with a hand-held electric whisk, or the whisk attachment, for 2 minutes. Break the eggs into a jug and beat with a fork just until combined. Gradually beat them into the dough, pouring them into the bowl in a thin, steady stream, and scraping down the sides of the bowl from time to time. When all the egg has been added, beat the paste-like dough for a further 2 minutes to make it very smooth and shiny. It should hold a shape when you lift the whisk out.

3. Transfer the choux paste to the piping bag fitted with the plain nozzle. Pipe 10 chubby fingers, each 12cm long, on the lined baking sheets, spaced well apart to allow for expansion. Bake in the heated oven for 15 minutes. Reduce the oven to 170°C/325°F/gas 3 and bake for a further 25 minutes. Remove the baking sheets from the oven. Using a cocktail stick or skewer, make a small hole in one end of each éclair to release the steam. Return to the oven and bake for 5–10 minutes until crisp and golden. Cool on a wire rack.

4. While the éclairs are baking, prepare the crème pâtissière. Heat the milk with the coffee in a medium pan until it is steaming hot but not quite boiling. Put the egg yolks, sugar, cornflour and vanilla into a heatproof bowl and whisk with a hand wire whisk for a minute or so until smooth and light. Set the bowl on a damp cloth so it doesn't wobble, then slowly pour in the hot milk in a thin, steady stream, whisking constantly. As soon as the mixture is smoothly amalgamated, tip it back into the saucepan. Whisk constantly over medium heat until the mixture boils and thickens to make a smooth, lump-free custard. Remove from the heat and whisk in the butter. Transfer the crème pâtissière to a heatproof bowl and press a sheet of clingfilm on to the surface (to prevent a skin from forming). Leave to cool, then chill thoroughly.

5. Meanwhile, make the fondant icing. Sift the icing sugar into a mixing bowl. Dissolve the coffee in the boiling water. Leave to cool for a minute, then stir into the sugar to make a very smooth icing with the consistency of thick cream – you should be able to spread it easily without drips. If it is too thick, work in few more drops of water. Cover if not using immediately.

6. To assemble the éclairs, split them in half horizontally. Give the crème pâtissière a good stir so it is very smooth indeed. Whip the cream* until it is floppy – the stage just before soft peak – and fold it into the crème pâtissière. Transfer the mixture to the piping bag fitted with the star nozzle and pipe a rope down the bottom half of each éclair. Stir the fondant icing, then spread or brush a thick coating over the top half of each éclair. Set the tops in place and decorate with the chocolate coffee beans, if using. Chill for about 30 minutes until firm – or for up to 3 hours.

7. To make chocolate tiles for decoration, gently melt the chocolate*. If you like, you can temper* it to give a glossy finish. Set the strip of acetate (or chocolate transfer strip) on a clean worktop. Pour the chocolate on to the strip and spread evenly (right over the edges) using an offset palette knife. Use the tip of a clean knife to gently lift up one corner of the acetate strip so you can peel it away from the worktop, then gently set it down flat (chocolate side up) on a clean space on the worktop. This will give the chocolate strip neat edges. Leave to firm up for a few minutes until almost set. Then, using a ruler and large sharp knife, cut the chocolate strip across into 10 rectangles, each 12 x 3cm. Leave until completely set before peeling these away from the acetate. Just before serving, set a chocolate tile on top of each éclair, shiny (or chocolate-transfer) side up.

LIME AND COCONUT MERINGUE PIE

A citrus pie with a twist: the case is a rich, coconut-flavoured pastry, made like shortbread, and is filled with a creamy citrus custard. It is topped off by a fluffy coconut Swiss meringue, prettily piped in swirls, and large shards of coconut flakes.

serves 8-10

FOR THE PASTRY

100g unsalted butter, softened
1 medium egg yolk, at room temperature
50g icing sugar
few drops of coconut extract
160g plain flour, plus extra for dusting
1 medium egg, beaten to mix, for brushing

FOR THE LIME CUSTARD FILLING

5 medium eggs plus 2 yolks, at room temperature
150g caster sugar
finely grated zest and juice of 5 unwaxed limes
finely grated zest and juice of 1 unwaxed lemon
150ml double cream, at room temperature

few drops of green edible food colouring (optional)

FOR THE SWISS MERINGUE

5 medium egg whites, at room temperature
250g white caster sugar
50g desiccated coconut
3 tablespoons flaked coconut, for decoration

you will need
1 x 20.5cm round, deep, loose-based sandwich tin, greased with butter; a baking sheet; a large piping bag fitted with a large star nozzle

1. To make the pastry put the softened butter and egg yolk into a mixing bowl. Sift the icing sugar into the bowl and add a few drops of coconut extract, then beat everything together with a wooden spoon until thoroughly combined. Sift the flour into the bowl and mix in, using the wooden spoon and then your hands to bring the mixture together to make a firm shortbread-like dough.

2. Turn out the dough on to a lightly floured worktop (if it is a very warm day, or the dough feels soft, wrap it in clingfilm and chill for 10–15 minutes until firm). Roll out to a disc about 27cm across and use to line the sandwich tin*. Prick the base well and chill for 15 minutes. Meanwhile, heat the oven to 180°C/350°F/gas 4.

3. Line the pastry case with baking paper, fill with baking beans and bake blind* in the heated oven for about 15 minutes until the pastry is set. Lift out the paper and beans and bake the case for a further 5 minutes.

4. Remove from the oven and lightly brush the base of the pastry case with beaten egg – this will help to seal it and keep the pastry crisp once the filling is added. Bake for another 5 minutes until the base is golden. Set the pastry case aside to cool while you make the filling. Turn down the oven to 150°C/300°F/gas 2, and put the baking sheet into the oven to heat up.

5. Put the whole eggs, yolks, caster sugar, lime and lemon zests and juice, and cream into a large bowl and gently mix using a hand wire whisk. Add a couple of drops of green food colouring, if you like, to give a light lime colour.

6. If your bowl is heatproof, set it over a pan of gently simmering water. Otherwise, transfer the mixture to a heavy-based pan and set over low heat. Stir the mixture until it warms up to the point where it is still just comfy when you dip in your little finger – don't let the mixture get hot or it will scramble. Transfer to a large jug.

7. Set the pastry case, still in its tin, on the heated baking sheet and pour in half the filling. Place the hot baking sheet back on the oven shelf, half pulled out, and slowly pour in enough of the remaining filling to come just below the pastry rim.

8. Carefully slide the shelf back into the oven and bake for 12–16 minutes until the custard filling is just set but still has a slight wobble in the middle when you jiggle the baking sheet – it is best to start checking after 10 minutes, then keep checking to avoid overcooking the custard (you don't want it to separate). Remove and leave to cool while you make the meringue. Turn up the oven to 180°C/350°F/gas 4 again.

9. To make the Swiss meringue, put the egg whites and sugar into the bowl of a free-standing electric mixer. Whisk with a hand wire whisk just until combined but not frothy. Set the bowl over a pan of gently simmering water (the base of the bowl should not touch the water) and whisk very gently – just to keep the mixture moving – until the sugar dissolves and the mixture reaches 60–70°C/140–160°F on a sugar thermometer (for more about making Swiss meringue, see Black and White Celebration Cake on page 64).

10. Place the bowl back on the stand mixer fitted with the whisk attachment and whisk on full speed until the mixture becomes a very thick and glossy, white meringue. Reduce the speed to medium and continue whisking the meringue until it is cold.

11. Transfer half the meringue to the piping bag fitted with the star nozzle. Sprinkle the desiccated coconut over the remaining meringue in the bowl and gently fold* in with a large metal spoon. Spoon this coconut meringue on top of the custard filling and gently spread it using an offset palette knife. Cover with piped swirls of meringue.

12. Bake for 10 minutes. Check and rotate the tart, if necessary, so it colours evenly, then bake for a further 2–3 minutes until the meringue is golden. Scatter the flaked coconut over the top and bake for 1–2 minutes until the flakes turn golden (watch carefully).

13. Set the tin on a wire rack and leave the tart to cool before unmoulding. Eat the same day, at room temperature or chilled.

CHAI PEAR CUPS

Here delicious home-made filo pastry, flavoured with cinnamon, is used to make tiny cups.
These are filled with a smooth, rich crème pâtissière infused with chai tea to give a warm
spicy taste, then topped with caramelised pears and shards of almond brittle.

makes 24 petits fours

FOR THE FILO PASTRY
185g plain flour
1 teaspoon ground cinnamon
¼ teaspoon fine sea salt
2 tablespoons olive oil
2 teaspoons cider vinegar
100ml warm water
cornflour, for dusting
40g unsalted butter, melted,
   for brushing

FOR THE CHAI CRÈME PÂTISSIÈRE
250ml full-fat/whole milk
½ vanilla pod, split open
1 chai teabag
2 medium egg yolks, at room
   temperature
45g caster sugar
15g cornflour

FOR THE ALMOND BRITTLE
40g toasted flaked almonds

100g caster sugar
2 tablespoons water
icing sugar, for dusting

FOR THE PEARS
2 just-ripe medium pears
   (preferably Anjou)
20g unsalted butter
1 tablespoons light muscovado
   sugar
sea salt flakes, to taste

you will need
1 x 6.5cm plain round
cutter; a 24-hole
mini-muffin tray, greased
with butter; a medium
piping bag fitted with a
round medium nozzle

1. To make the filo dough, sift the flour, cinnamon and salt into the bowl of
a free-standing electric mixer fitted with the dough hook attachment. Add
the oil, vinegar and water to the bowl and mix, using low speed, to make a
soft but not sticky dough (you may need to add a little more flour or water).
Knead* the dough in the bowl, still using the dough hook on slow speed,
for about 5 minutes until the filo dough is very smooth and elastic. Remove
the dough from the bowl, wrap it in clingfilm and leave it on the worktop to
relax for 1½ hours.

2. Meanwhile, get on with the elements to fill the pastry cups. To make the
crème pâtissière, put the milk, vanilla pod and chai teabag into a medium
pan, bring to the boil and simmer for a minute. Remove from the heat and
leave to infuse for 5 minutes. During this time, put the egg yolks, caster
sugar and cornflour into a heatproof bowl set on a damp cloth (to prevent
wobbling) and beat together thoroughly with a wire hand whisk until
smooth, light and creamy.

3. Remove the vanilla pod and teabag from the milk, then pour it on to the
yolk mixture in a thin, steady stream, whisking constantly. When thoroughly
combined, tip the mixture back into the pan. Set over medium heat and
whisk as the mixture comes to the boil to make a thick, smooth custard.
Transfer to a clean heatproof bowl, press a piece of clingfilm on the surface
of the custard and leave to cool.

4. To make the almond brittle, spread out the flaked almonds on a sheet of baking paper set on a baking sheet or board. Put the sugar and water into a small pan and heat gently, without stirring, until the sugar has completely dissolved. Turn up the heat and bring to the boil, then leave to boil rapidly (without stirring) for a minute or so until the syrup turns to a rich chestnut-coloured caramel. Quickly pour the caramel over the almonds and leave until cold and set.

5. Peel, quarter and core the pears, then cut into 1cm chunks. Melt the butter in a non-stick frying pan, add the pears and cook over medium heat for about 2 minutes until just softened, shaking the pan frequently. Add the sugar and gently stir in (you don't want to break up the pears), then turn up the heat and let the mixture boil rapidly for a minute to evaporate the excess liquid, leaving the pears with a thick, sticky coating. Transfer to a plate, sprinkle with sea salt flakes and leave to cool.

6. Weigh the filo dough and divide it in half. Rewrap one portion and set the other on a worktop dusted generously with cornflour. Lightly dust your rolling pin with cornflour, then roll out the dough as thinly as possible, checking frequently that it is not sticking. Now lightly dust your hands with cornflour and slide them under the pastry. Working very carefully, use your hands to gently stretch out the pastry until it is thin enough to see the worktop through it – aim for a rectangle about 60 × 40cm if possible.

7. Heat the oven to 180°C/350°F/gas 4. Dip the round cutter in cornflour, then use to stamp out a disc of dough (avoid the thick edges of the rectangle). Set it in one hole of the greased muffin tray to form a cup and gently brush with melted butter. Cut a second disc and press it on top of the first disc, then brush with melted butter. Repeat to make 12 filo cups – you will need to cut 24 discs from this sheet of dough, but there is enough extra to allow for tears/holes/mistakes. Make another 12 filo cups from the second sheet of dough in the same way.

8. Bake the filo cups in the heated oven for 14–15 minutes until crisp and golden – check after 10 minutes and rotate the tray, if necessary, so the cups bake evenly. Transfer the cups to a wire rack and leave to cool.

9. To assemble the petits fours, arrange the cups on a serving platter. Stir the crème pâtissière until smooth, then transfer to the piping bag. Pipe about 1½ teaspoons into each cup. Top each with about 1 teaspoon of caramelised pear. Dust with icing sugar. Break the almond brittle into small shards and set on top of the filling. Serve immediately.

BANOFFEE WHISKY CUPS

A much-loved dessert of rich caramel, bananas and whipped cream is elegantly presented in tiny filo cups for a mouthful of Scottish heaven. Here the home-made filo pastry is rolled into fine sheets using a pasta machine, but you can also stretch the pastry by hand.

makes 24

FOR THE FILO PASTRY
200g strong white bread flour
¼ teaspoon fine sea salt
100–120ml lukewarm water
1 tablespoon olive oil
cornflour, for dusting
60g unsalted butter, melted,
    for brushing
2 tablespoons apricot glaze OR
    sieved apricot jam

FOR THE CARAMEL SAUCE
90g unsalted butter

90g dark muscovado sugar
½ teaspoon vanilla bean paste
5 tablespoons double cream

FOR THE BISCUIT CRUMBLE
50g plain flour
25g ground almonds
60g unsalted butter, chilled
    and diced
20g demerara sugar
15g golden caster sugar
¼ teaspoon ground cinnamon

FOR THE BANANAS
2 large, just ripe bananas
25g dark muscovado sugar
25g unsalted butter
2 tablespoons whisky

FOR THE CREAM
200ml double cream, well chilled
1½ tablespoons caster sugar
½ teaspoon vanilla bean paste

you will need
1 shallow baking tin;
a pasta machine (optional);
1 x 24-hole mini-muffin
tray, greased with butter;
a piping bag fitted with
a star nozzle

1. To make the pastry, sift the flour and salt into the bowl of a free-standing electric mixer fitted with the dough hook. Mix 100ml lukewarm water with the oil, then add to the bowl. Mix together, on slow speed, to make a soft but not sticky dough. If the dough feels stiff or there are dry crumbs in the base of the bowl, work in more water a teaspoon at a time.

2. Knead* the dough, using the dough hook, for about 5 minutes until it feels smooth and pliable. Remove from the bowl, wrap in clingfilm and chill for about 1 hour to give the dough time to relax.

3. Meanwhile, make the filling elements. For the caramel sauce, put the butter and sugar into a medium pan and heat gently, stirring occasionally, until melted and smooth. Bring to the boil and cook to a rich, dark caramel colour. Carefully add the vanilla and cream, and mix in using a hand wire whisk. Pour the sauce into a heatproof bowl and leave to cool, then cover and chill for about 2 hours until thickened.

4. To make the biscuit crumble, put the flour and ground almonds in the bowl of a food processor and 'pulse' a few times to mix. Add the diced butter and blitz until the mixture looks like fine crumbs. Add both sugars and the cinnamon and 'pulse' until combined. Tip the mixture into a baking tin (or a rimmed baking tray) and spread evenly. Put on one side for now.

5. Cut the bananas into slices the thickness of a pound coin – you will need 48 slices. Combine the sugar and butter in a non-stick frying pan and heat gently, stirring occasionally, until melted and glossy. Add the sliced bananas and cook for a minute, gently tossing the bananas in the sticky sauce. Turn up the heat to medium. Carefully pour in the whisky and simmer for a few seconds, then remove from the heat. Transfer to a heatproof bowl and leave to cool.

6. Whip the cream* with the sugar and vanilla until soft peaks will form. Cover and keep in the fridge until needed.

7. To roll out the pastry using a pasta machine, unwrap the dough and cut it into 4 equal pieces, then rewrap 3 of them; set these aside on the worktop. Dust the centre of the worktop and the remaining piece of dough with cornflour, then flatten the dough on the worktop into a rectangle about 1cm thick. Dust the rollers of the pasta machine with cornflour too. Now roll the dough through the widest setting. Repeat, then roll through the next, slightly finer, setting. Continue rolling the dough, turning down the settings each time, until you reach the finest. By now you should have an almost transparently thin strip of pastry. (Alternatively, you can roll and stretch the dough by hand – see Salmon, Spinach and Feta Strudel on page 287 for details.)

8. Spread the strip of dough on another worktop well dusted with cornflour and cover with a sheet of clingfilm. Repeat with the other 3 pieces of dough, layering up the strips between sheets of cornflour-dusted clingfilm.

9. Heat the oven to 180°C/350°F/gas 4. Using a pasta wheel-cutter or sharp knife, cut the strips into 7.5cm squares (you will need 72). Keep the pastry you are not handling covered with clingfilm to prevent it from drying out (you may find it easier to work with one strip at a time).

10. To shape each cup, press one filo square into a hole of the muffin tray. Brush lightly with melted butter, then lay a second square on top at an angle. Butter this, then add a third square and brush it with butter. Make the other 23 cups in the same way.

11. Gently melt the apricot glaze in a small pan with 1 tablespoon water, then lightly brush on to the edges of the pastry cups. Bake in the heated oven for about 10 minutes until the pastry is golden and crisp – check after 5 minutes and rotate the tray, if necessary, so the pastry bakes evenly. Carefully transfer the cups to a wire rack to cool. Leave the oven on.

12. Sprinkle the crumble mixture with a little water, then bake for 5 minutes. Remove from the oven and stir the mixture, then bake for another 5 minutes until golden. Remove, stir gently to break up any clumps and leave to cool.

13. To finish the filo cups, spoon a little of the caramel sauce into each one, then add 2 slices of caramel-coated banana. Transfer the cream to the piping bag and pipe a small swirl on to each. Top with the crumble.

SWISS APPLE-ALMOND SLICE

A pastry to impress: dessert apples, quickly fried with nuts, cinnamon and rum-soaked sultanas, are piled high on a shortbread-like base, then decorated with a piped almond-paste lattice. It makes a handsome centrepiece for a celebration table, and the shape makes it easy to cut into neat slices. Take care with the final baking as it is easy to go from a lovely golden finish to scorched in a minute.

serves 8

FOR THE SHORTBREAD PASTRY BASE
120g plain flour
good pinch of fine sea salt
¼ teaspoon ground cinnamon
60g caster sugar
60g unsalted butter, chilled and diced
2 medium egg yolks

FOR THE APPLE FILLING
50g sultanas
3 tablespoons dark rum OR apple juice
600g tart dessert apples (about 5 medium)
35g unsalted butter
50g chopped almonds
1 teaspoon ground cinnamon

FOR THE TOPPING
350g white marzipan
1 tablespoon plain flour
1 medium egg white
2 tablespoons sieved apricot jam OR apricot glaze
1 tablespoon toasted flaked almonds, for sprinkling
crème fraîche, to serve

you will need
1 baking sheet, lined with baking paper; a large piping bag fitted with a 1cm plain nozzle

1. To make the pastry base, put the flour, salt, cinnamon and sugar into a food processor and 'pulse' several times to combine. Add the pieces of butter and blitz until the mixture looks sandy. Add the egg yolks and run the machine until the mixture comes together in pea-sized lumps.

2. Cut a sheet of clingfilm and spread it on the worktop. Tip out the dough lumps on to the clingfilm. Bring the lumps together with your hands to make a dough and shape into a thick disc. Wrap in the clingfilm and chill for about 15 minutes until firm but not hard.

3. Meanwhile, put the sultanas to soak in the rum or apple juice.

4. Unwrap the pastry and set it in the centre of the lined baking sheet. Lightly dust a rolling pin with flour, then roll out the dough to an 11.5 × 30.5cm rectangle. Using a pizza wheel-cutter, or a large sharp knife, trim the edges of the rectangle to make a very neat 11 × 30cm strip. Decorate the edges of the strip by fluting* them or pinching with your fingers, then prick the pastry strip all over with a fork. Chill for 15 minutes. Meanwhile, heat the oven to 180°C/350°F/gas 4.

5. Bake the pastry base in the heated oven for 12–15 minutes until a light golden brown with slightly darker edges. Leave to cool. Increase the oven temperature to 220°C/425°F/gas 7.

6. Peel, quarter and core the apples, then slice fairly thickly. Melt the butter in a large frying pan over medium heat, add the nuts and stir-fry for a minute. Add the apples and cinnamon. Stir well, then cook, stirring frequently, for about 5 minutes until the apples have started to soften and turn a pale gold colour. Add the sultanas and their soaking liquid to the pan and stir gently to mix. Cook, stirring now and then, until the base of the pan looks dry. Remove from the heat and leave to cool.

7. To make the topping, break up the marzipan into small pieces and put into the (washed) food processor with the flour and egg white. Run the machine, scraping down the sides from time to time, to make a smooth and thick yet pipeable mixture. Transfer the mixture to the piping bag.

8. To assemble the apple slice, spoon the apple mixture on top of the pastry base, leaving a 1cm border clear all around the edges. Use your hands to gently mound the filling and give it an even shape. Now pipe the marzipan mixture across the top of the apples in a zig-zag lattice pattern. Don't worry if there are gaps – you can easily go back and fill them in, or fix any mistakes. Make sure the lattice doesn't overlap the pastry base and become stuck to the baking paper (gently scrape it away if necessary).

9. Bake the apple slice for 8–10 minutes until the marzipan lattice is a good golden colour – watch carefully as it will quickly change colour and you don't want it to get too dark. Remove and leave to cool.

10. Once cold, carefully transfer the apple slice to a board or a serving platter. Gently brush with the warmed apricot jam or glaze, then immediately scatter the flaked almonds over the top. Serve at room temperature, the same or the next day, with crème fraîche.

FRESH APRICOT TATIN

Here fresh apricots with pistachios replace apples in a glorious twist on the traditional French upside-down tart. The apricot halves are set vertically and packed quite tightly in the tin to support the rich pastry covering. Special solid-based metal Tatin tins are now readily available but you can also use an ovenproof frying pan as long as it has a heavy base - cooking starts on top of the stove to caramelise the sugar/butter mixture before the pastry is added and the tart is baked.

serves 8

FOR THE PASTRY

175g plain flour
pinch of fine sea salt
2 tablespoons caster sugar
100g unsalted butter, chilled
    and diced
1 medium egg yolk
1½ tablespoons icy cold water

FOR THE FILLING

75g unsalted butter
100g caster sugar
about 1kg fresh apricots
40g unsalted pistachio nuts
    (shelled)

TO SERVE

vanilla ice cream OR crème
    fraîche

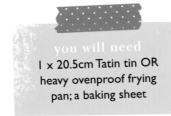

you will need
1 x 20.5cm Tatin tin OR
heavy ovenproof frying
pan; a baking sheet

1. To make the pastry in a food processor, put the flour, salt and sugar into the bowl and 'pulse' a couple of times to combine. Add the pieces of butter and blitz until the mixture looks sandy. With the machine running, add the egg yolk and water through the feed tube, stopping the machine as soon as the mixture comes together in a firm ball. (You can also make the pastry by hand: sift the flour, salt and sugar into a mixing bowl, rub in* the butter, and mix in the egg yolk and water using a round-bladed knife.) Flatten the ball of dough to a thick disc, wrap in clingfilm and keep in the fridge until needed.

2. Cut the butter for the filling into thin slices and arrange them on the base of the Tatin tin to completely cover it. Sprinkle the sugar evenly over the butter. Cut the apricots in half, following the slight indentation, and remove the stones. Press a pistachio into the hollow of each half (don't worry if some nuts fall out), then arrange the apricot halves in the tin so they are standing up vertically — pack them in tightly so the pastry lid won't collapse as the fruit cooks. Scatter the rest of the pistachios over the top.

3. Set the tin over moderate heat on the hob and cook and bubble for 12–15 minutes until the butter and sugar have melted and turned into a richly coloured caramel.

4. Meanwhile, heat the oven to 220°C/425°F/gas 7. Roll out the dough on a lightly floured worktop to a fairly thick disc that will fit the top of the tin. Roll up the dough loosely around the rolling pin.

5. Carefully remove the tin from the hob and set it on the baking sheet. Lift the rolling pin over the tin and gently unroll the dough so it drapes over the apricots to cover completely. Quickly tuck the edges of the dough down inside the tin using a round-bladed knife, then prick the pastry lid all over with a fork. Bake in the heated oven for about 20 minutes until the pastry is golden brown and crisp. Leave to cool for 5 minutes.

6. Run the round-bladed knife around the inside of the tin to loosen the pastry edges. Set an upturned large platter over the tin and, holding them firmly together, turn them over — the pastry will now be under the caramelised apricots. Eat warm or at room temperature.

MIL HOJAS

Very similar to millefeuille (*mil hojas* being the Spanish term), this impressive pastry uses flaked almonds to give the puff pastry layers extra crunch, making a perfect counterpoint to the creamy fillings. Both the pastry slices and the two fillings can be prepared up to a day ahead, ready to be assembled. Serve with raspberries.

serves 6

1. Lightly dust your worktop with flour. Scatter 25g of the flaked almonds over the flour. Roll out the pastry on the worktop to a thin 30 x 38cm rectangle. With a large sharp knife or pizza wheel-cutter, cut the rectangle across in half to make two 30 x 19cm rectangles – take care not to drag the knife or the pastry as you cut because this will distort the shape. Roll each pastry rectangle loosely around the rolling pin and gently unroll on to a baking sheet. Brush off the excess flour with a dry pastry brush, then prick the pastry well with a fork.

2. Beat the egg white with a fork until frothy, then lightly brush over the pastry rectangles. Mix the remaining flaked almonds with the caster sugar and scatter evenly over the top. Chill for 20 minutes. Meanwhile, heat the oven to 220°C/425°F/gas 7. Bake the pastry for 18–24 minutes until well risen, golden and very crisp. If undercooked, the middle will be soggy – it is better to slightly overcook if in doubt. Transfer to a wire rack to cool.

3. To make the filling, heat the milk with the lemon zest in a medium pan. Whisk the egg yolks with the caster sugar and cornflour in a heatproof bowl for a couple of minutes until thick and light. Set the bowl on a damp cloth (so it doesn't wobble), then gradually whisk in the hot milk. When thoroughly combined, tip the mixture back into the pan and stir briskly over medium heat until the custard boils and thickens. Remove from the heat and stir well to make sure the custard is very smooth before stirring in the butter and limoncello, if using. Pour and scrape into a clean heatproof bowl. Press a piece of clingfilm on to the surface of the custard to prevent a skin from forming. Leave to cool, then chill for about 2 hours until firm.

4. Whip the cream* with the icing sugar until it stands in soft peaks. Uncover the custard and give it a good stir so it is very smooth, then fold* in half of the whipped cream. Cover both the bowls and chill for about 4 hours until the fillings are firm enough to spread.

5. Use a sharp knife to cut each of the pastry rectangles lengthways into 2 equal strips, each about 9 x 30cm, then cut each strip across into 6 pieces (you will now have 24 pieces). Spread the lemon filling over 12 of the pastry pieces and whipped cream over 6 pieces. Layer them up, alternating the fillings and topping each stack with a plain piece. Dust with icing sugar.

75g flaked almonds
½ quantity Puff Pastry (see page 22) OR 375g ready-made all-butter puff pastry, thawed if frozen
1 medium egg white, at room temperature
1 teaspoon caster sugar
icing sugar, for dusting
raspberries, to serve

FOR THE FILLING

250ml creamy milk
finely grated zest of 1 unwaxed lemon
3 medium egg yolks, at room temperature
50g caster sugar
20g cornflour
30g unsalted butter, at room temperature
1 teaspoon limoncello (optional)
150ml double cream, well chilled
2 tablespoons icing sugar

you will need
2 baking sheets, lined with baking paper

GÂTEAU ST-HONORÉ

Named after the patron saint of pastry chefs, this is a truly spectacular creation, and a great challenge of skills. There's a puff pastry base, baked with a choux pastry ring, then topped with choux balls dipped in caramel. The ring is filled with crème St-Honoré (a crème pâtissière and meringue mix flavoured with orange liqueur) and finished with spun sugar.

serves 8-10

FOR THE BASE
½ quantity Puff Pastry (see page 22) OR 375g ready-made all-butter puff pastry, thawed if frozen

FOR THE CHOUX PASTRY
150g plain flour
115g unsalted butter
1 tablespoon caster sugar
¼ teaspoon fine sea salt
225ml water

4 medium eggs, at room temperature

FOR THE CRÈME ST-HONORÉ
200ml single cream OR 100ml each double cream and milk
1 vanilla pod, split lengthways
5 medium eggs, at room temperature
20g cornflour
100g caster sugar
good pinch of fine sea salt

20g unsalted butter, at room temperature
3 tablespoons orange liqueur

FOR THE CARAMEL
300g caster sugar
good pinch of cream of tartar
6 tablespoons water

TO FINISH
½ quantity Crème Chantilly (see page 18)

you will need
2–3 baking sheets, lined with baking paper; a large piping bag fitted with a 1.5cm plain nozzle; a piping bag fitted with a 0.5cm plain nozzle; a piping bag fitted with a St-Honoré nozzle (see recipe) OR an open star nozzle

1. To make the pastry disc for the base, roll out the puff pastry on a lightly floured worktop to a large round about 3mm thick. Using a cake tin or a plate as a template, cut out a 25cm disc, taking care not to drag the knife or stretch the pastry as you cut. Roll the pastry loosely around the rolling pin and transfer it to a lined baking sheet. Prick the pastry well with a fork, then chill for 20 minutes.

2. Meanwhile, heat the oven to 220°C/425°F/gas 7 and make the choux pastry. Sift the flour on to a sheet of greaseproof or baking paper. Put the butter, sugar, salt and water into a medium pan. Heat gently until the butter has completely melted, then turn up the heat and bring the mixture to the boil. Tip in the flour, in one go, then quickly draw the pan off the heat. Beat vigorously with a wooden spoon until the mixture comes together to form a heavy, paste-like dough.

3. Return the pan to low heat and beat the dough for a minute or so until it is very smooth and shiny and no longer sticks to the sides of the pan. Tip the dough into a heatproof mixing bowl, or the bowl of a free-standing electric mixer fitted with the whisk attachment, and leave to cool for a few minutes. Using a hand-held electric whisk, or the whisk attachment, beat the dough for a minute. Break the eggs into a jug and beat with a fork just to combine. Gradually beat the eggs into the dough, pouring them into the

SAVOURY BAKES

We cannot live on sweet stuff alone so it's a bonus that we can adapt and translate our baking skills to create good-looking and imaginative savoury snacks and party items, as well as to make the everyday meal just as interesting as a special-occasion dish.

Pastry is at the heart of this chapter, but there's more – from humble Yorkshire puddings jazzed up to transform your Sunday lunch (see page 294) to quick canapés (page 278), ideal for pastry-phobic bakers, where sliced bread makes tartlet cases easy work. For fans of sausage rolls there's a simple but irresistible spiced lamb version (page 282) using ready-made puff pastry – or home-made if you are in the mood. More intricate finger food recipes feature on pages 299 and 301 using home-made filo pastry to produce some very fine 'amuse-bouches'.

Sheets of ready-made filo make an easy crunchy topping for a pie, the perfect counterpoint to the creamy, rich coconut milk-based filling for the Thai-spiced Chicken Pie on page 285. You can also use bought filo for a savoury strudel, but making your own massive paper-thin sheet of strudel pastry – stretching out the dough over a floured tablecloth, with extra pairs of hands – is just so much fun. The Salmon, Spinach and Feta Strudel on page 287 is impressive enough for the most special of meals.

Another push-the-boat-out recipe is Duck and Pistachio Pâté en Croûte (page 307). Here, instead of the traditional British hot-water-crust hand-raised dough, a butter-rich, crisp French pâte brisée forms the pastry case. This pastry is made straight on the worktop, not in a bowl or processor, and is worked using the heel of your hand until pliable enough to lift off in one piece. Done well, this makes lining the loaf tin straightforward. The filling combines duck breast meat with rich duck liver and pork, all marinated overnight in wine and brandy. Thick slices of this glorious pie, eaten cold with a crisp, well-dressed salad, make the perfect warm-weather supper.

COTTAGE CHEESE PUFF BISCUITS

Crisp, mildly spiced cheese biscuits are always enjoyed when handed around with drinks, or served with dips or a selection of cheeses for a party. These are no trouble to make and they can also be used as the base for quick canapés (see ideas below).

makes 40

1 teaspoon nigella seeds
100g unsalted butter, at room
   temperature
¼ teaspoon sea salt flakes
⅛ teaspoon cayenne pepper, or
   to taste
100g natural cottage cheese
   (not fat-free or low-fat),
   well drained (see recipe)
140g plain flour

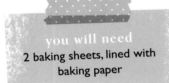

you will need
2 baking sheets, lined with
baking paper

1. Measure the seeds into a small, dry frying pan and gently toast over low heat for 1–2 minutes until aromatic. Tip out of the pan and leave to cool.

2. Cut the butter into chunks and put them into a food processor with the salt and cayenne pepper. Blitz until creamy. Before you weigh out the cottage cheese, drain it well by tipping off the watery liquid at the top of the tub, then drain the cottage cheese again in a sieve for a few moments. Add the cheese to the processor and 'pulse' until the mixture is very smoothly combined, scraping down the sides once or twice. Add the flour and toasted seeds and run the machine just until the mixture comes together to make a soft dough.

3. Scoop out the dough on to a sheet of baking paper. Flour your hands and shape the dough into a 22cm log that is 3cm thick, using the paper to help you. Wrap the log tightly in the paper and chill until it is firm enough to slice easily – at least 3 hours. (As long as the dough is wrapped well, it can be kept in the fridge for up to 48 hours.)

4. When ready to bake, heat the oven to 200°C/400°F/gas 6. Unwrap the log and, using a large sharp knife, cut across into 40 slices. Arrange the slices on the baking sheets, spacing them about 3cm apart to allow for expansion.

5. Bake in the heated oven for 12–15 minutes until golden with darker edges. Leave to cool and firm up on the baking sheets for 1 minute before transferring to a wire rack. Once cold, the biscuits can be stored in an airtight container for up to 5 days. If necessary, before serving reheat in the oven at 180°C/350°F/gas 4 for a few minutes to crisp them up.

some more ideas:

•   For really cheesy biscuits, mix 50g freshly grated Parmesan cheese with a good pinch of cayenne pepper and sprinkle over the slices before baking.

•   Use the baked biscuits as canapé bases. Top each with a slice of goats' cheese (for 40 biscuits, you'll need 3 x 150g goats' cheese logs, thinly sliced) and garnish with sliced pitted olives or slivers of sun-dried tomatoes. OR top the baked biscuits with thin slices of smoked chicken breast or turkey (for 40 biscuits, use 150g) and add a small dollop of finely diced spicy mango chutney to each. Avocado slices topped with a dollop of salsa are a vegetarian alternative.

DELICIOUSLY QUICK CANAPÉS

When preparing for a party, why not bake your canapé cases from bread slices instead of pastry? It's so easy and the results are impressive - crisp, good-looking and great-tasting as well as low in fat. They can be used for both warm and cold fillings - here there's a choice of a hot wild-mushroom-and-bacon mixture, or a cool, lively chicken salad flavoured with mango and sweet chilli sauce. Each of the fillings makes enough for 12 canapé cases.

makes 12

FOR THE CASES
50g unsalted butter
good pinch of cayenne pepper
12 thin slices slightly stale Soft
    Crust Sandwich Bread
    (see page 281) or bought
    sandwich bread

**FOR THE WILD MUSHROOM
FILLING (FILLS 12 CASES)**
5g dried porcini mushrooms
1 teaspoon olive oil

90g smoked back bacon
    (about 3 rashers), finely diced
1 small onion, finely chopped
50g button mushrooms
ground black pepper
3 tablespoons crème fraîche OR
    double cream
20g Parmesan cheese, freshly
    grated
fresh chives OR other herbs,
    to garnish

**FOR THE CHICKEN-MANGO SALAD
FILLING (FILLS 12 CASES)**
125g cooked skinless, boneless
    chicken (or turkey), well chilled
½ ripe mango
2 tablespoons mayonnaise
1 tablespoon Thai sweet chilli
    sauce, or to taste
finely grated zest and juice
    of ½ unwaxed lime
salad cress OR micro salad herbs,
    to garnish

you will need
1 x 12-hole jam tart/mince
pie/bun tin; a 7.5cm plain
round cutter

1. To make the bread cases, heat the oven to 220°C/425°F/gas 7. Melt the butter with the cayenne pepper, then use a little to brush the holes in the tart/mince pie/bun tin.

2. Using the cutter, stamp out a round from each slice of bread. Flatten the rounds by rolling with a rolling pin – this will compress the crumb (the bread will feel less 'bouncy'), making it easier to work with. Firmly press a round into each hole of the buttered tin, using your thumbs to press the bread on to the base and up the sides to line neatly (just as if you were lining with pastry).

3. Brush the bread cases thoroughly with the rest of the melted butter, then bake in the heated oven for about 10 minutes until golden – for best results, check the cases after 6 minutes and rotate the tin, if necessary, so they bake evenly. Remove and leave to cool. You can turn off the oven now if you are not serving the canapés immediately.

4. Once cold the cases can be stored in an airtight container for 24 hours. The fillings can be made and used immediately or prepared up to a day ahead and kept in the fridge until ready to finish.

5. For **wild mushroom canapés**, soak the dried mushrooms in a small bowl of warm water for 10 minutes. Meanwhile, put the olive oil into a non-stick frying pan, add the bacon and stir-fry over medium heat until crisp and golden brown. Reduce the heat and stir in the chopped onion. Leave to cook gently for a few minutes

6. Meanwhile, drain the soaked dried mushrooms and squeeze gently to remove excess water. Chop the dried and fresh mushrooms into small pieces about the same size as the bacon, then add to the frying pan. Fry, stirring frequently, for 2–3 minutes. Season well with black pepper and add the crème fraîche. Bring to the boil, stirring, then remove from the heat. If not using immediately, transfer the mixture to a heatproof bowl and leave to cool before covering tightly with clingfilm and keeping in the fridge.

7. To finish, heat the oven to 220°C/425°F/gas 7 and return the bread cases to the bun tin. Divide the filling mixture equally among the cases, then top with the grated cheese. Bake in the heated oven for about 8 minutes until piping hot. Arrange the canapés on a serving platter, garnish with chives or other herbs and serve warm.

8. For **chicken-mango salad canapés**, cut the chicken into 5mm dice and put into a bowl. Peel the mango and cut the flesh into dice about the same size as the chicken – you need 100g. Add to the chicken along with the mayonnaise, sweet chilli sauce and lime zest and juice. Mix everything together, then taste and add more chilli sauce if you like. If not using the filling immediately, cover the bowl with clingfilm and keep in the fridge.

9. To finish, stir the chicken-mango filling gently, then spoon into the cold bread cases. Arrange on a serving platter, garnish with cress or herbs and serve.

SOFT CRUST SANDWICH BREAD

This loaf is easy to slice thinly for canapé bases (see page 278). It makes good, crisp toast too.

makes a medium loaf

about 325ml milk
25g unsalted butter, plus a knob to finish
1 teaspoon golden syrup
500g strong white bread flour
7g fine sea salt
1 x 7g sachet fast-action dried yeast

1. Put the milk, butter and syrup into a small pan and heat gently until the butter has melted. Stir, then remove from the heat and cool until lukewarm. Meanwhile, put the flour and salt into a mixing bowl, or a free-standing electric mixer fitted with the dough hook. Mix in the yeast, then make a well in the centre. Pour in the lukewarm milk mixture and mix everything together with your hand, or the dough hook on the lowest speed, to make a soft dough. Leave to hydrate* for 5 minutes, then add more milk if needed.

2. Tip out the dough on to a lightly floured worktop. Knead* for 10 minutes, or 5 minutes with the dough hook on lowest speed, until the dough feels slightly firmer, silky smooth and very elastic. Return to the bowl, cover and leave to rise for about 1 hour until doubled in size.

3. Punch down the dough to deflate it, then tip it out on to the lightly floured worktop. Knead a couple of times to dislodge any large air bubbles, then flour your fingers and firmly press out to a 26 x 30cm rectangle of even thickness. Roll up fairly tightly from one short end, pinching the dough together with each roll. Pinch the seam firmly together.

4. Set the loaf in a greased 900g loaf tin (about 26 x 12.5 x 7.5cm), seam-side down with the ends tucked under. Gently press it right into the corners and flatten the surface to make a neat brick-like shape. Cover tightly and leave to rise for about 1 hour until doubled in size.

5. Towards the end of this time, heat the oven to 220°C/425°F/gas 7. Uncover the tin and bake the loaf in the heated oven for 15 minutes. Reduce the temperature to 180°C/350°F/gas 4 and bake for a further 20 minutes until the loaf is a good golden brown and it sounds hollow when tapped on the underside*. Turn out on to a wire rack. Rub the knob of butter over the top of the loaf to keep the crust soft, then leave to cool. Eat within 5 days or toasted. Once cold the loaf can be tightly wrapped and frozen for up to a month.

SPICY AND SIMPLE LAMB ROLLS

Super-easy to assemble and wonderful warm from the oven. These puff-pastry rolls, with their filling of minced lamb flavoured with aromatic spices and a touch of cayenne along with tangy soft-dried apricots, take very little time yet taste quite special.

makes 12 — | dairy free

FOR THE FILLING
450g lean minced lamb
1 small red onion
2 garlic cloves, crushed
2 teaspoons smoked sweet (mild) paprika
1½ teaspoons ground cumin
1½ teaspoons ground coriander
¼ teaspoon ground cinnamon
salt, ground black pepper and cayenne pepper, all to taste

TO ASSEMBLE
½ quantity Puff Pastry (see page 22) OR 375g ready-made all-butter or vegan puff pastry, thawed if frozen
100g soft-dried apricots
beaten egg, to glaze
sesame seeds, to sprinkle

you will need
1 baking sheet, lined with baking paper

1. To make the filling, put the lamb into a mixing bowl. Using the coarse side of a cheese grater, grate the onion on top of the lamb. Add the crushed garlic, paprika, cumin, coriander, cinnamon and a little salt, black pepper and cayenne. Mix everything together with your hands or a wooden spoon until thoroughly combined.

2. To check the seasoning, take a scant teaspoon of the mixture, shape it into a small 'burger' and quickly cook on both sides in a hot non-stick frying pan. Cool for a minute, then taste and adjust the flavourings in your lamb mixture as necessary – it can be as spicy as you like.

3. Roll out the pastry on a lightly floured worktop to a 34 x 32cm rectangle. Using a pizza wheel-cutter or a large sharp knife, cut the pastry in half down its length to make 2 rectangles, each 34 x 16cm. Divide the lamb mixture in half, then shape each portion into a thick sausage 34cm long.

4. Set one lamb sausage down the length of one pastry rectangle, placing it so it is 5cm from one long edge. Using kitchen scissors, snip each dried apricot in 2. Arrange half of the pieces along the top of the lamb sausage. Fold the nearest long pastry edge over the sausage. Brush the other long edge with beaten egg, then gently roll the lamb sausage over towards the egg-glazed edge until the 2 pastry edges are overlapping. The sausage will now be completely rolled up in the puff pastry and the join of the 2 pastry edges should be underneath. Repeat with the remaining pastry, lamb sausage and apricots.

5. Cut each long roll across into 6 equal pieces. Arrange these, slightly apart, on the lined baking sheet. Brush the pastry with beaten egg to glaze, then make 2 small cuts or scores across the top of each roll. Sprinkle liberally with sesame seeds. Chill the lamb rolls while you heat the oven to 220°C/425°F/gas 7.

6. Bake the rolls in the heated oven for about 25 minutes until the pastry is a rich golden brown. Transfer to a wire rack and leave to cool for about 5 minutes before serving.

THAI-SPICED CHICKEN PIE

The basis of this easy and temptingly spicy pie is cold roast chicken in a Thai curry sauce made with coconut milk. It's up to you to decide on the heat level. The topping is ready-made filo pastry, arranged so it bakes to a very crisp and light counterpart to the chicken and vegetable filling.

serves 6

1. To make the filling, put the shallots and garlic into the bowl of a food processor with the red Thai curry paste. Turn the can of coconut milk upside down and open it: the set thick coconut cream will now be at the bottom under a layer of clear liquid. Pour off the liquid into a small bowl, then measure 2 tablespoons of it into the processor. Blitz to make a thick purée, scraping down the sides of the bowl from time to time.

2. Heat the oil in a medium to large pan, then add the purée and stir-fry for a minute. Bash the lemongrass stick with a rolling pin to split it open, then add it to the pan along with the thick coconut cream left in the can (discard any remaining clear liquid). Mix well. Stir in the lime zest and juice, the fish sauce, sugar and lime leaves (if using). Bring to the boil. Reduce the heat and leave to simmer for 10 minutes, stirring occasionally.

3. Meanwhile, cut the baby corn into 2–3 pieces each, depending on size. Cut or pull the chicken meat into large chunks (discard any skin). Remove the filo pastry from the fridge and leave it to 'come to' (or follow packet instructions); keep the pastry wrapped.

4. Heat the oven to 200°C/400°F/gas 6.

5. Taste the coconut sauce and adjust the flavourings as necessary, adding more curry paste/fish sauce/sugar as needed. Discard the lemongrass. Stir in the corn, mushrooms and chicken and simmer for a further 5 minutes. Spoon into the pie dish.

6. Unwrap the pastry and unroll the stack of sheets on the worktop; keep the pastry covered with a slightly damp tea towel or sheet of clingfilm to prevent it from drying out. You will need 6 layers of pastry to cover the pie – the rest is for the crunchy topping. Check to see if the sheets are roughly the same size as the top of the pie dish: if they are much larger then they will need to be folded as you layer them. Remove one sheet, keeping the rest covered, and spread it flat on the worktop. Brush very lightly with melted butter, then lay a second sheet on top (or fold the first sheet over to fit the top of the pie dish with a little to spare). Brush with melted butter. Repeat until you have 6 layers of pastry.

FOR THE FILLING

2 banana shallots, quartered
4 garlic cloves, peeled and left whole
1½ tablespoons red Thai curry paste, or to taste
400ml can coconut milk
1 tablespoon rapeseed oil
1 lemongrass stick
finely grated zest and juice of 1 unwaxed lime
1 tablespoon Thai fish sauce, or to taste
½ teaspoon palm sugar OR light muscovado sugar, or to taste
2–3 fresh lime leaves, shredded (optional)
100g baby corn
500g cooked chicken meat
100g button mushrooms

TO ASSEMBLE

1 pack filo pastry (about 220g), thawed if frozen
50g unsalted butter, melted

you will need
1 pie dish, 1.25–1.5 litre capacity; a baking sheet

7. Brush the rim of the pie dish with water, then lift the layered pastry lid on top of the dish and gently press it on to the dampened rim. Trim off the excess pastry hanging over the rim using kitchen scissors or a sharp knife. Brush another sheet of pastry with a little melted butter, then tear it roughly into quarters. Drape these on top of the pie, rather like a dropped crumpled handkerchief. Repeat with the remaining sheets of pastry – the top of the pie will look like a mountain range.

8. Set the pie dish on the baking sheet and bake in the heated oven for 30–35 minutes until the pastry is a good golden brown and crisp. Serve hot, with steamed green vegetables and a basmati/wild rice mix.

SALMON, SPINACH AND FETA STRUDEL

Making strudel pastry really isn't as scary as it seems. It is much easier and quicker (and cheaper) to prepare than puff or even flaky pastry, and it is a lot of fun to make as you really do need at least 2 pairs of hands for the stretching part. You will also need a large clean sheet or tablecloth and a table or worktop you can walk around: the pastry gets big! (You can also use ready-made filo sheets of course.) The filling of lightly smoked salmon, spinach, feta and pine nuts cooks quickly in the strudel without making the pastry soggy.

serves 6-8

1. If making the strudel dough, sift the flour and salt into a large mixing bowl and make a well in the centre. Pour in the beaten egg, 20g melted butter and the water. Using your hand, mix together the ingredients in the well, then gradually work in the flour to make a very soft, paste-like dough. Slap the paste up and down in the bowl with your hand until it will leave the side of the bowl clean.

2. Turn out the dough on to a lightly floured worktop. Unlike other pastries, this paste-like dough is made from strong bread flour and it needs to be kneaded to develop the gluten – this is what enables it to become elastic enough to be stretched out to the thinness of a paper tissue. The easiest (and most enjoyable) way to knead the dough is to pick it up and throw it down on to the worktop, then gather it up again and repeat. Knead in this way for about 10 minutes until the dough feels silky-smooth and very supple. It should easily leave your hand and peel off the worktop. Cover the dough with the upturned bowl and leave to rest for 20–30 minutes while you prepare the filling.

3. It's essential to have the filling ready because the dough must be used promptly once it is stretched. Melt the butter in a frying pan, add the breadcrumbs and pine nuts, and fry, stirring constantly, until the crumbs are a rich golden brown. Tip into a heatproof bowl and leave to cool. Crumble the feta into large chunks. Cut the salmon into 2cm chunks.

4. When you are ready to start stretching the dough, heat the oven to 190°C/375°F/gas 5. Spread the cloth flat on a tabletop so there are no wrinkles. Lightly dust the cloth with flour. Set the ball of dough in the middle and very lightly brush the top with the remaining 15g melted butter. Using a rolling pin, roll out the dough to a square with sides about 30cm.

5. Now remove all rings, watches and bangles, and lightly flour your hands. Slip them, palms down, under the dough and gently move them apart so the dough is stretched over the back of your hands. Continue doing this,

FOR THE DOUGH
200g strong white bread flour
good pinch of fine sea salt
1 medium egg, at room
    temperature, beaten to mix
35g unsalted butter, melted
100ml water, at room temperature

OR 1 pack filo pastry (about 220g),
    thawed if frozen

FOR THE FILLING
50g unsalted butter
50g fresh breadcrumbs
50g pine nuts
150g good-quality feta cheese
4 x 125g lightly smoked skinless
    salmon fillets
100g baby spinach leaves
freshly ground black pepper

TO ASSEMBLE
75g melted butter, for brushing

you will need
1 large clean cloth or sheet;
a baking sheet, lined with
baking paper

another idea: Serve with Quick Herb Butter Sauce (see page 22) and some steamed asparagus or purple-sprouting broccoli for a pretty early-summer feast.

moving around the table as you work so the dough is evenly stretched on all 4 sides. Gradually it will become very thin – aim for a rectangular sheet of dough about 73 x 50cm. Don't worry too much if there are a few holes or tears because strudel pastry is easy to patch up. Trim off the thick edges with kitchen scissors. The strudel dough is now ready to use (if you have to leave it for a brief time, cover the whole surface with clingfilm topped with slightly damp tea towels).

6. If you are using ready-made filo sheets, arrange them slightly overlapping on a lightly floured cloth to make a rectangle about 70 x 48cm – again, because of the way the pastry is used, it doesn't matter too much if the pastry sheet is slightly larger, but if there is a lot over use kitchen scissors to trim off the excess.

7. The strudel or filo pastry rectangle should be lying vertically in front of you (i.e. with the shorter sides top and bottom). Brush the entire pastry rectangle lightly with melted butter. Spoon the breadcrumb/pine nut mixture on to the dough about 8cm in from the short side nearest to you, to make a band about 8cm wide that stretches 45cm from side to side (leaving a small gap at each end of the band). Arrange half the spinach leaves on top of this band and season well with black pepper. Distribute the salmon chunks evenly over the spinach. Season again with pepper (you won't need to add salt to the filling because of the feta). Cover with the rest of the spinach leaves, gently pressing and moulding the filling to an even shape. Scatter the feta on top and add another few grinds of black pepper.

8. Fold the 8cm-wide end flap of pastry over the filling, then lift up the cloth so the pastry-covered filling gently flops over away from you. Tuck in the ends to prevent the filling from escaping and use a dry pastry brush to remove as much of the excess flour from the roll as possible. Pull the cloth towards you so the pastry roll flops over again, then repeat, tucking in the ends and brushing away the excess flour as you go. When the strudel has been rolled up, use the cloth to tip it, seam-side down, on to the lined baking sheet – if necessary gently shape into a crescent or horseshoe to fit. Make sure the ends are neatly tucked under. Brush the roll (top, sides and ends) with the rest of the melted butter.

9. Bake in the heated oven for 30–35 minutes until the pastry is a rich golden brown and crisp. Transfer to a serving platter or board and serve hot.

ROAST VEGETABLE AND CASHEW PIE

Here's a simple dinner to prepare, needing nothing more than a green salad alongside.
It's perfect for using some of a glut of vegetables from the garden or allotment.

dairy free | —————————————————————— serves 4-6

1. To make the filling, heat the oven to 220°C/425°F/gas 7. Trim or peel the vegetables, then cut into 2cm chunks and put into the roasting tin (it will be quite full). Spoon over the olive oil and toss everything so the oil lightly coats the chunks. Roast in the heated oven for 20 minutes. Carefully toss and turn the vegetables using a fish slice, then roast for another 20 minutes.

2. Remove the tin from the oven and add the garlic and oregano. Season with salt, pepper and chilli flakes and toss everything together gently. Return to the oven and roast for a further 12–20 minutes until the vegetables are tender and lightly coloured but not falling apart or mushy.

3. Meanwhile, spread the cashews in a small baking dish or tin and toast in the oven for 5–7 minutes until golden. Set aside.

4. Remove the vegetables from the oven (you can turn it off for now) and stir in the toasted cashews and sun-dried tomatoes. Taste and add more seasoning – the mixture should be well flavoured. Leave to cool completely.

5. When ready to assemble, roll out the pastry on a lightly floured worktop to a 45 × 30cm rectangle. With a pizza wheel-cutter or large sharp knife, cut the pastry into 2 rectangles, one 25 × 30cm to form the lid of the pie, the other 20 × 30cm to form the base.

6. Roll up the smaller rectangle (the base) loosely around the rolling pin and unroll it on to the lined baking sheet. Brush beaten egg over a 1.5cm border all round the edges of the rectangle. Spoon the cold vegetable filling on to the central part of the pastry (leave the egg-glazed border exposed), mounding it up neatly in the middle – use your hands to gently press the vegetables into a slightly domed shape.

7. Roll up the pastry lid around the rolling pin and gently unroll and drape it over the top of the filling to cover. Use your fingers to press and seal the edges of the lid to the egg-glazed border around all 4 sides. Mark the pastry border with the back of a fork, pressing down neatly, then roll or curl the edge of the border inwards to make a neat band. Chill for 20 minutes.

8. Meanwhile, heat the oven to 220°C/425°F/gas 7. Brush the pastry lid with beaten egg to glaze, then cut 5 slits across the top on a slight diagonal. Bake the pie in the heated oven for about 25 minutes until the pastry is a rich golden brown and crisp. Serve hot with the butter sauce.

FOR THE FILLING
2 small to medium aubergines
2 courgettes
2 red peppers
1 red onion
1 small sweet potato (about 200g)
4 tablespoons olive oil
6 large garlic cloves, thinly sliced
leaves from a small bunch of fresh
   oregano
100g unsalted cashews
50g soft sun-dried tomatoes,
   roughly chopped
salt, black pepper and crushed
   dried chillies, all to taste

TO ASSEMBLE
½ quantity Puff Pastry (see page
   22) OR 375g ready-made
   all-butter or vegan puff pastry,
   thawed if frozen
beaten egg, to glaze

TO SERVE
Quick Herb Butter Sauce
   (see page 22)

you will need
1 roasting tin; a baking sheet,
lined with baking paper

another idea: You can boost the flavour of this pie by adding a tablespoon of pesto or some crumbled blue cheese along with the cashews.

SMOKED HADDOCK, CHEESE AND ALE PIE

Give a bit of a twist to a simple fish pie and it becomes fabulous enough for a dinner party. The creamy, Cheddar-rich filling in this pie has a bit of a bite from pale ale, and is packed with chunks of smoky fish, leeks and crushed small new potatoes. You can decorate the puff pastry top as extravagantly as you like. All you need with the pie is a crisp green salad.

serves 6

500g small new potatoes
500g undyed smoked haddock
    fillets
250ml double cream
4 black peppercorns
25g unsalted butter
200g trimmed leeks (about
    2 medium), thinly sliced
150ml pale ale OR 75ml fish stock
100g extra-mature Cheddar
    cheese, grated
½ teaspoon Dijon mustard, or
    to taste
1 medium egg yolk
salt and black pepper

TO FINISH
½ quantity Puff Pastry (see page
    22) OR 375g ready-made
    all-butter puff pastry, thawed
    if frozen
beaten egg, to glaze

you will need
1 pie dish, 1.25–1.5 litre
capacity, greased with
butter; a pie-raiser;
a baking sheet

1. Give the potatoes a good scrub (there's no need to peel them). Put them into a pan and add plenty of cold water to cover. Bring to the boil, then reduce the heat and simmer for 12–15 minutes until the potatoes are just tender when pierced with the tip of a small sharp knife. Drain thoroughly, then tip on to a chopping board. Lightly crush the potatoes with the back of a wooden spoon.

2. Set the pie-raiser in the centre of the pie dish. Spoon the potatoes around the raiser to make an even layer. Leave to cool until needed.

3. To cook the haddock (you can do this while the potatoes are boiling), put the fillets into a large pan in a single layer – use kitchen scissors to cut up a large fillet into pieces to fit your pan – pour over the cream and add the peppercorns. Bring just to a simmer, then cover the pan and cook very gently for 7–10 minutes until the fish will flake when pierced with the tip of a small, sharp knife. Remove the pan from the heat and carefully lift out the fish using a fish slice or slotted spoon to a heatproof plate (save the cooking liquid). When the fish is cool enough to handle, flake into large chunks, discarding the skin and any bones. Add any liquid that's accumulated on the plate to the cooking liquid.

4. Melt the butter in a medium pan, add the leeks and stir well. Cover the pan and cook over low heat, stirring now and then, for 8–10 minutes until the leeks are very soft. While the leeks cook, pour the ale into a small pan and boil until reduced by half (if using fish stock just bring it to the boil).

5. Uncover the leeks and add the reduced ale (or hot stock). Strain the fish cooking liquid into the pan. Bring to the boil, stirring gently. Remove from the heat, add the cheese and mustard, and combine thoroughly. Stir in the flaked fish, then season with salt and pepper to taste (the mixture should be well flavoured, so add more mustard if needed). Finally, gently fold in the egg yolk.

6. Spoon the fish mixture over the crushed potatoes in the pie dish and leave until completely cold before adding the pastry lid.

7. Roll out the puff pastry on a lightly floured worktop to the same shape – oval or round – as your pie dish but about 7cm larger all around. Cut around the shape to remove a strip of pastry about 1cm wide and long enough to fit the entire rim of the dish. Dampen the rim with water, then press the strip of pastry on to it, joining the ends neatly. Dampen the strip.

8. Make a small slit in the centre of the remaining pastry shape, then roll it up loosely around the rolling pin and gently unroll it over the pie dish; the pie-raiser should fit through the slit. Take care not to stretch the pastry as you cover the pie. Press the edge of the pastry lid on to the pastry strip on the rim to seal firmly. Trim off excess pastry with a sharp knife; save the trimmings for decoration.

9. Use the back of a small knife to 'knock up'* the pastry edge, then flute* it. Cut the pastry trimmings into decorative shapes (using a knife or small shaped pastry cutter) and stick them on to the lid with a dab of the beaten egg glaze. Chill the pie while heating the oven to 190°C/375°F/gas 5.

10. Set the pie on the baking sheet. Brush the pastry lid with beaten egg to glaze, then place the baking sheet in the oven and bake the pie for 30–35 minutes until the pastry is puffed up and a rich brown. Serve hot.

FILLED YORKSHIRE PUDDINGS

A great combination of crisp, well-risen Yorkshires, tender meat and well-flavoured sauce along with the crispiest crackling and a tart apple sauce too - this is the complete Sunday Roast Dinner in one neat package. The puddings must be completely cooked so keep checking - it's easy to assume that because they have risen well they are cooked through.

makes 24

FOR THE YORKSHIRE PUDDING BATTER
340g plain flour
½ teaspoon fine sea salt
few grinds of black pepper
6 medium eggs, at room temperature
500ml full-fat/whole milk, chilled
about 100ml sparkling mineral water, chilled
100ml sunflower oil, for brushing

FOR THE CRACKLING
100g piece trimmed pork skin

sea salt flakes, for sprinkling
good pinch of dried 'herbes de Provence'

FOR THE PORK FILLING
500g pork tenderloin (fillet)
2 tablespoons sunflower oil
1 medium red onion, peeled
1 celery stick
1 large carrot, peeled
1 medium dessert apple, peeled
430ml medium sweet cider
½ pork stock cube
1 bay leaf

1 teaspoon chopped fresh sage OR ½ teaspoon dried sage
1 tablespoon cornflour
wholegrain mustard and white pepper, both to taste

FOR THE APPLE SAUCE
2 medium cooking apples
3 tablespoons water
10g unsalted butter
1–2 teaspoons caster sugar, to taste
few drops of lemon juice, to taste

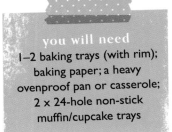

you will need
1–2 baking trays (with rim);
baking paper; a heavy
ovenproof pan or casserole;
2 x 24-hole non-stick
muffin/cupcake trays

1. Start by making the pudding batter as it needs time to stand. Sift the flour and salt into a mixing bowl, add some pepper and make a well in the centre. Break in one egg and whisk, using a hand wire whisk, so it is broken up and a little flour is mixed in. Repeat with the other 5 eggs, adding them one at a time, then slowly whisk in the milk, gradually drawing in the rest of the flour to make a smooth batter. Whisk in 50ml of the sparkling water. Transfer to a large jug, cover and chill for at least 30 minutes or until ready to bake.

2. Meanwhile, prepare the crackling. Trim off as much of the excess fat from the underside of the pork skin as possible and, if you like, score the surface to make serving easier (the butcher may have already done all of this). Sprinkle the skin side with salt and herbs and leave, uncovered, for 20 minutes. Meanwhile, heat the oven to 220°C/425°F/gas 7, and put the roasting tin into the bottom of the oven to heat up.

3. Wipe the salt and herbs off the skin and pat it dry between sheets of kitchen paper. Put the skin (skin-side uppermost) on a baking tray lined with baking paper and place a second baking tray or a baking sheet on top. Set a heavy ovenproof pan/casserole on the top (to weight it all down and keep the crackling flat). Pour cold water into the pan/casserole to fill it about 6cm deep.

4. Put the whole contraption into the oven. Pour cold water into the hot roasting tin (in the bottom of the oven) to create a burst of steam, then close the oven door quickly. Bake the skin for about 30 minutes until very crisp and golden. Remove and cool slightly, then chop into small shards. Set aside until needed. Remove the roasting tin from the oven but leave the oven on.

5. While the crackling is baking, make the pork filling. Trim the meat to remove all excess fat, then cut the tenderloin/fillet across into 3 pieces. Heat the oil in a large sauté pan and quickly brown the meat on all sides. Remove to a plate and take the pan off the heat. Cut the onion, celery, carrot and apple into 5mm dice. Reheat the oil in the pan, then add the onion, celery and carrot and cook gently over low heat, stirring occasionally, for about 8 minutes until softened. Stir in the apple along with 400ml of the cider, the stock cube, bay leaf and sage. Bring to the boil, stirring.

6. Return the meat to the pan (with any juices on the plate). Cover and simmer, stirring and turning the meat from time to time, for about 15 minutes until the pork is cooked through – no longer pink in the centre. Lift out the meat on to a chopping board. Mix the cornflour with the remaining cider in a small bowl, then stir into the hot vegetable mixture in the pan. Bring to the boil, stirring. Taste and add some mustard and pepper. Cut the meat into 5mm-thick slices, then cut the slices across in half. Return to the pan. Cover and keep warm until needed.

7. When the pork crackling comes out of the oven, return to the Yorkshires. Brush the holes of the muffin trays liberally with oil and put them into the oven. Heat for about 5 minutes until smoking hot. Meanwhile, give the chilled batter a good stir and mix in enough of the remaining chilled sparkling water to make the consistency like double cream. Using a small ladle, carefully pour the batter into the tins to half fill each hole. Bake for 25–35 minutes until well risen, very crisp and a rich golden brown – check to make sure the Yorkshires are cooked through. Unmould and keep warm until ready to fill.

8. While the Yorkshires bake, make the apple sauce. Peel, quarter and core the apples, then chop into even-sized chunks. Put into a medium pan with the water and cook over low heat, stirring frequently with a wooden spoon, until soft. Gently mash with the back of the spoon to make a thick purée. Remove from the heat and stir in the butter, sugar and lemon juice (if needed). Keep warm until ready to assemble.

9. To assemble the Yorkshires, arrange the puddings on serving platters and spoon a couple of pieces of pork and some vegetables into the centre hollow of each. Add a teaspoon of apple sauce to the top and garnish with shards of crackling. Serve any remaining apple sauce in a bowl, and any remaining vegetables and cider sauce in another warmed serving bowl.

SPICY CHORIZO AND SQUASH PARCELS

Impress your guests with these delectable morsels: neat bite-sized parcels of tissue-thin hand-stretched pastry filled with a tasty, juicy combination of chorizo and velvety-smooth roasted butternut squash.

makes 24

1. To make the pastry, first heat the water to 50°C/120°F (use a cooking thermometer). Sift the flour and salt into the bowl of a free-standing electric mixer fitted with the dough hook. Add the water and, using slow speed, mix until the dough just comes together. Still mixing on slow speed, slowly trickle the oil down the sides of the bowl. As soon as it is incorporated, stop the mixer and scrape down the sides of the bowl.

2. Now knead* the dough on medium/low speed for 4–5 minutes – it will still be very soft, and slightly sticky, but should leave the sides of the bowl clean (if necessary work in a little more flour or warm water as needed).

3. Dust the worktop and one of the lined baking sheets with cornflour, then scoop out the dough on to the worktop. Divide into 5 portions and set them on the baking sheets, slightly apart. Sprinkle the dough with more cornflour, then cover with clingfilm and chill for 1 hour to give the dough time to relax and firm up.

4. Meanwhile, make the filling. Heat the oven to 220°C/425°F/gas 7. Peel the squash and remove the seeds and fibres. Cut the flesh into 1.5cm cubes – you need 300g. Spread the squash cubes in a roasting tin and spoon over half the olive oil. Add a good pinch each of salt and pepper plus a few sprigs of thyme and toss everything together with your hands. Roast in the heated oven for 10 minutes, then stir gently. Roast for a further 7–10 minutes until the squash is just tender and starting to brown around the edges. Remove and leave to cool.

5. Peel and finely chop the onion and garlic. Heat the remaining olive oil in a non-stick frying pan, add the onion mixture and cook gently, stirring frequently, until soft and translucent. Strip the leaves from a couple of thyme sprigs and stir into the onion along with the wine and stock. Turn up the heat slightly and simmer until the liquid has reduced by half. Transfer the mixture to a food processor.

6. Remove the skin from chorizo and cut into 5mm cubes (you need 48). Put them in the frying pan (no need to wash it) and fry over medium heat, stirring frequently, until the fat runs and the cubes turn golden brown.

FOR THE FILO PASTRY

170ml water
225g plain flour
¼ teaspoon fine sea salt
1 tablespoon olive oil
cornflour, for dusting
50g unsalted butter, melted, for
  brushing

FOR THE FILLING

1 medium butternut squash
  (about 450g)
3 tablespoons olive oil
1 bunch of fresh thyme
1 white onion
2 garlic cloves
2 tablespoons dry white wine
5 tablespoons chicken or vegetable
  stock
125g chorizo cooking sausage
salt and black pepper, to taste

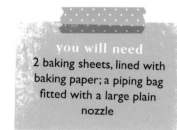

you will need
2 baking sheets, lined with baking paper; a piping bag fitted with a large plain nozzle

7. Remove the chorizo using a slotted spoon, draining the fat back into the pan, and leave to cool on kitchen paper. Pour the fat in the pan into the processor bowl on top of the onion mixture.

8. Set aside 24 cubes of roasted squash and add the rest to the processor bowl. Blitz to make a smooth, thick purée that will hold a shape. Stir in the leaves picked from 3 thyme sprigs. Leave the purée to cool, then transfer to the piping bag. Set aside.

9. To stretch the filo, dust the worktop, your hands and a rolling pin with cornflour, and have more at hand in a shaker or with a fine sieve – the dough is soft and delicate, but is easy enough to handle with sufficient cornflour. Take one piece of chilled dough from the fridge (it's easiest to work with one piece at a time) and roll it out on the worktop to a large, thin square. Now use your hands to stretch out the dough (see Salmon, Spinach and Feta Strudel on page 287 for details of how to do this) until it is so tissue-thin you can see the worktop through it. Trim off the thick edges with a pizza wheel-cutter or sharp knife, then brush the sheet very delicately with melted butter. Cut out 7.5cm squares – you can get about 10 perfect squares from each of the 5 portions. The dough is fragile, but there is plenty to allow for tears and holes, and mistakes.

10. Place one 7.5cm square, butter-side up, on a lined baking sheet, then lay a second square on top at an angle so the points do not meet. Pipe a small blob of purée in the centre (about ½ teaspoon). Top with 2 chorizo cubes and one squash cube. Draw up the points of the filo squares over the filling to form a neat parcel and pinch together about 1cm below the top edge.

11. Repeat using the rest of this batch of 7.5cm squares, then continue stretching and cutting the other portions of dough in turn until you have formed 24 parcels.

12. Bake for 12–15 minutes until the pastry is crisp and golden – for best results check after 6 minutes and, if necessary, rotate the sheets so the pastries bake evenly. Transfer to a serving platter, garnish with sprigs of thyme and serve warm.

CHINESE-STYLE PRAWN FILO TARTLETS

For these appealing and attractive *amuse-bouches*, crisp little tartlet cases fashioned from home-made filo are filled with stir-fried large prawns and colourful vegetables. The tissue-thin pastry rapidly dries and hardens when it comes into contact with the air, so be sure you have a just-damp tea towel or sheet of clingfilm ready to cover the pastry in case you are interrupted while shaping the cases.

makes 24

1. To make the filo pastry, sift the flour and salt into a mixing bowl and make a well in the centre. Mix the lukewarm water with the olive oil and pour into the well. Using your hand, gradually draw the flour into the liquid to make a soft but not sticky dough: if there are dry crumbs, work in more lukewarm water a few drops at a time.

2. Turn out the dough on to a lightly floured worktop and knead* it thoroughly for 10 minutes until very smooth and pliable. Wrap the ball of dough in clingfilm and chill for 1 hour to allow the dough to relax.

3. Meanwhile, prepare the filling ingredients (bear in mind the size of the tartlet cases). Finely chop the garlic, spring onions and ginger; put into a small bowl. Cut the carrot into fine needle-like shreds; put into another small bowl. Remove the black thread-like gut from the prawns, then chop each into 4 or 5 pieces; put into a third bowl. Stack up 4 of the mangetout and cut in half lengthways, then cut across to make fine dice. Repeat with the rest of the mangetout, then put all the dice into a fourth bowl. Finely chop the pak choy into pieces roughly the same as the mangetout. Add to the mangetout bowl along with the beansprouts. Cover all the bowls and keep in the fridge until needed.

4. Heat the oven to 200°C/400°F/gas 6. Unwrap the dough and divide it in half. Re-wrap one piece and set aside. Lightly dust the worktop, a rolling pin (use a long, thin one if possible) and your hands with cornflour, then roll out the portion of dough until it is about the size and thickness of an A4 sheet of paper. Now use your hands to stretch out the dough until it is so thin you can see the worktop through it (for instructions on how to do this, see Salmon, Spinach and Feta Strudel on page 287).

5. Using a pizza wheel-cutter or sharp knife, trim the stretched pastry to a neat 30 x 45cm rectangle. Brush the pastry very lightly with melted butter, then cut into 24 squares. Lift off one square and set it slightly apart on the worktop, then lay a second square on top (butter-side up), placing it at an angle to the first square so the points don't match up.

FOR THE FILO PASTRY
150g plain flour
¼ teaspoon fine sea salt
80ml lukewarm water
2 teaspoons extra virgin olive oil
cornflour, for dusting
50g unsalted butter, melted,
  for brushing

FOR THE FILLING
1 garlic clove, peeled
3 spring onions, trimmed
1 thumb-sized piece fresh root
  ginger, peeled
1 medium carrot, peeled
250g peeled raw tiger prawns
50g mangetout
60g pak choy
60g beansprouts, well rinsed
1½ tablespoons sesame oil
½ teaspoon Chinese five-spice
  paste, or to taste
¾–1 tablespoon light soy sauce,
  to taste
fresh coriander leaves, to garnish

you will need
1 x 24-hole mini-muffin tray,
ungreased

6. Turn the layered pastry upside down and gently press it into a hole in the muffin tray; the pastry edges will extend above the rim of the hole. Repeat with the other 22 squares. Then roll and stretch out the second piece of dough, and make more tartlet cases so you end up with 24.

7. Bake the filo cases in the heated oven for 7–10 minutes until a good golden colour and crisp – check after 5 minutes and rotate the tray, if necessary, so they bake evenly. Gently lift the cases out of the tray on to a wire rack and leave to cool.

8. When ready to serve, arrange the tartlet cases on a serving board, then make the filling. Heat the sesame oil in a wok or large sauté pan over high heat. Add the garlic mixture and stir-fry for a minute, then add the carrot strips and stir-fry for 2 minutes. Add the prawns and stir-fry for 4 minutes until they turn pink. Add the five-spice paste to the wok and stir in. Once thoroughly amalgamated, add the mangetout mixture and stir-fry for about 3 minutes until the vegetables are barely tender but piping hot. Mix in the soy sauce, then taste and add more if wanted.

9. Carefully spoon the filling into the filo cases, piling it as elegantly as possible. Quickly garnish with coriander leaves and serve.

LOBSTER AND GRUYÈRE TARTLETS

Glamorous and extravagant seafood tartlets are perfect for a very special meal on a summer evening, either as a first course, garnished with a few dressed salad leaves, or with new potatoes and steamed asparagus for a light supper. Lobster tails imported from Maine are available cooked and frozen or thawed from larger supermarkets - they work well in this savoury bake.

makes 8

FOR THE RICH SHORTCRUST PASTRY
300g plain flour
¼ teaspoon fine sea salt
3 good pinches of hot smoked paprika OR cayenne pepper
225g unsalted butter, chilled and diced
2 medium egg yolks
about 3 tablespoons icy cold water

FOR THE FILLING
225g white crabmeat, thawed if frozen
1 medium egg plus 5 yolks
1 tablespoon brandy
225ml double cream
3 cooked lobster tails (about 225g shelled weight), thawed if frozen
85g Gruyère cheese, grated
¼ teaspoon hot smoked paprika OR cayenne pepper, or to taste
fine sea salt and ground black pepper
fresh dill, to garnish

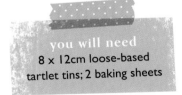

you will need
8 x 12cm loose-based tartlet tins; 2 baking sheets

1. To make the pastry, put the flour, salt and paprika into a food processor and pulse a couple of times just to combine. Add the butter and blitz until the mixture looks like fine crumbs. With the machine running, add the egg yolks through the feed tube, then gradually add enough of the cold water to make a soft but not sticky dough. (The dough can also be made by hand: rub* the butter into the seasoned flour, then work in the yolks and cold water with a round-bladed knife.) Shape the dough into a thick disc, wrap in clingfilm and chill for about 15 minutes until firm but not hard.

2. Unwrap the dough on a lightly floured worktop and divide into 8 equal portions. One at a time, roll out each portion to a 16cm disc and use to line a tartlet tin*. Press out any trapped pockets of air, then prick the base of the pastry case with a fork. Leave excess pastry hanging over the rims for now.

3. Set the tartlet tins on the baking sheets and chill for 20 minutes. Meanwhile, heat the oven to 190°C/375°F/gas 5.

4. Carefully trim off the excess pastry from the tartlet cases by rolling the rolling pin over the top of each tin. Neaten the rims with your fingers, then line each pastry case with baking paper, fill with beans and bake blind* in the heated oven for 12 minutes. Remove the paper and beans and bake the cases for a further 8–10 minutes until the pastry is cooked through and lightly golden. Slide the tartlet tins on to a heatproof surface, then return the baking sheets to the oven to keep hot.

5. Flake the crab into a mixing bowl, discarding any pieces of shell or cartilage. In another bowl, whisk the whole egg with the yolks, brandy, cream and seasoning. Add to the crab and mix well. Remove the lobster tails from the shell, if necessary, and cut each tail across into 8 slices. Season the slices lightly with salt and pepper.

6. Arrange 3 lobster slices in the base of each tartlet case. Set the tartlet tins on the hot baking sheets and spoon the crab and cream mixture into the cases. Mix the cheese with the paprika and scatter over the top of the filling. Return the baking sheets to the oven and bake the tartlets for 20–25 minutes until the filling is just set and golden. Carefully unmould the tartlets and serve warm (rather than piping hot), garnished with dill.

DUCK AND PISTACHIO PÂTÉ EN CROÛTE

One step up from the challenge of making a raised pork pie, here is an elegant pâté-filled pie for a celebratory lunch or a concert picnic in the park – a rich mix of duck breast meat and livers, pork fillet and minced pork plus pistachios and brandy, baked in a rich pastry crust. The pastry (pâte brisée) bakes to a crisp rather than crumbly texture, which is ideal for the moist, heavy filling. Plan to make this several days before slicing and serving.

serves 12

FOR THE PÂTÉ MIXTURE
2 duck breasts (about 400g in total)
100g duck (or chicken) livers
150g pork fillet
600g minced pork
1 small bunch of flat-leaf parsley
1 red onion, finely chopped
2 garlic cloves, crushed

5 tablespoons brandy
4 tablespoons white wine
60g unsalted pistachios (shelled)
salt and ground black pepper

FOR THE PÂTE BRISÉE
400g plain flour
1 teaspoon fine sea salt
200g unsalted butter, chilled

2 medium egg yolks
90ml icy cold water

TO FINISH
beaten egg, to glaze
3 leaves gelatine (from a 13g/8-leaf pack)
175ml good chicken stock
3 tablespoons white wine

1. Remove the skin and fat from the duck breasts, then cut the meat into 1cm cubes, discarding the silvery white sinews. Put into a large bowl. Trim the livers to remove any discoloured or white stringy bits, then cut into 1cm cubes and add to the bowl. Cut up the pork fillet into 1cm cubes and add to the bowl along with the minced pork.

2. Finely chop the parsley leaves and add to the bowl along with the onion, garlic, brandy and white wine plus some salt and plenty of ground black pepper. Mix everything together thoroughly using a wooden spoon or your hand. To test the seasoning, take a teaspoon of the mixture, shape it into a mini burger and fry on both sides in a non-stick frying pan until cooked through; when cool enough, taste the burger, then add more seasoning to the meat mixture as needed. Cover the bowl tightly and leave it in the fridge overnight so the flavours can develop.

3. Next day, put the pistachios into a small pan, add enough cold water to cover and bring to the boil. Drain the pistachios thoroughly, then tip on to a clean, dry tea towel and gently rub them to loosen their brown papery skins. Cover and leave on the worktop until needed.

you will need
1 x 900g loaf tin, about 26 x 12.5 x 7.5cm, greased with butter and lined with a long strip of foil-lined baking paper or baking paper*; a baking sheet

4. To make the pâte brisée, sift the flour and salt on to a clean worktop and make a large well in the centre. Put the butter between sheets of clingfilm and pound with a rolling pin until the butter is pliable but still cold. Cut into pieces and add to the well along with the egg yolks and cold water. Put the fingertips of one hand together to form a beak shape and use to mash together the ingredients in the well. Once they are thoroughly combined, gradually work in the flour with your fingers, using a plastic dough scraper or a metal spatula to help you draw the flour in. When the mixture looks like coarse crumbs, gather the whole lot together with your hands to make a ball of dough. Be patient – it will take a few minutes for the dough to come together. If there are dry crumbs and the dough just won't come together, add more water a teaspoon at a time; if the dough feels really sticky, work in a little more flour.

5. Lightly dust the worktop with flour and gently start to work the dough – this is known as the *fraisage* and prepares it for rolling out: press down on the ball of dough with the heel of your hand and push it away from you, then gather up the dough into a ball once more (using the scraper) and repeat. Continue working the dough for a couple of minutes – no more – until it is silky-smooth and very pliable, so pliable it can be peeled off the worktop in one piece. Tightly wrap the dough in clingfilm and chill for about 20 minutes until firm but not hard.

6. When you are ready to assemble, cut off 200g of the pâte brisée for the lid, wrap and put on one side for now. Roll out the rest of the dough on a lightly floured worktop to a neat 45 × 30cm rectangle (or large enough to line the base and all 4 sides of your tin plus a little over to make the rim). Roll the dough loosely around the rolling pin, then gently unroll and lower into the tin. Using your thumbs, gently press the dough on to the base and up the sides, pressing out any air bubbles and the gathers at the corners. Leave the excess dough hanging over the rim. Make sure there are no holes or gaps in the dough lining (if necessary, patch with little pieces of the excess dough). Roll out the reserved dough to a rectangle to fit the top of your tin, plus a little extra for the rim.

7. Mix the pistachios into the meat mixture until evenly distributed, then pack the filling into the dough case. Make sure the tin is evenly filled – right into the corners – and that there are no gaps or air pockets. Bang the tin on the worktop a couple of times to settle the contents. Brush the rim of the dough case with beaten egg. Lift the dough lid and lay it in place, then firmly press the edges together to seal. Using a sharp knife, trim off the excess dough (save for the decorations), then 'knock up'* the edges with the back of the knife. Flute* the edges to give a scalloped effect and at the same time gently roll the pastry rim inwards – it will be easier to remove the baked pie from the tin if the pastry edge is not firmly attached to the rim.

8. Make a large steam hole in the centre of the lid and set a small foil 'chimney' in it. Re-roll the dough trimmings and cut out small decorations. Attach these to the top of the pie with dabs of beaten egg. Chill the pie for 15 minutes while the oven heats to 180°C/350°F/gas 4. Put a baking sheet into the oven to heat up.

9. Brush the lid of the pie with beaten egg to glaze. Set the tin on the hot baking sheet in the oven and bake for about 1½ hours until the pastry is a rich golden colour. Check the pie after an hour – if you think the pastry is browning too quickly, lightly cover the top with a sheet of baking paper or foil. To test if the filling is cooked through and piping hot, insert a metal skewer into the centre of the pie through the steam hole and leave it for 10 seconds, then withdraw the skewer and gently touch it to the back of your hand. If the skewer feels very hot indeed then the pie is cooked. If it feels comfortably hot, then return the pie to the oven and test again after a further 5 minutes of baking.

10. Remove the pie from the oven and leave it to cool in the tin. Once the pie is cold, lift out the foil chimney.

11. Soak the gelatine in a small bowl of cold water for 5 minutes. Meanwhile, bring the stock and wine to the boil, then remove from the heat. Lift the gelatine out of the water and squeeze out the excess, then add to the hot stock and whisk well until melted and smooth. Pour into a jug and leave to cool until starting to thicken.

12. Carefully insert a large piping tube or small funnel into the steam hole in the pie. Slowly pour in the thickening stock. Now and again, gently tilt the tin so the stock can reach the sides and ends – you may not need all of it. Leave to cool, then cover the pie and chill overnight, preferably for 24 hours. To serve, carefully remove the pie from the tin and cut into thick slices.

CONVERSION TABLES

WEIGHT

METRIC	IMPERIAL
25g	1oz
50g	2oz
75g	2½oz
85g	3oz
100g	4oz
125g	4½oz
140g	5oz
175g	6oz
200g	7oz
225g	8oz
250g	9oz
280g	10oz
300g	11oz
350g	12oz
375g	13oz
400g	14oz
425g	15oz
450g	1lb
500g	1lb 2oz
550g	1lb 4oz
600g	1lb 5oz
650g	1lb 7oz
700g	1lb 9oz
750g	1lb 10oz
800g	1lb 12oz
850g	1lb 14oz
900g	2lb
950g	2lb 2oz
1kg	2lb 4oz

LINEAR

METRIC	IMPERIAL
2.5cm	1in
3cm	1¼in
4cm	1½in
5cm	2in
5.5cm	2¼in
6cm	2½in
7cm	2¾in
7.5cm	3in
8cm	3¼in
9cm	3½in
9.5cm	3¾in
10cm	4in
11cm	4¼in
12cm	4½in
13cm	5in
14cm	5½in
15cm	6in
16cm	6¼in
17cm	6½in
18cm	7in
19cm	7½in
20cm	8in
22cm	8½in
23cm	9in
24cm	9½in
25cm	10in

VOLUME

METRIC	IMPERIAL
30ml	1fl oz
50ml	2fl oz
75ml	3fl oz
125ml	4fl oz
150ml	¼ pint
175ml	6fl oz
200ml	7fl oz
225ml	8fl oz
300ml	½ pint
350ml	12fl oz
400ml	14fl oz
450ml	¾ pint
500ml	18fl oz
600ml	1 pint
725ml	1¼ pints
1 litre	1¾ pints

SPOON MEASURES

METRIC	IMPERIAL
5ml	1 teaspoon
10ml	2 teaspoons
15ml	1 tablespoon
30ml	2 tablespoons
45ml	3 tablespoons
60ml	4 tablespoons
75ml	5 tablespoons

INDEX

A

ale: Smoked haddock, cheese and ale pie 292–3
almonds:
    Armagnac, prune and almond tart 244–5
    Bakewell tart 228
    Chai pear cups 255–6
    Five nut caramel tart 241–2
    Lemon and lemon confit tart 238–9
    Linzer sablés 100
    Marjolaine 211–12
    Mil hojas 267
    Swiss apple-almond slice 261–2
apples:
    Apple sauce 294–6
    Blackberry and apple buckle 182
    Mulled wine, cranberry and apple crumble 191
    Roasted apple brown sugar pie 230–1
    Swiss apple-almond slice 261–2
apricots:
    Fresh apricot Tatin 264
Armagnac, prune and almond tart 244–5
aubergines: Roast vegetable and cashew pie 291

B

babka: Chocolate, cardamom and hazelnut babka
    159–60
bacon: Wild mushroom canapés 278–80
Bakewell tart 228
baklava: Pistachio chocolate baklava 233–4
bananas:
    Banana split ice-cream cake 199–200
    Banoffee whisky cups 258–60
Banoffee whisky cups 258–60
beer:
    Bitter chocolate stout cake 40–2

Crunchy beer bread 120–2
    Malt, chocolate and orange iced 'beer' biscuits 103–4
    Smoked haddock, cheese and ale pie 292–3
Bhaa bara brith biscuits 105–6
biscuits:
    Bhaa bara brith biscuits 105–6
    Bitter extremely rich chocolate cookies 97
    Cottage cheese puff biscuits 276
    Crisp spiced wafers 96
    Linzer sablés 100
    Malt, chocolate and orange iced 'beer' biscuits 103–4
    Maple walnut biscuits 92
    Mexican wedding cookies 84
    Peanut butter, chocolate chip and oat cookies 94
    Viennese whirls 113
Black and white celebration cake 64–7
Black olive flatbread 123
blackberries:
    Blackberry and apple buckle 182
    Forest fruits strawberry mousse cakes 219–20
breads:
    baking tips 16–17
    Black olive flatbread 123
    Cardamom pear plait 162–5
    Chocolate, cardamom and hazelnut babka 159–60
    Chocolate orange swirl bread 150–2
    Cobbled chocolate loaf 137–8
    Crunchy beer bread 120–2
    Dampfnudeln 139–40
    Deliciously quick canapés 268–81
    Fresh herb fougasse 149
    Greek country bread 130–2
    Mallorcas 167–8
    Orange pain aux raisins 170–2
    Pain d'épices 124
    Parmesan prosciutto ciabatta 153–5

This book is published to accompany the television series entitled The Great British Bake Off, broadcast on BBC ONE in 2016
This series was produced for BBC Television by Love Productions

First published in Great Britain in 2016 by Hodder & Stoughton
An Hachette UK company

1

Hardback ISBN 978 1 473 61544 1
Ebook ISBN 978 1 473 61545 8

Editorial Director: Nicky Ross
Project Editor: Sarah Hammond
Author of Baker Profiles: Ramona Andrews
Copy Editor: Norma MacMillan
Designer & Art Director: Nikki Dupin
Photographer: Rita Platts
Food Stylist: Emma Marsden
Assistant Food Stylist: Sam Dixon
Props Stylist: Kate Wesson
Production Manager: Laura Oliver
Art Editor: Kate Brunt
Art Director: Sarah Christie

Typeset in Gill Sans, Brandon, Orpheus Pro and Mostra Nuova

Printed and bound in Germany by Mohn Media GmbH, Gütersloh

Hodder & Stoughton Ltd
Carmelite House
50 Victoria Embankment
London EC4Y 0DZ

Love Productions would like to thank the following people:

Producers: Jane Treasure, Claire Emerson
Challenge Producer: Chloe Avery
Food Team: Anna Horsburgh, Monika Frise
Home Economist: Becca Watson
Executive Producer: Sarah Thomson-Woolley
Commercial Director: Rupert Frisby
Publicist: Amanda Console
Commissioning Editor: Clare Paterson

Thank you to Mel, Sue, Mary, Paul, Andrew, Benjamina, Candice, Jane, Kate, Lee, Louise, Michael, Rav, Selasi, Tom and Val.

ON YOUR MARKS... GET SET... BAKE!

Continue on your journey to star baker with tips and advice on how to *Bake It Better* from **THE GREAT BRITISH BAKE OFF** team.

Inspirational ideas for a *showstopping* birthday party.

Get even more of THE GREAT BRITISH BAKE OFF in the step-by-step app.